Facebook Friendship Groups as a Space for Peace

A Case Study of Relations between Libyan and American Citizens

Lisa Gibson

Washington and Jefferson College

Series in Politics

VERNON PRESS

www.vernonpress.com

In the Americas:	*In the rest of the world:*
Vernon Press	Vernon Press
1000 N West Street, Suite 1200,	C/Sancti Espiritu 17,
Wilmington, Delaware 19801	Malaga, 29006
United States	Spain

Series in Politics

Library of Congress Control Number: 2024937439

ISBN: 979-8-8819-0116-5
Also available: 979-8-8819-0026-7 [Hardback]; 979-8-8819-0087-8 [PDF, E-Book]

Cover design by Vernon Press with elements from Freepik.

Table of Contents

List of Figures and Tables

Figures

Tables

Acknowledgements

I would like to thank my family, friends, and advisors that have supported me in the process of writing this book. I especially would like to thank the Libyan people who participated in the interviews and their desire to foster more peaceful relations between the US and Libya. You taught me a lot about what it is like to carry the legacy of the bad decisions of your government and how, despite years of isolation and oppression, you still recognize your own agency to change the narratives. I was inspired by so many of your stories and convinced that not only can average citizens make a difference, but they also have an obligation to. Regular citizens can be ambassadors of their countries and the simple processes of socializing and interactions on social media is the first step in building trust and respect, which is the necessary foundation for long-term peaceful relations.

Chapter 1

Introduction

'Do I not destroy my enemies when I make them my friends?'
– Abraham Lincoln

1.1 Background and context

Historically, the study of International Relations (IR) was principally concerned with how to attain peace, security, justice and order between sovereign states, which many scholars conceived of as competing in an anarchic international arena. This state of anarchy is seen as fixed and unchanging. This book challenges the premise that anarchy is the natural state of international relations and instead contends that interactions impact the quality of relations. This book was inspired by years of working as a citizen diplomacy practitioner in Libya and a desire to understand what kind of impact citizen exchanges have. This is what led me to study friendships during my PhD program and this book is an edited version of my dissertation. The premise of this book is that, to some extent, world peace is dependent upon whether states and citizens of states view each other as friends or enemies. The central tenets of this book are that views of friend and enemy in international relations are socially constructed. This book builds upon existing scholarship, which problematises distinctions between friend and enemy. The most notable and earliest proponent of the socially constructed nature of relations within the international arena was Alexander Wendt in his book *Social Theory of International Politics.* In this book, Wendt (1999) argued that the language used and the way states relate to one another affects the quality of relations and that if states refer to one another as an enemy, then that language will likely result in enemy behaviour and conflict. He argued that views of friend and enemy are based on 'self' and 'other' distinctions and that these views are a social construct. However, Wendt limited his argument to relations between states in the context of security. In arguing as such, he avoided any discussion of the important role that people have in both causing conflict and facilitating peace. This is influenced by his support for the conventional perspective among many IR[1] scholars, which focuses on the state as agent in international relations. Oelsner and Koschut (2014) appropriately question the purely structure-focused definition of

---

[1] IR is used for the field of International Relations and international relations deals with the activity.

friendship that Wendt used. This book extends Wendt's arguments to relations between people, *as agents of states*, in international relations. This book argues that these 'self' and 'other' distinctions and the differences that exist between states and citizens of states do not necessarily have to result in conflict. Instead, if views are socially constructed, then people as agents of states should be able to choose to relate differently, which means that enmity is not inevitable between states, and it should be possible to reconstruct relations based on friendship. Nordin and Smith suggest that what is missing in International Relations is the constructivist view that relations can be transformed through interaction (Nordin and Smith, 2018b, p. 11). Viewing friendship this way requires an understanding of more relational approaches to friendship, which involve people. As such, this book diverges from Wendt's (1994) argument which suggests that the state is the primary facilitator of peace in international relations. Instead, it argues that people are the key agents in reconstructing relations, and the various ways and spaces they interact can provide useful insights into these relational processes.

This book contributes to the study of the concept of friendship in IR by exploring the human side of friendships and how relations between people influence relations between states. To do this, this book focuses on the role of citizens as actors in IR and argues that just as citizens are often the ones perpetrating many recent international conflicts, citizens also have a key, although often neglected, role to play in facilitating peace in international relations. Part of the way citizens are engaged in fostering peaceful relations in international relations is through a variety of citizen diplomacy initiatives that promote understanding and trust, and which are designed to help people change the way they see one another and one another's states. These initiatives promote behavioural and language practices where citizens are actively engaged in the practice of redefining identity narratives that they have for one another.

As Figure 1 (see below) shows, this study sits at the intersection of several different research areas with their main connecting point being the agency of citizen actors in constructing peaceful relations between states in the international arena. Friendship studies is an interdisciplinary area of research which involves the 'investigation and theorization of horizontal ties of affinity, concern and action' (Amity, n.d.). Peace and conflict studies go hand in hand. Conflict studies have historically involved the process of exploring the concept of peace through the lens of preventing war, so-called negative peace (Beer, 1990). Peace studies involves studying the nature of conflicts and attempts to address these conflicts through peaceful solutions (Richmond, 2012). These efforts focus on what is described as positive peace, which deals with peace creation instead of conflict prevention exclusively (Galtung, 2012). Public diplomacy involves a variety of communication activities designed to inform and influence public opinion in other countries. The purpose of public diplomacy is to influence views on both formation and execution of foreign policy (Cull, 2006). Public diplomacy also involves helping diverse citizens efforts to understand one another; this is sometimes called citizen or people's diplomacy (PD Alumni Assoc, 2008). Cultural diplomacy is a subset of public diplomacy and involves a variety of activities designed to promote cultural understanding between people (Lenczowski, 2011, p. 19). All these areas involve the role of people in attempting to prevent conflict and foster more peaceful relations between states.

Figure 1.1 People as agents.

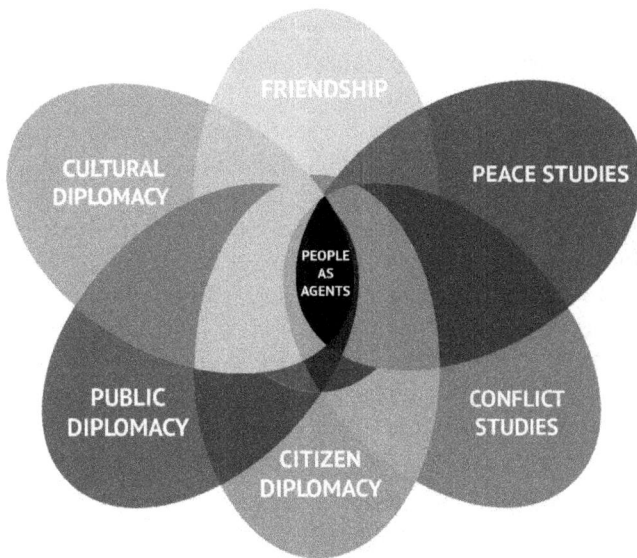

Source: Author.

Epistemologically this book draws upon three critical approaches: critical social constructivism, critical peace studies and practice theory to explore how citizen agents engage in the practice of reconstructing relations between both citizens and states in international relations. All three of these approaches recognise the agency of people in constructing international relations. These critical approaches are valuable because 'critical contributions to IR theory provide a more sophisticated conceptualization of peace' (Richmond, 2008b, p. 121). They also offer a more normative and emancipatory view of peace, where transformation should be the objective (Richmond, 2008b, p. 126). All three of these approaches involve some exploration of the role of behaviour and language in understanding social reality. They also use similar methodological approaches to understand how collective sense is constructed by actors. As such, they emphasize the importance of language and suggest that social facts exist only because of 'human agreements manifest as collective understanding of discourse' (Wallis and Richmond, 2017, p. 424; Searle, 1995). To understand social reality, it is necessary to uncover the social facts that are constructed by and through language, rules and speech acts (Onuf, 1998, p. 66 and Kratochwil, 1989).

The first approach, critical social constructivism, examines how cultural processes are used to construct meaning between actors (Das, 2009; Cho, 2009). There are positivist and interpretivist variants of constructivism within IR. 'Critical constructivism focuses on narratives, discourse and texts as well as everyday micropolitics and practices' (Wallis and Richmond, 2017, p. 423). Constructivists challenge the perception that relations in the international system are fixed with unchanging interests and defined in terms of power. They do not believe conflict and enmity are inevitable (Wendt, 1999). Instead, they see relations in the international system as being socially constructed and continually changing through social processes (Cho, 2009, p. 90). Ideational factors such as culture, norms and ideas play a role in the way actors define their interests (Wendt, 1994) and their policy decisions. Pouliot argues that social facts are central to constructivism. Therefore, social facts constitute the only foundation of reality upon which knowledge can be understood in global politics and social life in general (Pouliot, 2004, p. 320). Critical constructivists see theory as practice and they support research approaches that seek not only to understand the world but to change it. 'By disturbing comfortable understandings of the world and revealing their arbitrariness, can open up an awareness of new possibilities—of our ability to make the world anew' (Gusterson, 1993, p. 8; Weldes et al., 1999, p. 21).

The second approach, critical peace, also focuses on the role of communication and is described as 'post-sovereign peace' which transcends realist notions of territorial sovereignty and which revolves 'around forms of communication designed to facilitate emancipation for both the individual and for others' (Richmond, 2008b, p. 129). This form of emancipatory peace involves communication designed to facilitate empathy between actors through dialogue, ensuring that no person is excluded (Richmond, 2008b, p. 452). Critical peace studies recognise the agency of citizens in reconstructing identity narratives (Richmond, 2008a; MacGinty, 2019). Most of the current scholarship on critical peace explores intrastate conflicts, but it also applies to interstate conflict. Critical approaches 'point to everyday practices, local and social dynamics and other discursive formations of order' (Wallis and Richmond, 2017, p. 424). Critical peace and conflict studies involve 'the role of citizens to reconfigure citizenship rights in order to overcome dominant narratives within relational space' (Williams, 2015, p. 1). This view of peace focuses on care, empathy, solidarity and reconciliation (Jabri, 2007; Keller, 2006; Richmond, 2008a). It is described as an 'everyday form of peace, offering care, respecting but also mediating culture and identity, institutions and customs, providing for needs, and assisting the most marginalised in the local, state, regional and international contexts' (Richmond, 2011, p. 4). The concept of everyday peace moves beyond negative forms of peace towards everyday diplomacy and people-to-people activities (MacGinty, 2014, p. 550). 'Everyday peace is dialogic in the sense that it relies on interaction, social recognition and social responses' (MacGinty, 2014, p. 554; Skeggs, 1997, p. 4). Critical peace theorists emphasize the need for 'bottom-up and people-centric approaches to peace that are contextually sensitive and aware of the possibilities of local agency' (MacGinty, 2019, p. 5). The concept of local includes the diversity of communities and individuals within political society beyond liberal perspectives of elites and civil society (Richmond, 2011, p. 14). This approach desires to understand citizens' perspectives and analysis of conflicts that 'emphasise emotional intelligence, adaptability and agency' (Fregonese, 2012; Mitchell, 2011; Williams, 2015). This is a more sociological and human-focused approach to peace and conflict (MacGinty, 2014, p. 549; Brewer, 2010). Critical peace and conflict studies are 'primarily concerned with the quality and nature of peace in cultural, social, economic, and political terms, ranging from the international system to the state and communities' (ECPR, 2010). This kind of peace draws upon notions of hybridity where there can be multiple identities and ideas presented which are not delineated by states (Walker, 1994; Richmond, 2008b, p. 457). Hybrid peace recognises that multiple ideas can be developed in alternative spaces, including the internet, and through social movements which are not 'patrolled by the state' (Walker, 1994, p. 669-700; Richmond, 2008b, p. 147). As a result, theorists believe that gaining local perspectives requires using ethical, ethnographic and active research methodologies that allow someone to research people where they live and do life (Richmond, 2011, p. 15). This can include everyday activities that happen in the online world.

The third approach, practice theory, suggests that the way actors relate to one another in regard to ideas, culture and norms plays a significant role in how relations are constructed (McCourt, 2016). The practice turn in IR is consistent with the move toward more interpretivist methods of research because it is a reflexive approach, which sees knowledge as socially constructed (Cornut, 2015). The premise of what is considered practice is quite broad and can look at states, social movements and even 'personhood as practices' (Cornut, 2015, p. 1). Central to the practice theory is agency. The concept of agency deals with the ability of people to act independently and make their own choices (Barker, 2005, p. 448). It also recognises the capacity of agents to construct and reconstruct their worlds (Gauntlett, 2004, pp. 93-96). Historically, the dominant perspective among IR scholars is that states are the primary actors in world politics. However, others contend that 'ontologically only individuals can express agency and therefore states are structures rather than agents' (Wallis and Richmond, 2017, p. 424; Wight, 1999; Wight, 2006). As members of political societies, citizens are seen as having agency to be involved in political life. In his book *Politics As a Vocation*, Max Weber recognised the agency of citizens to engage in political activities and took a behaviourist approach to determine whether someone was engaging in politics (Weber, 1919). It is not a person's job description or title that determines whether someone is involved in politics, it is what they are doing. This same idea can be applied to people engaged in international political practices and is often positioned within what is called the 'practice turn in IR'. This approach recognises that not only is the personal political but that the political is also personal (Humphrey et al., 2019). Studies show that a variety of non-state actors have agency to engage in the practice of socially constructing international relations (Finnemore and Sikkink, 1998; Keck and Sikkink, 1998). It is the purpose and practice of the relations and interactions that determine whether there is agency rather than the source of those actions (Bially Mattern, 2011, p. 72; Duvall and Chowdhury, 2011, p. 337-43). Previously, these behavioural approaches were positioned in constructivism by theorists like Wendt, Kratochwil and Onuf and given only peripheral investigation, whereas under practice theory it is the practice of constructing relations that is put front and centre (Cornut, 2015). It is through the practice of interaction and dialogue that one can observe 'socially meaningful politics of action, which in being performed more or less competently, simultaneously embody, act out, and possibly verify background knowledge and discourse in and of the material world' (Adler and Pouliot, 2011 p. 4; Braun, Schindler, Wille, 2018, p. 795). It is through the practice of interaction and social communication that actors promote shared understandings (Risse, 2000; Wallis and Richmond, 2017). These practices of interaction among people are described as a 'social artefact' (Navari, 2011, p. 614; Cornut, 2015, p. 5) that is 'always linked to a collective' (Bueger and Gadinger, 2014, p. 19; and Cornut, 2015, p. 5). These collectives consist of groups of citizens within societies that engage in the practice of international relations through social processes of knowledge creation.

In this study, I show that citizens are using transnational Facebook friendship groups as a forum to reconstruct the narratives they have of one another and one another's states with the hope that these activities will foster more peaceful relations. If it is true that the language used and the way states relate to one another can have an impact on the quality of relations between those states, then it is beneficial to explore how constructs of friendship can result in improved relations between states and citizens that historically have engaged in conflict. The best way to explore whether constructs of friendship result in improved views of a state and citizens of a state is to explore relations between people. Since states are not just institutions but also collectives of their citizens, there is a need to explore whether constructs of friendship between citizens result in improved relations between states. Therefore, a useful way to explore a social construct of friendship is through studying a friendship group between citizens that are from countries that have a history of conflict.

It is my argument that transnational citizen-led friendship groups can serve as a kind of diplomacy. In international relations, diplomacy is one of the main tools used to foster peaceful relations between states. Many things fall under the auspices of diplomacy. This includes everything from formal negotiations to more soft power initiatives like cultural exchanges and public diplomacy. At the heart of diplomacy is promoting goodwill. Acts of goodwill help to foster understanding and trust, which are foundational to good relations between states and citizens of states and can mitigate conflicts. Thomas More said that 'men are bound more adequately by goodwill than by pacts, more strongly by their hearts than by their words' (More reproduced by Wolfers and Martin, 1956, p. 6). There is likely no better gesture of goodwill than friendship. Transnational citizen friendship groups can be a forum for promoting understanding and goodwill between citizens and states.

Public diplomacy is one method used to promote goodwill between states and involves efforts to influence foreign publics' views of states. Views are influenced by language and narratives. In recent years, public diplomacy has been seen as more akin to propaganda (Pigman, 2010). However, it also includes efforts to help people understand a country's history and culture with the hope that it will result in better views and improved relations between the people of those states (Schneider, 2005, p. 147). In recent years, there has been a shift from purely state-centric one-way messaging forms of public diplomacy to two-way dialogic forms of public diplomacy involving a variety of non-state actors, including individual citizens (Nye, 2004). These two-way approaches focus on cultural exchanges and activities that foster conversations between people from different countries. However, there is still little research into what impact these activities have on improving the way transnational citizens view one another and the governments of foreign countries. There has been a lot written about what public diplomacy is, how states are using public diplomacy and how public diplomacy is evolving from a purely one-directional messaging-centred format to a two-way dialogic process. However, there seems to just be an assumption that public diplomacy does what it is designed to do, namely improving a foreign public's views of states and the people of those states. Therefore, there is a need to study what meaning foreign publics give to public diplomacy-type activities and how it impacts them. In recent years, scholars and governmental leaders have begun to question the effectiveness of public diplomacy efforts and call for performance indicators and a means of measuring impact (Carter, 2005; LBJ School, 2010; Banks, 2011). The most helpful way to understand how public diplomacy initiatives affect foreign publics is to ask them. This book seeks to understand what meaning citizens give to transnational citizen-led friendship groups, whether they see these activities as a helpful diplomatic activity and in what ways these activities affect their views.

This study explores people-to-people friendships in the context of transnational Facebook friendship groups and the ways these groups serve as a form of public diplomacy. This book uses the Aristotelian friendship typology to explore what friendship means in the context of transnational citizen Facebook friendship groups and how friendship can serve as a social process of identity construction used by people to foster peaceful relations in the international arena. This book shows that the Facebook friendships in this study have both personal and political purposes and draw upon attributes of utility and pleasure of friendships and can serve as a medium to bridge the differences that exist between people of different cultures by promoting understanding and trust. Seeing friendships this way allows one to observe how efforts to facilitate friendship between states can have a transformative effect. 'The process of building and maintaining friendships actually transforms small pockets of the international system by revealing alternative forms of order as well as alternative patterns of interaction among particular actors' (Koschut and Oelsner, 2014, p. 1).

This research is necessary because the study of friendship in IR is still in its infancy. Alexander Wendt argues that, 'relative to the "enemy", the concept of friend is undertheorized in social theory, and especially in IR where substantial literature exists on enemy images but little on friend images, on enduring rivalries but little on enduring friendships, on the causes of war but little on the causes of peace, and so on' (Wendt, 1999, p. 298). Since Wendt first problematised the prominence of enemy themes in IR, scholars like Smith (2014), Nordin (2018), Oelsner (2014), Koschut (2014), Eznack (2013), Berenskoetter (2014), Van Hoef (2017) and others have begun to research friendship in IR. Most of the literature is still largely theoretical and focuses on reconceptualising and applying the views of 'classical' theorists like Aristotle and Kant to the concepts of friend and enemy in international relations. In addition, much of the literature on friendship in IR still takes state-centric views of friendship. 'Friend' in IR is discussed in much the same way that alliances and security communities are, or in reference to 'special relationships' such as that between the US and the UK. There are still very few scholars exploring the role of citizens in promoting good relations between states. Ignoring the role that citizens play in international relations overlooks the increasing role that citizens have in both perpetrating conflicts and promoting peace between countries. However, more critical and post-structuralist scholars like Nordin and Berenskoetter have led the way in focusing on friendship as a social process involving people as agents. This book extends the boundaries of current scholarship on friendship in IR by exploring the agency of citizens in defining and facilitating positive relations between states and citizens of states. In this capacity, citizens are exercising a complementary agency to states in fostering peaceful relations.

As the nature and types of actors involved in international conflicts change, the types of actors involved in peace and diplomacy must also change. Conflicts in international relations are no longer perpetrated only by sovereign states. The increasing role of non-state actor groups, such as global terror networks, in conflicts all over the world indicates that borders and state sovereignty can no longer be the only focus of IR. Large multinational organisations like the United Nations are struggling to foster peace in the global sphere on their own as is evidenced by ongoing conflicts around the world. Instead, there is finally a recognition that the world is changing and as a result so must the types of actors involved in facilitating peace in international relations.

In this book, critical peace theory is being drawn upon to study bottom-up and people-centric approaches to fostering peaceful relations in interstate conflicts while arguing that the process of reframing identity narratives is happening through a kind of citizen-led public diplomacy in the context of Facebook friendship groups. The findings show that these groups serve as a kind of virtual cultural exchange where people socialise and learn about each other's culture with the intention of countering negative stereotypes, promoting understanding and trust. The goal is to promote more peaceful relations between Libya and the US.

1.2 Aim

This book explores the role that citizens have in improving relations between states through citizen-led friendship groups. In particular, it investigates constructs of friendship between states that historically have been in conflict. If the system is socially constructed rather than fixed, it should be possible to reconstruct relations based on how actors relate. Constructivists see both structure and agency as being important factors in understanding how the international system is constructed (Wendt, 1987). This book is most concerned with the role of citizens as agents in constructing relations between states, rather than focusing on structural relations. It does this by exploring the role that citizens have in improving relations between states through citizen-led friendship groups. This book argues that these citizen-led friendship groups serve as a kind of citizen-led public diplomacy where actors attempt to promote understanding and redefine identity narratives that they have for one another. It is through this process of reframing identity narratives that more peaceful relations are developed. These relational processes are positioned under the umbrella of public diplomacy, because these activities focus more on improving views and images rather than on any negotiation or formal conflict resolution. However, the purpose of improving views between people is not only to give foreign publics a good image of states but ultimately to improve relations between citizens of those states. Improving the foreign publics' image of the US and relations with its people was the main rationale for the US government ramping up its public diplomacy efforts following the terror attacks on the World Trade Center and Pentagon on 9/11 and specifically encouraging citizen diplomats to be a part of the process. The US government recognised the need to counter extremist and anti-American narratives. Enlisting the assistance of citizen diplomats showed a recognition that people have a role in how identity narratives are framed between states. This will be discussed in more detail in the next chapter.

This book involves a case study of relations between American and Libyan citizens and what impact citizen-led Facebook friendship groups have on Libyans' views of the American people and US foreign policy. The practice of engaging in public diplomacy is not done simply to improve foreign publics' views for its own sake, but instead, there is a belief that improved views should translate into improved relations. A study of relations between Libya and the US is interesting because these countries' recent history has been marred by conflict. The country of Libya has historically held an important place in US foreign relations. Years of sanctions against Libya precipitated by Muammar Gaddafi's involvement in state-sponsored terrorism caused years of strained relations between Libya and the US and impacted the views of Libyan citizens. Following the Libyan revolution and the people's overthrow of Gaddafi, there was a hope that relations between Libya and the US would be improved. However, following the revolution, there was a disintegration of the security situation in Libya with the country spiralling into more internal conflict. After the attack on the US Consulate in Benghazi and escalating violence, the US Embassy moved its location to Tunisia and significantly decreased its engagement in Libya.

Although the US government continues to provide limited security assistance in the ongoing conflicts within Libya, there is a significant need for both the government and non-state actors to engage in more effective practices of promoting peaceful relations between people of these states, including activities which confound stereotypes, promote understanding and focus on reframing identity narratives between citizens. The kinds of activities that are utilised in practice should be informed by research and what is seen as most beneficial by the people in that country. While we know very little about what works in terms of state-centric public diplomacy, we know even less about what works in terms of citizen-led public diplomacy. As will be discussed in the coming chapters, the US government recognises that citizen diplomats have an important role to play in improving the views of foreign publics. There is also a perception that citizen-led public diplomacy should be focused on promoting an understanding of values and showing that American values are not necessarily different from the values of people in the Middle East and North Africa. However, there seems to be an assumption that the process of citizens interacting and sharing about one another's culture, religion and history will automatically translate into improved views of the US government and its foreign policy. This book suggests that this is not necessarily the case. However, this book does argue that everyday peacemaking activities like friendships between citizens can and do have some impact on changing the way participants see one another. As such, this research study answers the following questions:

1. What meaning do Libyans give to Facebook friendships?
2. How and through what modes of reasoning/narratives do transnational citizen-led Facebook friendship groups between Libyans and Americans affect Libyans' view of Americans?
3. How and through what modes of reasoning/narratives do transnational citizen-led Facebook friendship groups between Libyans and Americans affect Libyans' views of US foreign policy?

The rationale for exploring these questions is that historically, the US has been one of the forerunners in public diplomacy, partly because as the perceived hegemon in the world arena, it has been the object of criticism and anti-American sentiment around the world. Since 11 September 2011 and the attacks on the World Trade Center and Pentagon, American leaders and critics have suggested that America has an image problem, especially in the Middle East and North Africa (Peterson, 2002). As a result, there has also been a recognition that the US needs to do more to improve its image abroad, especially in the Middle East and North Africa. Following 9/11, the US government began to increase its public diplomacy efforts after allowing them to lapse following the end of the Cold War. Much of the increase in public diplomacy funding in the US happened during the George W. Bush administration. President George W. Bush believed that US image problems, especially in the Middle East, were because America was perceived to have different values than the people of the Middle East (Bush, 2001). Previous surveys of people in the Middle East and North Africa have not confirmed these suspicions. Instead, researchers have found that values were less important than US foreign policy to people's image of the US (Zogby, 2004). Despite these findings, the US government continues to focus its efforts on improving its image abroad. The US State Department is leveraging the soft power of a variety of non-state actors, including individual citizens, for this task. A former undersecretary for the US Department of State, Jim Glassman, was one of the leading proponents of engaging a variety of actors in public diplomacy efforts. 'It is a lot easier to be influential if other people are making the pronouncement and joining the conversation' (Glassman, 2011). He believed the role of the US in convening conversations about different views was a way to 'influence to meet strategic goals' (Glassman, 2011). As a result, the US government began a shift from messaging-centred public diplomacy to more relational-centred public diplomacy, involving citizens and civil society leaders.

With the increasing focus on public diplomacy in recent years has come a shift from what scholars call 'old' public diplomacy to 'new' public diplomacy (Melissen, 2005). Old public diplomacy was characterised by one-directional messaging, while new public diplomacy involves two-directional dialogue and involves citizens and civil society actors. At the centre of this two-directional dialogical approach are efforts to build relationships between citizens through a variety of cultural, educational and business exchanges. Through these exchanges, both face-to-face and virtual, citizens wield a form of soft power. A country's soft power rests with its culture, its political values and its foreign policies (Nye, 2011, p.84). As such, relationships are the new currency of public diplomacy.

If relationships are now seen as an important component of public diplomacy, then fostering friendships between people of different nations could have more impact on the public's views than existing efforts. Friendship groups are a powerful mechanism of goodwill. However, building friendships between people from different countries was much more difficult before the advent of the internet. In addition, social media, in particular, has changed the way friendships are made and has helped to bridge the geographical divide that previously existed between people from different countries (Saudi Gazette, 2012; Digital Age, 2017). Through social media platforms like Facebook, Twitter, Instagram and others, the world truly is within people's reach.

It is not uncommon for people to have Facebook friends and other social media connections with people all over the world. In these online worlds, people can explore, socialise and develop friendships with people who live a world away. But how beneficial are these connections? Are Facebook friendships the same as face-to-face friendships? If not, how are they different, and what value do people place on these online friendships? Do they help promote understanding between people from different cultures, and if so, in what way? In the end, as an IR scholar, one also must ask, what impact do these friendships have on relations between states? This is the rationale for conducting this research project. Research needs to be done into understanding what meaning participants give friendship diplomacy efforts between people of different states, especially with those that have a history of strained relationships like the US and Libya. Exploring friendship diplomacy in the context of everyday activities like transnational citizen-led friendship groups provides rich insights into how social media platforms are being used as both a messaging and dialogic form of public diplomacy. It also provides insights into the value of citizen-led initiatives and how these initiatives impact the way people view another country, its people, its values and whether these cross-cultural friendships translate into better views of a country's foreign policies.

1.3 Methodology

This research is designed to explore how Libyans understand friendship in the context of Facebook friendship groups with Americans and the ways that discussing things like history, religion, current events and culture improve relations. There is also an interest in determining the way in which these everyday social activities are viewed by participants as a form of diplomacy which translates to improved views among participants. This study is interested in what meaning Libyan citizens give to their interactions with American citizens in the context of Facebook friendships, especially Facebook friendship groups that were specifically created to foster more positive and peaceful relations between Libyans and Americans. The intention is to see in what ways the narratives that take place in these groups impact on the attitudes and views of Libyans toward the American people and US foreign policy and whether the participants see these activities as impacting relations between their states.

Following the Libyan revolution, two Facebook friendship groups were started by Libyan and American citizens to promote understanding and friendly relations between Americans and Libyans. These groups are the Libya American Friendship Association and Libyan and Americans United for Friendship and Peace. These groups, and similar friendship groups between people of other cultures, serve as fora for a kind of virtual cultural diplomacy. However, what is unique about these groups is that they are not created under the auspices of any governmental organisation. Some things shared in the group, like information about holidays and exchange opportunities, are similar to the kinds of things that the US Embassy posts on their Facebook page as part of their public diplomacy efforts. However, the difference seems to be the dialogic nature of the friendship groups and the lack of any overt governmental political agenda. The purpose of these groups is more about promoting cultural understanding and friendly relations and a sense of solidarity between Libyans and Americans. This research study involves conducting exploratory qualitative case study research into how Libyans construct meaning around their history of strained relations with America and their purposes for participating in Facebook friendships with Americans. This case study was chosen because there is a need for a better understanding of how public diplomacy impacts the views and attitudes of foreign publics, which would allow state and non-state actors to engage in public diplomacy initiatives from a more informed perspective. We know very little about what kinds of activities are most beneficial in influencing attitudes of foreign publics and cultivating more peaceful relations. In addition, there is even less known about citizen diplomacy, and there are currently no known empirical studies attempting to understand how Facebook friendships between citizens can be used as a form of public diplomacy to improve relations between states in international relations.

This research uses a qualitative research design with a critical social constructivist and interpretivist approach because central to this research is the view that actors have a role in constructing meaning about others, including states and their citizens. This is sometimes referred to as 'meaning-making'. This idea suggests that meanings are negotiated and identities are elaborated through the process of social interactions between people (Hare-Mustin and Marecek, 1990; West and Zimmerman, 1991). This study is interested in what meaning Libyan citizens give to their interactions with American citizens in the context of Facebook friendships, especially Facebook friendship groups that were specifically created to foster more positive and peaceful relations between Libyans and Americans.

The intent of qualitative research involving human subjects is for the researcher to examine a social situation or interaction by allowing the researcher to enter the world of others and attempt to gain a holistic understanding (Merriam, 2009; Maxwell, 2013; Patton, 2015; Bloomberg and Volpe, 2016). Qualitative research allows for deeper exploration of a phenomenon and the meaning that participants give to that phenomenon through a process of extracting and interpreting the meaning of experience (Merriam, 2009; Denzin and Lincoln, 2013a and 2013b). Within social science more broadly, qualitative research is most closely aligned with the social constructivist paradigm. However, within the discipline of IR, constructivism can be both positivist and rely upon quantitative methods or interpretivist and use qualitative methods in its research. Interpretivist researchers tend to prefer qualitative research methods that foster conversation and reflection, which allows the researcher and participants to reflexively explore the nature of things. This research uses an interpretivist methodology to understand how actors engage in identity construction. Interpretivists see meaning as being constructed socially and experientially through a dialogic process (Schwartz-Shea and Yanow, 2012). Interpretivists emphasize the role of language and discourse in understanding how actors construct meaning together. Interpretivists desire to explain and understand the social meanings that 'underpin political activity, especially "how the processes of social representations are formed and internalized" in the realm of the international' (Bevir and Daddow, 2015, p. 275). Part of the way sense is made of a social phenomenon is through studying the language used between actors, because language shapes society and society shapes language. Discourse is a 'social activity of making meaning with language and other symbolic systems in some particular kind of situation or setting' (Lemke, 1995, p. 8). Discourse analysis sees the process of understanding discourse as a social practice (Fairclough and Wodak, 1997). Therefore, this approach tends to use narrative research methods that focus on interpreting discourse in text and talk.

Interpretivists also see the qualitative research process as inherently subjective and see the researcher and participants as being linked together in a reflexive process of knowledge creation (Schwartz-Shea and Yanow, 2012). Reflexivists contend that the very character of knowledge is inseparable and dependent upon the social position and organisational practice of the researcher (Jackson, 2016, p. 174). This process of reflexivity makes 'truth' situational, and part of the research process involves recognising that multiple truths by the individual actors can be conflicting and contradictory (Schwartz-Shea and Yanow, 2012). Furthermore, 'they see all talk through which people generate meaning' as contextual (Dahlgren, 1988, p. 292). The reflexivity is particularly necessary in research involving human subjects where the researcher is present within the research process and the co-construction of meaning happens between both participants and the researcher. Even when researchers use a semi-structured approach to interviewing, they still make decisions about which topics to cover in the interview and guide the dialogue, including making decisions on when to continue down the path of discussion on a particular subject and when to move on. In addition, the process of interpreting the data is also reflexive and quite subjective. However, by using a systematic process of coding and theme identification, the research process becomes more rigorous and thereby allows researchers to show how they identified the particular themes that they did (Braun and Clarke, 2013). These themes will be directly related to the research question and topic being discussed. Interpretivist research also integrates well with more critical research designs, because scholars using critical research approaches in IR research have a desire to engage more marginalised voices, including gaining the perspectives of non-western actors, as is happening in this study.

Before the project was started, the process of ethical review was carried out and approved by the Ethics Committee in the School of Politics and International Relations at the University of Nottingham. In addition, before the interviews took place, the participants gave their informed consent to participate in the interviews and for their comments to be included in publications.

This research makes an original contribution to the study of IR by using the little-used methodology of focus group interviews for the empirical portion of the research. Focus groups are a beneficial method for exploratory qualitative research. Focus groups can be particularly helpful in research that explores everyday narratives in international politics (Stanley, 2016). Focus groups represent a kind of dialogical research method. In this method, the goal of the researchers is to facilitate the production of knowledge by and for the subjects (Padilla, 1993). Through this process, researchers can observe the 'commonsense conceptions and taken-for-granted assumptions they share' (Gamson, 1992, p. 193). Schultz calls this intersubjectivity and suggests that others see the world the same way and meaning is defined socially, not individually (1967, p. 192). Focus groups are the most beneficial way to learn how actors construct meaning together around a given phenomenon. 'Focus groups are group discussions exploring a specific set of issues' (Kitzinger and Barbour, 1999, p. 4). Barbour and Kitzinger suggest that focus group interviews allow researchers to explore how accounts are explained, censured and changed through social interaction based on group norms (1999, p. 5). They argue further that focus groups are better for exploring how points of view are constructed or expressed within a group compared to other methods (1999, p. 5). In focus groups, 'collective sense is made, meanings are negotiated and identities are elaborated through the process of social interactions between people' (Kitzinger and Barbour, 1999, p. 65; Hare-Mustin and Marecek, 1990; West and Zimmerman, 1991). Focus groups are also especially useful for critical researchers who are cognizant of power dynamics in the research process. 'Compared with most traditional methods, including the one-to-one interview, focus groups inevitably reduce the researcher's power and control' (Wilkinson, 1999, p. 70). Since central to this book is understanding the role that dialogue has in friendship groups and how the dialogue impacts Libyans' views of Americans and US foreign policy, it makes the most sense to use a dialogical research method to explore this topic.

Some researchers differentiate between focus groups and group interviews, suggesting that the former has more interaction between participants (Barbour and Kitzinger, 1999, p. 4). Bloor et al. (2001, pp. 42-43) suggest that the primary objective of focus groups is not to elicit the group's answers but to stimulate discussion and then, after subsequent analysis, to understand the meanings and norms which underlie the group's answers. Much of the interaction is perceived through nonverbal behaviour, which becomes less clear in online focus groups. Some scholars have suggested that the lack of nonverbal communication in online forums affects the quality and depth of data (Graffigna and Bosio, 2006; Greenbaum, 1998). However, Lijadi and van Schalkwyk (2015) disagree with this perspective in their study, arguing that many linguistic characteristics were mirroring the spoken word such as photos, songs, videos, emoticons and links to other websites.

Both the face-to-face focus group and the Facebook focus groups that I conducted included some level of interaction between participants, including discussion on some answers, building upon one another's answers, disagreements, comments and interactive gestures. In addition, in the online focus group, some participants posted photos of historical and cultural significance and that were unique to the region of Libya they were from. They also posted links to news articles and emojis such as happy faces and thumbs-ups, while one participant even posted a short survey as a follow-up to one of my questions, reflecting that it was not a passive process but an interactive process of knowledge creation. These 'speech acts in the participant's responses alerted the facilitator to the mood in the group and helped with interpreting the group dynamics, processes, and meanings' (Lijadi and van Schalkwyk, 2015, p. 7; Stewart and Williams, 2005). Based on all these factors, the focus group interviews conducted for this research meet the definition of focus groups.

There are several advantages of using focus groups over other research methods. The first is that they have proven to be a particularly useful research method in accessing groups that are considered hard to reach, such as members of ethnic minority groups or people considered marginalised (Chiu and Knight, 1999). The second is that the most common purpose for focus group interviews is 'for an in-depth exploration of a topic about which little is known' (Stewart and Shamdasani, 1990, p. 102). Since this study involves both a hard-to-reach group and an in-depth exploration of Libyan perspectives on Facebook friendships with Americans, it is a suitable research method.

Both face-to-face and Facebook focus group interviews were done with Libyans to explore the impact of friendships between Libyans and Americans. One pilot face-to-face focus group was conducted with Libyans in Denver, Colorado, and another focus group interview was organised and held on Facebook. Denver was chosen to be the location of the face-to-face focus group because the founder of the Libyan American Friendship Association lived in the Denver area a the time of the interviews. In addition, because of the unstable security situation in Libya, I was unable to travel to Libya to conduct interviews. However, I wanted to be sure to gain the perspectives of Libyan's living in Libya, so I needed another approach. Since this study deals with interactions on Facebook, it made the most sense to conduct the focus group as well. This research is also interesting because it doesn't just study how social media is useful in improving relations, it also uses social media to conduct some of the focus group interviews. It uses an innovative form of data collection by using a Facebook focus group interview, which is conducted completely online through a private group on Facebook. The decision was made to interview Libyans about their perspectives because there is an increasing call for insights into non-western perspectives and Libyans are especially interesting because they are an under-researched demographic. In addition, this research provides helpful insights for the US State Department on ways to improve their practice of public diplomacy towards Libya. This research also provides helpful information for policymakers to understand how citizen initiatives are received and how Libyans' views of the American people and the American government are affected through Facebook friendship groups with Americans. In addition, the information elicited in the focus group interviews also includes Libyans' perspectives on the types of activities they find most beneficial to improving their views and why those are beneficial. Furthermore, gaining the perspectives of Libyan citizens is also valuable because it can have an emancipatory effect by empowering a neglected population to share their views. This book does not include the perspectives of the American participants in these friendship groups because the decision was made to focus on a deeper exploration of the Libyan perspectives rather than focusing on a shallower exploration of both the American and Libyan perspectives. As such, this study does not provide a comparative approach of views of both American and Libyan citizens. In addition, because Libya is still suffering from internal conflict and does not have one centralised government, there is little happening in terms of foreign policy toward America. As such, gaining the perspectives of the American participants is left for future research.

Figure 1.2 Language escalation framework.

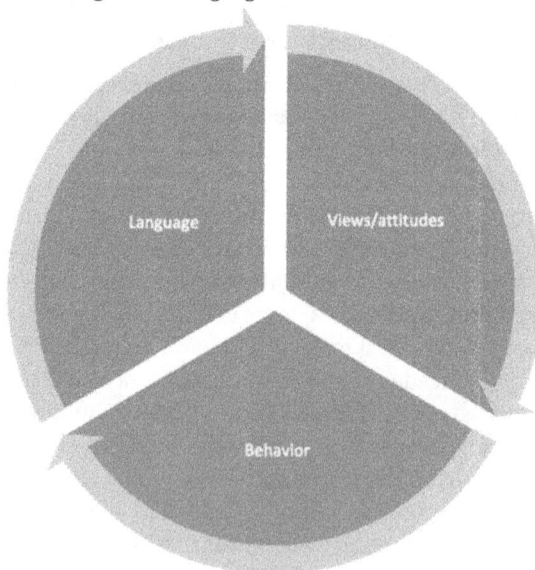

Source: Author.

The analytical framework guiding this research is the premise that language affects views/attitudes and views/attitudes affect behaviour. These concepts suggest that the language and behaviours used in interactions between people actually reinforce certain behaviours and impact the quality of relations. When one actor treats another as an enemy, the most common response is for the other actor to see them as a threat and respond in kind. This enemy behaviour becomes a cyclical process with each actor treating the other as an enemy which can culminate in a full-blown interstate conflict, which is reflected in Figure 4 (see below). If it is true that treating another as an enemy can lead to conflict, then actors treating one another as friends should be able to contribute to more positive or peaceful relations.

Libyans were recruited through a structured snowball sampling method. Snowball sampling is sometimes referred to as a 'network or chain sampling' and refers to a situation where participants are asked to refer other individuals whom they know that fit the criteria of the study (Miles and Huberman, 1994; Patton, 2015). Snowball sampling can be particularly suited to gain a diversity of perspectives through an 'in-depth and contextualised exploration of a central phenomenon' (Maxwell, 2013, p. 327). The criteria for this study were as follows:

- All participants were Libyans.
- All participants participated in Facebook friendship groups with American citizens.

The research approach involved recruiting participants from two Facebook friendship groups. The research sample included 38 individuals. Included in the sample were individuals who lived in Libya, the US and other locations. In qualitative research, researchers do not attempt to include a certain percentage of the population being researched, as is the case in quantitative research. Instead, efforts are made to use case selection approach to find participants who represent a cross-section of the population. In this research, a short survey was used as an effort to find both female and male participants from a variety of adult age groups and include participants from the largest areas and population centres in Libya. The purpose of qualitative case selection is to reflect the diversity within the population being studied rather than attempting to recruit a representative sample (Kuzel, 1992; Mays and Pope, 1995). It is helpful for group members to share at least one important characteristic (Barbour, 2007). Rather than focusing on random sampling techniques, the researcher interviews as many participants as necessary to reach what is known as the saturation point. The saturation point is the point at which no new answers are being given. In this research, focus group interviews were continued until the data reached a saturation point.

This study included participants from the two largest cities of Tripoli and Benghazi and individuals from other smaller cities like Derna, Shahhat, and Sabratha. All these cities are located in the north of Libya, along the coast. Unfortunately, there were no participants from the more rural areas of Libya which are located in the south. However, those areas are sparsely populated by comparison to the north. Since the largest percentage of the ethnic minorities like Tuareg and Amazigh in Libya live in the south, this research is limited because it did not gain their perspectives. To recruit participants, a message was posted on the Facebook walls of the Libyan and American Friendship Association and Libyans and Americans United for Friendship and Peace. The message included a link to a short survey through Google forms which asked demographic questions and included the information sheet providing the details and purposes for the project, which informed participants about their right to refuse to participate or withdraw from the study. The participants were asked to include their names and email address if they consented to participate. The demographic questions included sex, age, where they were from in Libya and whether they have American friends.

1.4 Structure of the book

This book consists of eight chapters where the concept of friendship relations between Libyans and Americans is conceptualised and empirically investigated. This book positions transnational citizen-led Facebook friendship groups as a kind of citizen-led public diplomacy designed to improve relations between states by promoting understanding between citizens and by improving the way these citizens see one another and one another's states. These friendship groups serve as a social process of identity construction where, through processes of interaction and dialogue, the members of these groups reframe the identity narratives they have of one another. It also explores the question in what ways these groups have any impact on the way citizens view the foreign policy of the states. In addition, it discusses this research in the context of a dialogic form of diplomacy rather than purely a messaging form of public diplomacy. There is a brief discussion of the historical context of conflictual relations between Libya and America. There is also an explanation of the research design including methodological framework, data collection methods, case selection, contextual nature of data and process of data analysis.

The second chapter is a literature review around the evolution of public diplomacy from what is called 'old' to 'new' by highlighting the change from a pure state-centric messaging-centred activity to a dialogic activity involving a variety of both state and non-state actors. The strands of discussion include public diplomacy as a form of soft power, US public diplomacy, the importance of understanding culture and the shift from pure message-centric media to social media platforms.

In the third chapter, there is a discussion of the socially constructed nature of views of friend and enemy and ways that treating others as enemy can actually lead to conflict. There is also a discussion of how friendship can serve as a conduit of peaceful relations by allowing people to bridge the divide that exits between people of different cultures. This chapter draws upon the Aristotelian friendship typology to discuss the different types of friendship and how those can serve as a social process of identity construction that allows people to promote understanding, dispel stereotypes and foster trust. There is finally a discussion of the ways that the Aristotelian view of friendship and a shared life can be observed in the context of social media platforms.

The fourth chapter provides a case description of the historical conflict between Libya and the US. This chapter starts with a discussion of relations between Libya and the US during the time of King Idris Senussi and how Muammar Gaddafi's coup in 1969 resulted in the severe degradation of US and Libya relations. There is a discussion of Gaddafi's involvement in several acts of state-sponsored terrorism, including the LaBelle Disco bombing and Lockerbie bombing, which resulted in the loss of American lives and caused a further decline in Libyan and American relations. The resulting sanctions from the US and the UN against Libya for many years caused Libya to be relegated to outsider status in the world community. The chapter also includes a discussion of the international community's efforts to reform Libya, including eventually welcoming Libya back into the world community. Furthermore, there is a discussion of the subsequent Libyan revolution and Libya's current ongoing military skirmishes for power and its failure to fully transition to a democratic state. This chapter also includes a discussion of the recent security situation in Libya and the Trump administration's decision to include Libya on the list of countries banned from travelling to the US and its impact on ongoing relations between the US and Libya.

In the fifth chapter, the findings from the focus group interviews are reported. The chapter starts with an explanation of the topics covered in the interviews and the designation system used to delineate participants in the face-to-face focus group interview from the Facebook interview. This includes a discussion of the overarching themes identified. These themes are: meaning of friendship; differences between same-culture and cross-cultural friendships; open-mindedness and respect are key; online versus face-to-face friendships; impact of media on views; cultural exchange promotes understanding; trust-building and inclusive communication; capacity-building and educational programmes; civil society is more important than government; US foreign policy is the problem. Under each theme, the actual quotes and paraphrases from the focus group interviews are shown with an accompanying explanation of the answers.

In the sixth chapter, the findings and themes are identified, interpreted and analysed in relation to the theoretical literature on public diplomacy and friendship. Since this research process is inductive, the reliance on the theoretical literature serves to help explain the answers given by focus group participants in relation to the greater understanding of the topics of public diplomacy and friendship in IR literature. The purpose is not to test an existing theory but to attempt to understand how friendship groups are being used in a citizen-led public diplomacy capacity. This is particularly important because both the topics of public diplomacy and friendship in IR are in a state of flux and this research is intentionally pushing the boundary of these topics. There are quite divergent perspectives on how to define public diplomacy and friendship, which I discuss at length in the two literature chapters. The culmination of the iterative process involves interpreting what the participants say about the topics of public diplomacy and friendship between countries that have a history of conflict and translating that into conclusions about whether these activities help improve participants' views and promote understanding between states. As such, the findings are organised in a narrative way under the respective research questions. The participants discuss that there are different kinds of friendships with some being more useful and others because people enjoy them. They also discuss the fact that deeper friendships are possible between people of different cultures but that they require some face-to-face time to develop. The Facebook friendships do not generally rise to the level of deeper forms of friendship but instead include attributes of friendships of utility and pleasure, where participants use it as a forum to socialise and learn about the US and the American people. They also have attributes of political friendships where participants use these groups to promote understanding between people with the hope that these friendships will result in improved relations between Libya and the US They additionally serve as a social process of identity construction where participants actively engage in a process of dialoguing and educating one another with the intent to dispel stereotypes, reframe narratives and foster more trust and respect between their countries. The participants note that these friendships serve as a kind of virtual cultural exchange and have some impact on their views of the American people, but they find face-to-face interactions as much more helpful in promoting understanding, improved views and more positive relations. They see cooperative civil society and educational projects as more impactful in improving their views. However, they do not see exchange programmes or friendships as having any impact on their views of American foreign policy, but instead they separate their views of the American people from US foreign policy.

Finally, in the seventh chapter, there is a review of the overall book, including the literature chapters, methodology, case description of the conflict between Libya and the US, findings from the focus group interviews, synthesis of the findings with the theoretical literature, conclusions drawn and recommendations for further research. The overall conclusions are that the Libyan participants in these Facebook friendship groups do see these groups as serving a kind of peacemaking and diplomatic function, where they engage in a process of cultural understanding with the intent to dispel stereotypes and promote trust and understanding which are seen as essential to improving relations between Libya and the US. They recognise their own agency in the social process of identity construction and the need for more concerted efforts to facilitate education among more Libyan citizens because they see these types of cultural exchanges as valuable in promoting open-mindedness.

The participants recognise that cultural differences can serve as somewhat of a barrier to relations between Libyans and Americans, but only if people are not open-minded in the midst of the difference. Therefore, they recognise the need for more citizens to be engaged in these kinds of cultural diplomacy activities that promote understanding and open-mindedness. A lack of open-mindedness is what tends to create negative perceptions. Online friendships serve as a kind of first step and virtual cultural exchange between Libyan and American citizens. It is a forum to promote general understanding about history, culture and religion, which can foster trust and respect. Trust and respect are essential to fostering more positive relations. However, they recognise that online and Facebook can only take people so far, so they value face-to-face over online activities and would like to see more face-to-face exchanges being facilitated by civil society organisations. These activities are viewed as helpful in improving the Libyans' image of the US and its people, but do not necessarily translate into improved views of US foreign policy. Instead, the US government must recognise that their image is tainted by its foreign policy priorities, including both past and current. The most pressing issue for Libyan citizens is the travel ban, which is not seen as something impacting the Libyan government but instead as directed at the Libyan people, lumping all Libyan citizens into a category of enemy simply because they are from Libya. So, it is important that the US government not just focus its efforts on promoting a positive image of US culture and values while neglecting its foreign policy. In the end, the implication for US foreign policy is that the US government could do more to engage in foreign policy priorities that are not seen as arbitrary and unfair toward the Libyan people. In addition, the US government should consider investing more in cultural diplomacy and civil society projects, which bring Americans and Libyans face-to-face which provide opportunities to cooperate on shared initiatives because, in the end, these are the kinds of activities the Libyan people see as most valuable to improving their views and relations between Libya and the US.

In the next chapter, there will be a discussion of the literature on public diplomacy, including its evolution from messaging to dialogue and a discussion of how social media networks can be a useful medium for engaging in public diplomacy.

Chapter 2

Public Diplomacy

2.1 Introduction

Public diplomacy is targeted communication with people in other countries with the intention of influencing their attitudes and views. There are a variety of things that fit within the definition of public diplomacy with some scholars focusing more on messaging approaches under the auspices of terms like "branding" or "image". While others focus more on relational public diplomacy approaches involving dialogue and interactions. In addition, some scholars explore public diplomacy purely through a state-centric lens. However, nonstate actors also play a key role in public diplomacy but still remain largely neglected in public diplomacy research. However, there is increasing recognition for the important complimentary role they provide to state-centric approaches, and therefore should not be neglected in terms of research and scholarship. Some see citizen engagement as a new phenomenon. However, this chapter will show that citizen engagement in public diplomacy is not new, and citizen involvement has been a part of the definition from its earliest conceptualisations. Instead, there has been little evaluation done of public diplomacy in general, and the scholarship that does exist has been primarily focused on state-centric approaches. What is needed is more engagement in scholarship on the role of nonstate actors and some understanding of how effective nonstate actor or citizen public diplomacy is.

This chapter explores the evolution of public diplomacy from being a purely state-centric messaging activity to a more dialogic activity involving a host of actors. Central to this mode of public diplomacy are non-state actors. Non-state actors include a variety of civil society leaders, celebrities, business leaders, education leaders and private citizens. This chapter seeks to explore the role of independent citizens in public diplomacy efforts and discusses the role that social media has in facilitating and reinforcing the agency of citizens in these kinds of efforts. This chapter lays the foundation for an upcoming discussion of friendship as a form of relational public diplomacy and whether citizen-led Facebook friendship groups between Libyans and Americans are a form of public diplomacy which impacts Libyans' views toward Americans and US foreign policy.

This chapter is organised around the following subtopics: (a) definition of public diplomacy, (b) public diplomacy as a form of soft power, (c) US public diplomacy, (d) shift from messaging to dialogue, (e) role of non-state actors, (f) importance of understanding culture, (g) new media, (h) understanding the impact. This chapter culminates with a concluding summary.

The review of the literature in this chapter shows that the kind of Facebook friendship groups that are explored in this study fit within the theoretical discussion of the role of citizens, networks and social media to public diplomacy efforts discussed in the literature. The new public diplomacy paradigm recognises that interaction and citizen involvement have always been intended as a part of public diplomacy efforts from its earliest conceptions (Brown, 2010). The purpose of public diplomacy is to improve foreign public views of a state's people, culture and foreign policy through efforts designed to promote understanding. The purpose of public diplomacy is ultimately to foster more peaceful relations between states and citizens of states. This is facilitated through a variety of messaging and exchange activities that foster communication, dialogue and interaction. This process of interaction and dialogue is important to promoting understanding, helping to dispel myths and reframe identity narratives. This chapter also shows that social media, networks and virtual exchanges between citizens can and do have an important role to play in public diplomacy efforts. However, the literature also indicates that there is a need to understand whether these kinds of virtual public diplomacy initiatives, like Facebook friendships, contribute to improving foreign publics' views. Therefore, this research study fills an important gap in the research by gaining the insights of Libyan citizens on how citizen-led Facebook friendship groups impact their views.

2.2 Definition of public diplomacy

Like much of diplomatic practice, public diplomacy has gone through changes both in definition and practice. Under the Westphalian system, traditional diplomacy was seen as a set of activities that take place entirely between sovereign states. Public diplomacy is different from traditional diplomacy because in public diplomacy citizens of foreign publics are the primary targets of messaging and influencing. Some scholars look at public diplomacy through a more communication-centric lens, seeing it as overlapping with public relations and public affairs (Cull, 2006). Public diplomacy overlaps with the disciplines of International Relations, Communications, Public Relations, and Event Marketing. This diversity of disciplines studying public diplomacy contributes to a lack of consensus on how public diplomacy is to be defined (D'Hooghe, 2015). The purpose of public diplomacy is to promote a positive and attractive image of the values, culture and policies of a state. However, it is not about promoting a good image for its own sake but instead facilitating positive relations and preventing conflicts. The purpose is to improve the image or reputation of the sending country as a way to shape the policy of the receiving country (USC Center for Public Diplomacy, n.d.). One could suggest that the hope is that if the receiving country likes the sending country and sees them in a positive light, then they are less likely to engage in a conflict with them. In the end, effectiveness of public diplomacy is measured by minds changed (Nye, 2019).

During the 1960s, Edmund Gullion of the Fletcher School of Law and Diplomacy was credited with coining the term public diplomacy to characterise the informational and educational programmes that were instituted by government and non-governmental organisations. People-to-people interactions were central to Gullion's views of public diplomacy. Gullion said, 'What is important today is interactions of groups, peoples and cultures beyond national borders to think about foreign affairs' (Gullion quoted in Brown, 2010). Even from its earliest definitions, there was a recognition of the importance of people influencing one another through interactions. The relational side of public diplomacy has been reinforced by US State Department Under Secretary for Public Diplomacy and Public Affairs Judith McHale when she said:

> I think that the more we can have people having direct conversations with each other — and through those conversations and initiatives, through history of cultures we can learn about each other and if we do that, at the people-to-people level, that will provide us with a path to a more peaceful and prosperous future. So it's a key part of what we're trying to do, to really have people engage with each other, to learn about each other (Brown, 2010).

Both in the past and present, public diplomacy has had the underlying purpose of fostering more peaceful relations between states with interactions between people as being foundational to those efforts. This is the approach to public diplomacy that this book takes.

Despite its earliest focus on interactions, much of public diplomacy in recent years has been positioned as a messaging-centred activity and described as a state-centric activity often difficult to distinguish from propaganda because it was one-directional. Pigman (2010) suggests that the purpose of both propaganda and public diplomacy is to attempt to influence people's attitudes and opinions. However, today, many see propaganda as a 'deceitful and dangerous' practice (Pigman, 2010, p. 123). In addition, he suggests that the key difference between the two is trust (Pigman, 2005, p. 123). Whether foreign publics develop trust often depends upon whether they see the language used as being in the service of propaganda (Chomsky, 1992).

There is a fine line between information and propaganda. People tend to be wary of propaganda (Nye, 2004). In 1937, Britain's foreign secretary, Anthony Eden, said 'it is perfectly true, of course, that good cultural propaganda cannot remedy the damage done by bad foreign policy, but it is no exaggeration to say that even the best of diplomatic policies may fail if it neglects the task of interpretation and persuasion which modern conditions impose' (quoted in Nye, 2004, p. 101). Therefore, the ultimate purpose must be to change foreign publics' views. This is the reason that one-directional messaging is less effective than interactions. In interactions, people make judgements on whether they believe the people who are communicating with them are trustworthy. It the hearer perceives the speaker as trustworthy, they are more likely to believe and be influenced by what is said.

This book takes the position that public diplomacy is distinct from propaganda because it involves a variety of activities. In current practice, public diplomacy can be state- or citizen-led, with a variety of activities falling under the auspices of public diplomacy as set out in Figure 2 (see below). Things like media messaging, cultural programmes, language programmes, and even civil society projects can all be used to improve foreign publics' views. However, historically, public diplomacy has been viewed primarily as a top-down process that governments use to influence the attitudes of foreign publics due in part to the view of state as actor in international relations. It is seen as an important tool of statecraft that involves explaining a country's foreign policies to foreign publics (Van Ham, 2005). Melissen suggests that a more precise definition is one given by Paul Sharp, where he posits that public diplomacy is a process 'where direct relationships with people in a country are pursued to advance the interests and extend the values of those being represented' (2005, p. 11; Sharp, 2005, p. 106). This definition is more consistent with Gullion's views of public diplomacy as being about interaction rather than just messaging. This is also the perspective that this book takes. Melissen's choice of Sharp's definition is consistent with his argument that relationships are now the preferred method for public diplomacy.

Although citizens are primarily involved in influencing other citizens, at times, their behaviour involves engaging with foreign state leaders as well, especially when the citizens are participating in a cultural exchange programme and are being hosted by a foreign government. This study is concerned with the people-to-people activities of citizens that are using social media to impact the views of other citizens.

Public diplomacy can look different in diverse cultural contexts, and the way it is used varies from state to state. For example, Melissen (2005) notes that in Germany, public diplomacy is focused on increasing approval levels. In China, it is primarily focused on economics and image (D'Hooghe, 2015). In the global south, meanwhile, economics is the primary motivation for public diplomacy (Melissen, 2005).

Figure 2.1 Public diplomacy processes.

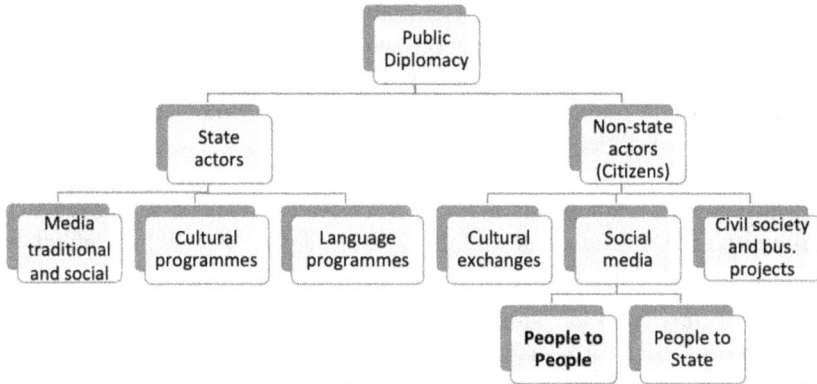

Source: Author.

There are a variety of activities that can fall under the auspices of public diplomacy. Both state and citizens have a role to play in public diplomacy. Public diplomacy is not just designed to improve a country's image for its own sake but to foster foreign publics' views of a state's foreign policy, its culture and people, with the intention of fostering more peaceful relations between states.

2.3 Public diplomacy as a form of soft power

Public diplomacy is founded on the belief that knowledge and information are power. The best way to empower people is to provide them with clear information so they can make informed judgements. Public diplomacy is seen as a form of soft power because it focuses on attraction by promoting positive images rather than on coercion or fiscal incentives (Nye, 2008). Soft power is defined as 'the ability to get what you want through attraction rather than coercion or payments' (Nye, 2004, x). Policies do not produce soft power if they do not attract others (Nye, 2019). While at the same time, domestic and foreign policies that appear hypocritical, arrogant or are based on a narrow view of national interest can actually undermine soft power (Nye, 2019). Attraction depends not only on official policies but also activities of civil society and other actors (Nye, 2019). Some would suggest that both hard and soft power are important to foreign policy because they both influence behaviour. 'The distinction between them is a matter of degree' (Henrikson, 2005, p. 73). However, soft power is like the carrot, and hard power is the stick (Nye, 2004). Arguably, when speaking of efforts to influence foreign publics, using a carrot is likely to be more effective than a stick, because citizens are not bound by strategic priorities that governments are. So in this way, using soft power to attract is much more valuable. Soft power is viewed differently according to cultural contexts. Further, each country has very different views on how they perceive another's soft power. How a country uses its soft power affects the way a country is perceived in terms of its culture, political values and foreign policy. Nye (2004) suggests that when people see a country's policies as legitimate, their soft power increases. Advocates of soft power suggest that seduction can have more of an impact than coercion (Nye, 2004). However, its subjective nature makes it difficult to measure effectiveness (McClory, 2017). As such, there are limits on how impactful one can say soft power is because its effectiveness largely depends on how it is received by audiences. This is why it is important to do studies like this, which ask foreign audiences how initiatives impact them.

The new currency of soft power is building networks and fostering collaboration (McClory, 2017). It is through these networks that interaction and communication happen best. 'Narratives become the currency of soft and attractive power' (Nye, 2010). Sharing about culture and values is part of what creates interest and attraction to another culture. This is what makes exchanges, both face-to-face and virtual, more effective than broadcasting (Nye, 2011, p. 111). The digital revolution has eroded traditional borders and allowed a variety of actors to use soft power to engage in public diplomacy through a variety of communication mediums (McClory, 2017). This book shares this view and explores soft power that is used in the context of online social networks.

Soft power can be leveraged in both positive and negative ways by both state and non-state actors. 'Those actors affect both the general public and governing elites in other countries and create an enabling or disabling environment for government policies' (Nye, 2011, p. 101). From an American perspective, these soft power efforts and interactions are strategically important in advancing the goals of democracy, liberty and development (Nye, 2011, p. 102). However, some note a decline in US soft power. For example, Nye (2004) suggests that the US government's use of language condemning all Muslims after 9/11 has also been a factor and certainly has not served to bolster the US government's persuasive impact in Muslim countries. Instead, it has stirred up anti-American sentiment and even has been leveraged by extremist groups in their claims that the US is against them. Further, Trump's travel ban of individuals from eight countries, including six Muslim-majority countries, often referred to as the Muslim ban, has only further exacerbated the situation.

McClory asserts that other factors are contributing to the decline of US soft power. One of them is the US ending free trade and open markets (McClory, 2017, p. 17). Another is the Trump administration's questioning of the value of traditional security alliances such as NATO, including challenging America's commitment to Article 5 of the NATO treaty, which deals with collective defence (McClory, 2017, p.17). Trump's zero-sum worldview and reliance on the hard power of trade tariffs are also eroding US soft power (Whelan, 2017; Nye,

2019). Trump also decided to pull out of the Paris Climate Accord. In addition, Trump's daily criticisms of groups such as the United Nations and other world leaders, including long-term allies, only further exacerbated a perception that the soft power is on the decline. Despite the exodus of several diplomatic staff and cuts in the diplomacy budget, the US Embassies still tried to promote a positive and welcoming image abroad. It was certainly an uphill battle when compared with the constant negative rhetoric being tweeted or shared by Trump on a daily basis. Diplomatic staff cannot do it alone. Instead, more than ever, the use of soft power to promote a positive image of a state is as much a job of non-state as state actors, and citizens can and are involved in using their soft power in diplomacy in order to foster more peaceful relations within the international community.

Non-state actors play a significant role in leveraging their soft power as norm entrepreneurs in redefining norms through social relationships. As norm entrepreneurs, they help define moral codes in the international arena (Colonomos, 2001). This process of redefining norms involves reframing narratives and changing the way people relate with one another. It is through social relationships that non-state actors, including citizens, leverage their soft power to engage in social processes of identity formation, which includes processes of reframing identity narratives that they have of one another and one another's states.

Norms guide, inspire and explain expected behaviour and create mutual expectations about behaviour between actors (Ruggie, 1998, p. 97). 'Actors not only reproduce normative structures, they also change them by their very practice, as underlying conditions change, as new constraints or possibilities emerge, or as new claimants make their presence felt' (Ruggie, 1998, p. 99). Recent literature has expanded the idea of soft power to what some theorists call social power. The idea is that power is non-linear and moves through relationships and communication (Van Ham, 2013, p. 18). The study of social power looks beneath the surface at social relationships, institutions, discourses, and media (Van Ham, 2005, p. 3; Sterling-Folker and Shinko, 2005). Social power depends upon 'the ability to set norms and values that are deemed legitimate and desirable without resorting to coercion' (Van Ham, 2013, p. 19). Central to the idea of social power is norm advocacy, where actors actively engage in a process of redefining language and norms (Van Ham, 2013, p. 20). This literature reinforces the idea that people have the ability to change the way they relate with one another, and it is through the process of language communication and social interaction that they change and reinforce behavioural norms that encourage more peaceful interactions.

2.4 US public diplomacy

Central to this book is US public diplomacy because it deals with how the participation of American citizens in Facebook friendship groups with Libyan citizens impacts Libyans' views of the American people and US foreign policy. The US system has traditionally favoured more hard power policies over soft power policies, especially during the Cold War when the US became one of the global superpowers (Wiseman, 2012). However, the US has also historically focused a great deal on public diplomacy. The peak of US public diplomacy happened during the Cold War when the United States Information Agency (USIA) regularly engaged in public diplomacy activities around the world. These included a variety of broadcast-focused activities such as the Voice of America radio show, WorldNet Television, Radio Free Europe and others. It also focused on exchanges, cultural programmes and other educational and foreign press programmes (USIA, n.d.).

Cultural diplomacy is a vital component of US public diplomacy. For example, during the Cold War, the State Department sent the Brubeck Quartet as jazz ambassadors to several countries with the intent of exposing people to American culture and as an attempt to 'win them over as ideological allies in the cold war' (Perrigo, 2017). Cultural diplomacy involves 'exchange of ideas, information, and other aspects of culture among nations and their peoples to foster mutual understanding' (Schneider, 2005, p.147). Cultural diplomacy includes art, language exchanges, ceremonial visits, sports, religion and the giving and receiving of gifts. It is believed that such sharing about culture builds familiarity and comfort with people from other cultures (Pigman, 2010). This approach involves persuading through values, culture and ideas.

The Cold War was as much a cultural war as it was a war of military strength. Even the CIA was involved in leveraging the power of culture. In fact, during the Cold War, the CIA used modern American art, such as the works of Jackson Pollock, Robert Motherwell, Willem de Kooning and Mark Rothko, as a 'weapon' (Saunders, 1995). 'In the propaganda war with the Soviet Union, this new artistic movement could be held up as proof of the creativity, intellectual freedom, and the cultural power of the US. Russian art, strapped into the communist ideological straitjacket, could not compete' (Saunders, 1995). During this period, the US government had over one hundred Information Resource Centers around the world, with some equipped with libraries to encourage 'in-depth study and understanding of American society and institutions' (USIA, n.d). In 1999, following the end of the Cold War, the USIA merged with the Department of State. The elimination of the USIA seemed to suggest that public diplomacy and soft power were no longer as important to the US government's overall diplomatic agenda. During the 1990s, after the end of the Cold War, the US government also cut many of its cultural diplomacy programmes. However, Schneider (2005) argues that cultural diplomacy must be fully utilised in the war on terror and those programmes that exist, like the Alhurra TV station, aren't nearly enough. 'Soft power requires hard dollars' (Schneider, 2005, p. 163).

Since 9/11, US public diplomacy has focused on promoting national interests and security through informing and influencing foreign publics by seeking to encourage and broaden dialogue between American citizens and the citizens of other states. The re-emergence of the primacy of public diplomacy in US foreign policy has largely been influenced by the terrorist attacks of 9/11 (Fitzpatrick, 2011; Snow, 2009). Those attacks served as a wake-up call to the US government and catalysed a revamping of the US public diplomacy programme. Former President George W. Bush surmised that those attacks were the result of the US having an image problem in the Middle East and based on the perception of different values between Americans and people of the Middle East (Bush, 2001). As a result, the US government increased efforts to promote a positive image of the US abroad, especially in the Middle East. The US government funds cultural exchanges, English language teaching programmes, media campaigns, television shows and other programmes as part of its public diplomacy efforts.

In 2003, the US government attempted to reform its perceived image problem in the Middle East through a media campaign called the *Shared Values Initiative*, which was a series of videos designed to showcase American cultural diversity and religious tolerance. These videos depicted the positive everyday experiences of American Muslims. The videos were supposed to be shown in the Middle East. However, many media outlets in the Middle East, including government-run channels in Egypt, Lebanon and Jordan, refused to show the advertisements (Rampton, 2007). By most accounts, this campaign was a failure. Focus-group interviews, conducted after the advertisements, were shown indicated that 40% of the viewers had negative first impressions of the advertisements (Fullerton and Kendrick, 2006, p. 180). Fullerton suggests that this initiative failed because the US government did not understand the complexities of cross-cultural communication and did not research Muslim values (2006, p. 180). Considering the initial motivation around the initiative was to create a better understanding of values, this disregard for Muslim values in the process was more than just an oversight. It was perceived as blatantly disrespectful. This failed initiative reinforces the need for two-directional dialogic approaches to public diplomacy that are focused on promoting cultural understanding and respect rather than one-way messaging.

Campaigns focused on improving views of a country's culture and values do not necessarily translate into improved views of its government and foreign policy. For example, surveys of individuals in the Middle East tend to suggest that the issues people have with the US are not about values at all, but instead about US foreign policy. A survey of individuals in the Middle East found that despite what world leaders believed, values were considered less important to an individual's image of the US. Instead, US foreign policy was mentioned as the main reason for negative images for 79% of respondents in Morocco, 86% in Saudi Arabia, 76% in Jordan, 89% in Lebanon and 75% in the United Arab Emirates (Zogby, 2004). These findings suggest that much of the US government's perceived image problem is based on negative views of its foreign policy, and therefore, public diplomacy campaigns which are focused exclusively on promoting cultural understanding and positive views of American values will only go so far in terms of improving relations between states.

Although during the post-9/11 period US public diplomacy was revitalised, many of those advances have declined since Trump came to power. (Nye, 2019; Whelan, 2017; McClory, 2019). Rather than focusing on promoting a positive image abroad, Trump's America First rhetoric has done little to foster trust or promote positive relations with other states. Ongoing conflicts and terror attacks against both state and non-state actors have continued to plague the US since 9/11. As such, there is a need for more concerted efforts by both citizens and state officials to promote more positive images and narratives among foreign publics and to counter the negative images of the US. A Pew Research Center survey of people in thirty-seven countries found low confidence levels in Trump in regard to international affairs with only a median of 22% of respondents having confidence in Trump (Wike et al., 2017; PDAA, 2017). His character and foreign policies are viewed with doubt and apprehension. In comparison, 58% of respondents have a favourable opinion of the American people and popular culture (Wike et al., 2017; PDAA, 2017). The 'America First' rhetoric, coupled with Trump's very critical statements on Twitter and in the media, suggests that the Trump administration has little concern about how the country is perceived. Whelan suggests that 'Trump has done public diplomacy a favour' by showing that rhetoric does matter and has a real impact on security interests (2017, p. 65). The protectionist rhetoric and Trump's lack of personal diplomacy continue to undermine the efforts of US diplomats around the world. Further, Whelan argues that the Trump administration's rhetoric has affected the economy and had a direct impact on US alliances (2017, p. 65). In the same vein, she takes her argument one step further by claiming that Trump has made America a 'laughingstock' in the world community. Instead of generating goodwill, Trump's election has had the opposite effect (Whelan, 2017, p. 65). Two concrete examples of this decline in public diplomacy since Trump's election were the decrease in exchange student applications and a decrease in US tourism (Whelan, 2017). The further decline of US image under the Trump administration shows why it is important to understand how foreign audiences' views are impacted by foreign policy and how these views should impact the way the US engages in public diplomacy.

Critics of the US post-9/11 public diplomacy approach argue that the US has used a one-way messaging approach while neglecting to do any research into Muslim values (Zaharna, 2010). Nye (2004) suggests that anti-American sentiment is largely a result of American foreign policy and the US being seen as an imperialist. Part of the challenge of the US-focused public diplomacy as it relates to the Arab world has been the focus on image over substance (Nye, 2004, p. 121). Much of the focus has been on promoting democracy and the benefits and values of democratic society. This approach is influenced by democratic peace theory. Nye notes that this is a problematic approach in the Arab world when half the world's countries are democratic, while none of the twenty-two Arab countries are democratic (Nye, 2004, p. 118). As a result, misunderstandings have arisen. So, Nye urges the US to become more aware of how their policies are perceived by others (2004, p. 125). This can only happen when people listen and ask questions rather than bombarding other people with messages. Zaharna criticises America's post-9/11 diplomacy approach as well. She takes issue with using the one-way messaging approach while neglecting to do any research into Muslim values. Further, like other critics, she argues that this approach has left Muslims 'feeling neither understood nor respected' (Zaharna, 2010, p. 130). 'Feeling neither understood nor respected, the audience repeatedly described the US communication attempts as "patronizing," "condescending," or "insulting"' (Nye, 2004, p. 130). Comments like these make it clear that the US public diplomacy efforts toward the Middle East are insufficient and, in some ways, could actually be making things worse. Since 9/11, terrorism has not decreased, and the frequency and locations of terror attacks have expanded while the world has seen an increase in the scope and efficacy of terror networks such as ISIS. This has resulted in a general mistrust of all Muslims in the belief that they hate and want to destroy America (Nye, 2004). This sentiment has deteriorated further under the Trump administration with the Muslim travel ban. Nye correctly argues that to be successful in the global communication age, America needs to change attitudes at home as well as abroad (2004, p. 125).

Many in the world have a love/hate relationship with the US. In particular, Arab states tend to feel a sense of powerlessness and humiliation from the US (Van Ham, 2005, p. 55). Van Ham poses a very important question that should be seriously pondered by the US government. That question is 'if US hard *and* soft power create resentment, how can the US ever be successful in winning the "hearts and minds" of its foes and rivals and keep the allegiance of its allies?' (Van Ham, 2005, p. 56). This question is especially important for states like Libya, which have a history of conflict with the US and whose citizens have been impacted by years of sanctions and are now subject to the travel ban, both of which have an impact on citizens views of US foreign policy.

The US approach to public diplomacy has also been criticised by some scholars. Part of the criticism centres around what is seen as an overemphasis on the study of the US government's public diplomacy approach since 9/11. At the centre of this criticism is the perception that the US is behaving as a liberal imperialist power using military strength and ideology to sell democracy, liberty and prosperity as the answer to all the world's problems (Van Ham, 2005, p. 48). Part of Van Ham's critique concerns the historic US role as hegemon which has often involved the state behaving as the global police. However, arguably, in many situations, this is a role that the world community has called upon America to fulfil, rather than the US government just arbitrarily policing the world community. This critique is why it is important for the US government to understand how foreign audiences view the US and its foreign policy.

Although the US government has publicly stated their commitment to the importance of a dialogic form of public diplomacy, they still primarily rely on a messaging-focused approach. This one-way communicative approach of sharing their message through TV shows and exchanges has its limits. Van Ham argues that the problem with this approach is that it is marketing, and in marketing, it is not what is said, but what others hear that is important (2005, p. 61). Van Ham argues that the Arab world hears 'domination, chaos and cynicism' (2005, p. 61). In addition, he asserts that the Arab world will not accept US public diplomacy so long as US foreign policies continue the way they are. Van Ham also suggests that the US public diplomacy approach underestimates the role of radical Islam, which he believes underpins anti-Americanism (2005, p. 61). This view has proven even more relevant since the emergence of ISIS.

The strongest criticism of US public diplomacy has been focused on the failure to listen carefully to the concerns of people in the Muslim world. This continues to be a problem when the US government often disagrees with some of the narratives being communicated by terror groups, instead choosing to convey its own narrative of the situation. As such, 'True dialogue, rather than mere one-way communication, is therefore seen as the essential starting point to fix the US's serious—but probably not yet fatal—image problem around the world' (Van Ham, 2005, p. 62). This will continue to be a challenge so long as the US government has a policy of not engaging in dialogue with terrorists or extremist groups.

More than ever there is a need for more strategic public diplomacy by the US. However, there are significant concerns that any positive steps that have been made to improve the US image abroad were unravelled under the Trump administration. His transactional leadership style and disregard for multilateral relations show a blatant disregard for the way America is perceived around the world, and no concern for the long-term implications. Rather than focusing on attraction and improving the US image abroad, his constant critical tweets and reckless words are having the opposite effect. In addition, banning individuals from certain Muslim-majority countries only hurts the US image in the region, while only going so far in protecting the country. This, coupled with the decision by Trump to recognise Jerusalem as the capital of Israel, only further exacerbated already tense views in the Middle East. The lack of leadership and diplomacy of this administration left a void that non-state actors must fill.

2.5 Shift from messaging to dialogue

The emergence of the new public diplomacy has been characterised by a shift from a pure messaging-centric public diplomacy to a dialogic form of public diplomacy. Early public diplomacy was primarily focused on conveying an image. However, states like the US have begun to move away from a messaging model of public diplomacy to a relational form of public diplomacy that involves the devolution of power from state to non-state actors (Nye, 2011; Kirkpatrick, 2011, p. 31; McClory 2017). Nevertheless, there is still some debate among those that see the purpose of public diplomacy as being to exert some power over a target audience and those who desire to engage or empower a community (Fisher, 2011, p. 271). This book takes the view that empowering a community of actors to influence one another is a more favourable approach to improving relations between states and citizens.

Dialogic public diplomacy involves creating long-term relationships through activities and exchanges (Nye, 2004). 'This evolution of public diplomacy from one-way communication to a two-way dialogue model treats publics as peer-to-peer cocreators of meaning and communication' (Nye, 2010). Saunders argues that 'the relational paradigm assumes that politics is a cumulative, multilevel, open-ended process of continuous interaction among significant clusters of citizens in and out of government and the relationships they form to solve public problems in whole bodies politic across permeable boundaries' (2013, p. 137). Citizens are at the centre of the relational paradigm of public diplomacy (Saunders, 2013, p. 137). These citizens get power by building relationships. The more relationships, the more power (Saunders, 2013, p. 137).

Mutual agreed-upon expectations for behaviour are necessary in relational approaches to diplomacy. Thomlison suggests that a relationship is a 'set of expectations two parties have of each other's behaviour based on their interaction patterns' (2000, p. 178). The relationship-centred approach focuses on 'message exchange, relationship building, and network creation, with the result being that communication not only moves at a greater speed but is also

much more flexible and adaptable than in the informational approach'
(D'Hooghe, 2015, p. 20). The relational shift in diplomacy is a result of a
'growing interest from public diplomacy theorists in dialogue, transparency,
trust and commitment' (Zaharna, 2009, p. 86). For public diplomacy to be truly
relational, it requires a worldview that supports the need to achieve mutual
understanding (Fitzpatrick, 2013, p. 30). These ideas are not new and have
always played a role in diplomacy, especially in international negotiations.

Mark Leonard is credited as being one of the earlier proponents of a more
relational form of public diplomacy (Leonard et al., 2002). He suggests that
public diplomacy begins with understanding other countries' needs and
cultures and finding areas of 'common cause' (Leonard et al., 2002; Zaharna et
al., 2013, p. 5). In this way, public diplomacy has less to do with branding and
image and more to do with building bridges of understanding between
countries. However, Zaharna argues that the changes in 'public diplomacy are
as much a communication phenomenon as a political one' (2009, p. 86).
Actions tend to speak louder than words. 'Effective public diplomacy is a two-
way street that involves listening as well as talking' (Nye, 2004, p. 111). Listening
to what people have to say and what they think is also an important part of
public diplomacy (Melissen, 2005). Relationships are what matter most in
public diplomacy.

Dialogue is the most effective way to learn what others think and believe.
Dialogue refers to situations where ideas are exchanged and communication is
multidirectional (Cowan and Arsenault, 2008, p. 18). It is through the process
of asking questions and sharing views with one another that individuals
influence one another. Habermas (1990) refers to this deliberative process
as communicative action. In this approach, Habermas (1990) suggests that
undistorted communication is necessary to establish an ideal speech community
where normative visions of a 'good life' can occur. There is a difference between
technical dialogue and real dialogue. However, both can be tools for advancing
diplomatic goals, and the very act of exchanging information can create a
foundation for deeper attachment in the future (Cowan and Arsenault, 2008, p.
18). Dialogue is a cooperative activity focused on building respect, social
capital and community while promoting human flourishing (Freire, 1972).
Cowan and Arsenault argue for a more relational dialogue, suggesting that
reciprocal communication is very important to lasting friendships between
individuals, and that 'many of the most effective and esteemed leaders are
those who listen more than or as much as they speak' (2008, p. 18.). Further,
they argue that 'dialogue should focus primarily on improving relationships
and understanding rather than changing opinions' (Cowan and Arsenault,
2008, p. 19). While dialogue between cultures is the end goal, it begins with a
dialogue between individuals (Cowan and Arsenault, 2008, p. 17). Cowan and

Arsenault further assert that when individuals, whether government officials or private citizens, meet face-to-face or in an online forum, the relationships that are formed provide the building blocks in which a 'broader dialogue between civilizations can evolve' (2008, p. 17). This assertion is consistent with the argument of this book. Ultimately, the end goal of dialogue is improving understanding and fostering better relations.

Real dialogue can also be referred to as authentic dialogue. Lyotard and Thebaud assert that in authentic dialogue, one speaks only as much as one listens (1985, p. 4). The process of striving for authentic dialogue should be the goal because it is through the process of listening to one another that understanding happens. However, this authentic dialogue is not always easy to achieve. Linklater (2001, p. 29) argues that 'authentic dialogues can never be anything other than an ideal to be aimed for, a goal that can be approximated, because there may always be forms of exclusion that human beings have still to discover'. Nevertheless, if society has any hope of facilitating better relations between states and citizens of states, every effort to engage in authentic and real dialogue must be made. To do this, 'faith in people is an a priori requirement for dialogue' (Freire, 2014, p. 65). 'Without this faith in people, dialogue is a farce which inevitably degenerates into paternalistic manipulation. Founding itself upon love, humility, and faith, dialogue becomes a horizontal relationship of which mutual trust between the dialoguers is the logical consequence' (Freire, 1972, p. 64). All dialogues must start somewhere. Dialogues do not always start out at the deeper, more authentic level. Instead, the value is in the process of relating to one another and building toward increasing levels and authenticity and transparency.

Authentic dialogue is not always comfortable. Nelson (1973) argues that to have authentic dialogue there needs to be an extreme expansion of what are perceived as permissible expressions and disagreements. This kind of dialogue must be heartfelt and honest. In situations of conflict, dialogue can be painful and difficult. Linklater argues that dialogic commitment requires 'the development of societies that regard the differences between human beings as less important than their shared experience of pain and suffering' (Linklater, 2001, p. 30; Rorty, 1989, ch. 9). Seeing dialogue as a process of promoting understanding and trust between people and societies is essential. It is through this intentional process that people can start to engage in more superficial forms of dialogue, which is more typical in friendship groups. The goal is that these shallower forms of dialogue will serve as building blocks for more authentic dialogue as trust is established.

All types of actors have a place in the dialogue process. Linklater (2001) argues that through a dialogic process, truth can be discovered by consensus of the participants and where irrelevant, truth is excluded so that a better argument can come through. This perspective sees truth as contextual. This is the process that happens in a conflict mediation, where parties work through their divergent perspectives until they reach some type of agreement on how to move beyond the conflict. Of special consideration to Habermas is the nature of the dialogic process and whether certain voices are heard louder than others (Brown, 2001, p. 198). Habermas sees dialogue as being essential to emancipation. It is through the process of empowering all actors in this dialogic process that emancipation can happen. 'Habermas and his IR followers no longer think in terms of revolution as the precondition for emancipation… their dialogic commitment extends to all comers of all genders, continents, and cultures' (Brown, 2001, p. 201). Habermas (1994, p. 120) argues that it is also important that communities not attempt to erase the human differences in search of agreement and understanding. Instead, the end goal is to seek understanding within the differences. From this approach, Linklater surmises that Habermas prefers understanding over emancipation (1994, p. 104; 2001, p. 30). It is through the process of dialogue and communication that citizens are empowered to interact with one another in a way that promotes understanding, and through this process, they reframe narratives they have of one another. As people gain an understanding of one another within their differences, they can begin to recognise that differences should not be seen as a threat. Through changing these narratives, they can foster more peaceful relations.

The dialogic form of public diplomacy is especially important in preventing and resolving conflicts. It is through these dialogic relationships that people are able to heal wounds and build trust. 'Dialogue as a tool of public diplomacy is critical both as a symbolic gesture that emphasises that reasonable people can find reasonable ways to disagree and as a mechanism for overcoming stereotypes and forging relationships across social boundaries' (Cowan and Arsenault, 2008, p. 20). Cowan and Arsenault suggest that dialogue is not guaranteed to change opinions of foreign policy decisions but can go a long way in showing respect for alternate voices and facilitating understanding of policies (2008, p. 19). Building trust between people is essential to improving relations.

The US government's approach to public diplomacy emphasises building trust and respect but makes clear that it will not tolerate 'extremist' views and will do everything in its power to denigrate those views (Boyd-Judson, 2011). This approach shows the difficulties that exist in attempting to engage in genuine dialogue where there are seemingly incompatible moral values between nations and peoples, or, as Boyd-Judson (2011) put it, 'understanding the enemy's moral universe'. The challenge with this position is that it appears that the US government is interested in genuine dialogue so long as it is dialogue with which they agree. Sadly, this view prevents them from understanding the divergent views that are at the very heart of terrorist attacks such as 9/11. Lynch

(2000, p. 323) criticises this approach because he says the US is missing out on an unprecedented opportunity for 'a new kind of dialogue focused on the question of the relations between Islam and the West'. He emphasises that 'some conflicts and hatreds are real and cannot be talked away'; however, 'others are not and dialogues might be helpful to determine which are which' (Lynch, 2000, p. 323). Citizen diplomats stand uniquely positioned to fill the gap in convening dialogue around tough issues because they are not held back by the political and ideological constraints that hamstring traditional diplomats.

Central to the dialogic approach to public diplomacy are transnational networks. Zaharna (2009) argues that these networks can help to overcome cultural differences, foster credibility and control narratives. This argument is consistent with the perspective of this book that transnational social media networks can serve as a forum to bridge the cultural divide. These networks transcend traditional boundaries, both geographically and politically, and include everything from terrorist networks to global financial networks (Hocking, 2005). Zaharna argues that these networks add a level of complexity to information flow and have implications for views of identity, information dominance and soft power (2013, p. 1). Within these networks is a strong public dimension that plays a vital role in fostering communication and trust (Hocking, 2005). Hocking (2005, p.37) defines these global networks as 'a set of relatively stable relationships which are of a non-hierarchical and interdependent nature linking a variety of actors, who share common interests with regard to a policy and who exchange resources to pursue these shared interests acknowledging that cooperation is the best way to achieve common goals'. This cooperation often includes collaboration on projects that have concrete goals to benefit the collective good. Zaharna et al. (2013, p. 7) suggest that collaboration in public diplomacy is the equivalent of traditional diplomatic negotiation. NGOs have a moral edge over government and businesses because their brands are forces for good 'unencumbered by the trappings of sovereignty and untainted by realpolitik' (Hocking, 2005, p. 39).

The role of dialogue is central to public diplomacy efforts aimed at preventing and resolving conflicts because it allows citizen actors to promote cross-cultural understanding, build trust and control narratives through dialogue in transnational networks.

2.6 Role of non-state actors

The shift from old public diplomacy to new public diplomacy has resulted in an increasing role for non-state actors. In modern diplomatic efforts, the involvement of non-state actors in public diplomacy is often called citizen diplomacy and includes a variety of citizen actors, including members of civil society, business, education, sports, and even independent citizens. Historically, public diplomacy was a method used by governments to influence public attitudes on the formation and execution of foreign policies (Cull, 2006). However, this definition has changed. D'Hooghe's definition of public diplomacy recognises the role of citizens as 'an instrument used by states, associations of states, and some sub-state and non-state actors, to influence thoughts and mobilise actions to advance their interests and values abroad by building and managing relationships and developing an understanding of cultures, attitudes, and behaviour' (2015, p.6). This definition of public diplomacy is broad and focuses on a variety of actors and activities that foster positive and peaceful relations between states and citizens of states. Sometimes citizens engage in public diplomacy activities under the auspices of the state, while other times they are involved in activities completely on their own initiative. In addition, since many of these non-state actors are engaging in these activities with no direct connection to the government, the messages communicated can be quite diverse. As a result, citizen diplomacy can potentially complement official diplomacy or subvert it. This is, of course a risk, especially for more authoritarian regimes which desire to tightly control the views shared by their citizens (Nye, 2004). This is why some countries ban citizen diplomacy efforts when they run counter to official foreign policy.

The diversity of actors engaged in diplomatic activities has resulted in an attempt to develop a framework for the diverse tracks of actors involved. Initially, they were simply classified into two tracks. Joe Montville, a former US Foreign Service officer, is credited with popularising the terms Track I and Track II diplomacy to distinguish between state and non-state actor diplomacy ((McDonald, 1991, p. 8). Track I diplomacy deals with government-to-government relations in the field of foreign affairs, while Track II deals with everything outside of formal government relations between people from around the world (McDonald, 1991). Initially, Track II focused on de-escalating conflict by 'reducing anger, fear, and tension and by improving communication and mutual understanding' (McDonald, 1991, p. 1). Now citizen diplomats are involved in public diplomacy activities focused on promoting understanding with other citizens and even government officials where there has not necessarily been any previous conflict.

To capture the diversity of actors involved in diplomatic activities the Institute for Multi-track Diplomacy established a model of nine tracks of diplomacy. These tracks are focused on activities that foster peacemaking and listed in Table 2.1 below.

Table 2.1 Multi-track diplomacy.

Track 1	Government
Track 2	Professional conflict resolution programmes by non-state actors
Track 3	Business
Track 4	Citizen diplomacy activities like exchanges through NGOs and other interest groups
Track 5	Research, training and education
Track 6	Peace activism
Track 7	Religious groups
Track 8	Fundraising
Track 9	Media and public opinion

Source: Institute for Multi-track Diplomacy.

Although this model provides an interesting framework to see the variety of actors that are involved in diplomacy, all but Track 1 diplomacy involves citizen diplomats acting in some non-governmental capacity. Further, there is quite a bit of overlap between the types of activities that actors are involved in. For example, someone could be involved in activism, fundraising and communications activities while at the same time being a private citizen diplomat. So, rather than providing a clear distinction on where someone fits in the process, it tends to muddy the waters further. So, for purposes of this book, I will use citizen diplomacy to contrast with state diplomacy rather than focusing on one of the tracks listed here.

Two areas where non-state actors are most often involved are citizen diplomacy and cultural diplomacy. Citizen diplomacy involves contacts between publics of different nations and tends to be highly relational. These contacts include exchanges, visitor programmes and sports and cultural activities (D'Hooghe, 2015). Whereas cultural diplomacy can be practised by both state and non-state actors and is defined as 'a course of actions, which are based on and utilize the exchange of ideas, values, traditions and other aspects of culture or identity, whether to strengthen relationships or enhance socio-cultural cooperation, promote national interests and beyond' (ICD, n.d.). As can be seen by the definitions, there is quite a bit of overlap between the descriptions of citizen and cultural diplomacy. With these somewhat nuanced distinctions what is most important is the kinds of activities that the actors are engaged in, rather than what the actors are called. Implicit in both these kinds of diplomacy is promoting relationships and understanding. I would argue that in both citizen and cultural diplomacy, the underlying purpose can be to promote a better image of the country and improve relations between people. In either case, cultural diplomacy is very important when relations between countries are strained and where it is necessary to bridge the divide that exists between states (Ellis, 2012; D'Hooghe, 2015, p. 43). When cultural diplomacy is done in practice, it is uniquely suited to have an impact on interfaith and intercultural understanding and be effective in promoting reconciliation (ICD, n.d.). However, it is necessary for cultural exchange to go beyond just arts and music. It should involve activities that get to the heart of people's identity and how people think, behave and communicate, which is socially constructed and impacts narratives (D'Hooghe, 2015, p. 43). Zaharna (2012) appropriately notes that culture is often neglected in public diplomacy initiatives, and when public diplomacy initiatives fail, it is because culture has been neglected. Therefore, considering the important role that culture can play in terms of perceived impact of public diplomacy, more attention should be paid to what the targets of the intended public diplomacy find to be helpful and influential to them. This is the reason that friendship groups designed to promote cultural understanding like the groups in this study are important.

The most notable citizen diplomats have included actors and sports figures. A couple of recent examples include actress Angelina Jolie's work in Africa and former NBA basketball player Dennis Rodman's effort in North Korea, which is particularly noteworthy because of his relationship with North Korean leader Kim Jung Un. There are also cases where average citizens are involved in building bridges between their country and others.

The increasing role of citizens in public diplomacy efforts comes as a result of a recognition of the agency of citizens as actors in their own right. This recognition is slowly evolving into more scholarship on citizen diplomacy. Hocking (2005) sees this shift to involving non-state actors in international relations as so great that they are calling for changing the name from 'statecraft to actor craft'. Part of the reason for this shift in language could be attributed to the increasing role of non-state actors in international relations and transnational peacemaking. This comes as a result of a diffusion of power from state to non-state actors (Nye, 2011, xvi). The increase in conflicts that are being perpetrated by non-state actors is also a significant factor. For example, non-state actors killed more people in New York on 9/11 than the state of Japan killed in the bombing of Pearl Harbor in 1941 (Nye, 2011, xii). In addition, the emergence of global terror networks such as Al Qaeda and ISIS has challenged the purely state-centric view of international relations, because now global conflicts are not perpetrated merely by state actors. Hocking (2005) suggests that terrorism has tested the boundaries of diplomacy as citizens are finding themselves caught up in terrorist acts. In acts of terror, harm to citizens is not just collateral damage. Instead, citizens are the ones intentionally being targeted in these attacks. So, if terrorism is being perpetrated by non-state actors and the victims are non-state actors, no longer can anyone claim that international conflicts occur merely between states. If non-state actors are victims of conflicts, then they have an important role to play in preventing conflicts and engaging in diplomacy.

Although, in recent years, there has been an increasing emphasis in the literature about non-state actors in diplomacy, non-state actors' role is not new. 'Such unofficial diplomats have, of course, existed as long as there have been (self-)designated communities interacting with each other across some form of a (non-)recognized border' (Scott-Smith, 2014, p 2). However, the presence and influence of non-state actors within international relations were largely neglected 'due to the overarching shadow of "the state" as the official representative of all things diplomatic' (Scott-Smith, 2014, p. 2). What is most significant is that 'by dislocating the state as the prime adjudicator of diplomatic legitimacy, New Diplomatic History accepts the individual as an international political actor in their own right' (Scott-Smith, 2014, p. 3).

Much of the public diplomacy involving non-state actors has involved NGOs. Nye (2004) suggests that non-state actors help to develop new norms by pressing governments to develop new policies. Norms function in not only a 'causal sense, but in a broader communicative and constitutive sense' (Ruggie, 1998, p. 85). Nye (2010) contends that selling a positive image can best be accomplished by private citizens because the 'soft sell may prove more effective than the hard sell'. In fact, some have suggested that NGOs might have more credibility than governments and are, therefore, better able to communicate with civil societies in other countries (Leonard et al., 2002). This book supports the view that civil society actors have a very important role to play in promoting positive images.

According to one study, NGOs tend to be viewed more positively than governments (Zatepilina-Monacell, 2012). A multi-case study of American NGOs looked at whether the way they are perceived by states had an impact on the way the US was perceived and attitudes toward foreign relations. The research found that NGOs that are privately funded are seen more positively, especially when they see their role as advancing the interests of the international stakeholders and where they are willing to publicly oppose the US government on matters concerning US interests (Zatepilina-Monacell, 2012). The fact that NGOs and civil society actors are perceived as more trustworthy shows that they may be in a better position to influence foreign publics. Nye says 'postmodern publics are generally sceptical of authority and governments are often mistrusted. Thus, it often behoves governments to keep in the background and to work with private actors. Some NGOs enjoy more trust than governments do. And though they are difficult to control, they can be useful channels of communication' (2004, p. 127). However, the independent nature of these actors indicates that they are not necessarily involved in a pure public diplomacy function.

States are increasingly recognising and supporting the role of non-state actors in public diplomacy. The US State Department has a section of their website dedicated to encouraging citizen diplomacy with the label 'You are a citizen diplomat'. This website defines citizen diplomacy as a political concept of average citizens engaging as representatives of a country or cause, either inadvertently or by design (State Department, n.d.). It is communicated as a responsibility of citizens to help shape foreign relations 'one handshake at a time', by engaging with the rest of the world in a meaningful and mutually beneficial dialogue (State Department, n.d.). This view of the important role that citizen diplomats play is central to this book and my argument that citizens have an important role in building relations between both citizens and states.

One of the earliest recorded US attempts to involve citizen diplomats in foreign affairs happened after the US Congress passed the Informational and Educational Exchange Act, which allowed for participation of laypeople in the informational and cultural relations of the State Department (Marshall, 1949, p. 8). In 1945, the State Department launched a pilot project to engage citizen diplomats. They invited several non-profit organisations to send representatives to the Chapultepec Conference held in Mexico City. Marshall suggests 'that this was the first hesitant experiment in citizen diplomacy' (1949, p. 4). Later, UNESCO came out of this project. Marshall argued that participation in these events must be voluntary because it would provide a more accurate picture of the people themselves rather than handpicked individuals (1949, p. 8). Further, there was a recognition that it is 'in the minds of men that defences of peace must be constructed' (Marshall, 1949, p. 9). At the heart of democracy is the belief that people rather than states are the ultimate foundations of goodwill, and as such, every means must be explored to enable men to plan and participate in the expression of international goodwill (Marshall, 1949, p. 9). 'But to be effective in maintaining peace, they must now speak the minds of citizen diplomats, of great masses of people, rather than of dynasties, political parties, or ruling groups' (Marshall, 1949, p. 9).

McClory (2017) suggests that non-state actors have two primary means of influencing global events. One is by providing direct services such as capacity-building and development; in addition, he suggests they can 'mount advocacy campaigns designed to change behaviour or to bring about changes to norms, conventions, and international law, or national policy' (McClory, 2017, p. 25). The second approach is more akin to international lobbying than what has traditionally been viewed as public diplomacy. Further, small NGO actors and even individual citizens can quickly mobilise others and engage in transnational events. However, McClory does agree with other scholars that individual citizens are most effective when they work collaboratively and in networks (2017, p. 25). This can even include online networks where citizens quickly use social media to support one another or even dispel negative messaging around significant global events like terrorist attacks. For example, following the terrorist attacks on the Christchurch mosque in New Zealand in March 2019, members of the Facebook friendship group called Libyans and Americans United for Friendship and Peace engaged in dialogue and support around their feelings about such attacks. Similar kinds of dialogue and behaviour happened following the attack on the US Consulate in Benghazi, Libya, in 2012, where Libyan members of the Libyan American Friendship Association Facebook group condemned such acts, and some of the members shared how they joined a street demonstration against the act in Benghazi the day after it happened. The Libyan members also communicated their sorrow and condemnation for what had happened to US Ambassador Chris Stevens and the four other victims and shared how many of the Libyan people had deeply appreciated Ambassador Stevens's efforts in Libya. In response, some of the American members of the group shared appreciation for the support and comments. These efforts were helpful in dispelling negative perceptions that all Libyans were supporting the attacks and reinforcing the perspective that many Libyans were opposed to what happened, which is an important gesture of peace during times of conflict.

State officials recognise the valuable complementary role that citizens have to state public diplomacy efforts. In the US, support for citizen involvement in public diplomacy has been welcomed by both Republican and Democratic officials. Former Secretary of State Condoleezza Rice said, 'Public diplomacy cannot be an American monologue; it must be a dialogue with people from around the world. The dialogue must be sought out and conducted, not only by people like us in government, but by committed Americans from all walks of life' (quoted in Hughes, 2005; Pigman, 2010). Previous policy statements by the US State Department indicate a support for developing productive people-to-people relationships around the world and acting quickly to counter misinformation about US society and policies (D&CP, n.d., p. 57). Former US Secretary of State Hillary Clinton was also a strong proponent of citizen diplomacy and the need to 'leverage civilian power by connecting businesses, philanthropists, and citizens' groups with partner governments to perform tasks that governments alone cannot' (Clinton, 2010). Former President Barack Obama also supported leveraging citizen power in global engagement (Gregory, 2012, p. 118). The strong bipartisan support of US government officials for citizen involvement in public diplomacy indicates that these state officials recognise that public diplomacy is not only a state-centric messaging activity but also involves a variety of activities that bring the American people together with people from other countries. They also recognise that fostering peaceful relations between states is as much a function of citizenship as it is of governance and that a variety of everyday activities conducted by individuals in day-to-day life can serve as a conduit of peaceful relations between states and citizens and states.

Citizen diplomacy has also been recognised as valuable in other ongoing international intractable conflicts. In 2013, former Iranian and US diplomats discussed the important role that citizen diplomacy could play in the Iran nuclear talks and the important role citizens play in rebuilding trust between the US and Iran after 34 years of strained relations (Miller and Mousavian, 2013). The diplomats noted that in order for any agreements by two governments to be supported by the populations of both countries, there must be opportunities for Iranians and Americans from all walks of life to meet face-to-face and work together (Miller and Mousavian, 2013). 'Facilitating tourism, academic, humanitarian, media, cultural, economic and social activities, and parliamentarian exchanges will lay the foundation for a durable and sustainable relationship based on mutual respect and common interests' (Miller and Mousavian, 2013). Face-to-face exchanges are an essential part of the process of fostering positive relations between states and citizens of states.

In situations where there has been conflict, elite diplomacy is generally not sufficient in bringing about long-lasting change (Handlemann, 2012). The reason is that the absence of public involvement makes the process unstable and fragile, because it lacks the ability of people on both sides to overcome psychological barriers such as fear, mistrust and prejudice (Handlemann, 2012, p. 163). Since this book specifically looks at public diplomacy between the countries of Libya and the United States, which have experienced years of conflict, this recognition of the important role of non-state actors in the process is even more persuasive.

Citizen diplomats play a complementary but not exclusive role in diplomatic efforts. In some situations, civil society actors and citizens engage in more informal dialogues, while in others, citizens have actually engaged in more structured negotiations where there has been conflict. Josselin and Wallace (2001) suggest that non-state actors also have a significant role in 'developing structures of global governance'. Diplomatic actors 'will increasingly function as facilitators and social entrepreneurs between domestic and foreign civil society groups as they operate in global policy networks' (Hocking, 2012). Historically, religious groups have played a large role here. However, now competing groups of citizens are becoming involved in defining norms in the international community.

Cosmopolitanism promotes the concept of global citizenship (Smith, 2017). Colonomos (2001) argues that the development of transnational networks favours cosmopolitanism and the globalisation of norms and growing interaction between states and non-state actors. These actors engage in moral agency in the international arena while dealing with very important topics such as human rights and peace (Colonomos, 2001). The process of globalisation has further advanced the ability of non-state actors to gather networks of diverse allies and promote their causes and messages in a variety of channels (Colonomos, 2001). This process of influencing norms is happening in a variety of settings, including in online Facebook groups like the ones investigated in this study.

There is resistance among some people to the increased role of non-state actors in international relations and diplomacy. Scholars and practitioners who support the realist paradigm of IR tend to be critics of non-state actors, seeing them as potential revolutionaries or as disguising state interests (Josselin and Wallace, 2001). Some scholars even argue that the role of non-state actors has threatened foreign ministries and weakens governmental authority by loosening the bonds between governments and populations (Langhorne, 2005, p. 333). The roles of non-state actors are unclear. As such, this creates a crisis of authority and legitimacy (Langhorne, 2005, p. 334). In addition, the change of actors in diplomacy impacts the language used to describe actors involved in international relations. The words 'non-state actors' imply that these actors can only be conceptualised in relation to states, which may prove misleading in the future (Langhorne, 2005, p. 335).

Another critique of the engagement of non-state actors is that non-state actors are not really perceived as acting independently because they often receive government funding (Josselin and Wallace, 2001). Arguably, there is a clear distinction between being independent and receiving funding. NGOs that receive funding in the US are not told what they can and cannot do. However, in order for NGOs to receive funding, the government would certainly want to know what they are doing and would make the decision to fund projects based on whether they are perceived as valuable to diplomatic efforts. So whether these NGOs are truly acting independently is unclear.

As the nature of transnational conflicts changes, so do the types of actors involved in efforts to foster positive and peaceful relations through diplomacy. Although some scholars and practitioners have concerns about non-state actors being involved in diplomacy because of fears that they might undermine state efforts, other democratic states like the US government not only accept the increasing role of citizens in diplomacy, they support this role as an essential part of citizenship in a democratic society and strongly encourage citizen participation. Citizens have a vested interest in promoting peaceful relations between states and play an invaluable complementary role to governmental diplomatic efforts in international relations.

2.7 Importance of understanding culture

Cultural differences can be a source of misunderstanding and contribute to transnational conflict if actors are not able to successfully build a bridge over those differences. Cultural understanding can be facilitated at both the state and non-state level. Therefore, states often support cultural diplomacy initiatives and exchanges between citizens as an effort to promote understanding and more peaceful relations. Current cultural diplomacy initiatives focus on cultural engagement on a more superficial level. Activities like art exhibits, music concerts and other cultural programmes can only go so far in breaking down barriers and promoting understanding. What relational public diplomacy allows an opportunity for people to engage in cultural learning on a deeper level. It is through processes of intentional cultural learning that people build bridges with one another. Long-term dialogic forums and friendship groups provide excellent mediums for cultural learning and building trust. It is through the process of promoting understanding and respect that citizens recognise that differences in culture do not necessarily have to result in conflicts.

Culture affects the way we build relationships, how we communicate information and how that information is interpreted. Zaharna (2012) argues that the new public diplomacy should recognise the role of culture in public diplomacy's relational context, because she believes that this is an important step in accounting for the reciprocal agency of the targets of public diplomacy. Cultural considerations will be helpful in understanding the way relationships are perceived in a particular culture. In addition, because cultural norms and beliefs tend to be socially constructed, one cannot take a one-size-fits-all approach to public diplomacy (Seo, 2013, p. 162). This is why case study research like this project is important. It is designed to understand how public diplomacy efforts are perceived by people from a particular cultural context. This study does not recommend a one-size-fits-all approach to how a state like the US engages in public diplomacy, but instead suggests that it is important for a state to adapt its public diplomacy efforts to the particular context it is targeting while taking into account the unique culture and historical relations.

The challenge of public diplomacy efforts is that it is unclear whether these activities achieve their intended purpose. For example, Proedrou and Frangonikolopoulos (2012) argue that the cultural and educational approach to public diplomacy has not worked sufficiently and that what is needed is a systematic way to collect and analyse the opinions of foreign publics. Without asking people who are on the receiving end of public diplomacy what they think, one can only speculate as to why these efforts are not seen as sufficient. As such, more evaluative efforts are necessary. Proedrou and Frangonikolopoulos (2012) suggest that states should create official sites where foreign publics can express their opinion and ask questions. This is one way to learn what foreign public thinks about public diplomacy efforts. However, another way is studies like this one, where researchers ask foreign publics what they think about existing efforts and what they think might be more beneficial. It should become a reflective process that helps states to understand the shortcomings of their policies while also building trust with foreign publics (Proedrou and Frangonikolopoulos, 2012). This approach extends public diplomacy significantly by actually allowing foreign publics to have input on the policies of states. It also allows states to learn where misunderstandings might exist and provide clarification on policies. 'This strategic discursive PD works in the trajectory of enhancing transparency, legitimacy and thus also the efficiency of states and other international actors' foreign policies' (Proedrou and Frangonikolopoulos, 2012, p. 737). An example of this approach was when former US Secretary of State Colin Powell held a 90-minute interview with young people from 146 countries on MTV in 2002. This type of interactive engagement with foreign publics is a place where states could partner with NGOs (Proedrou and Frangonikolopoulos, 2012, p. 737). These efforts to ask foreign publics what they think are the most helpful way to really understand how messaging and other public diplomacy initiatives are being received. As such, citizen-led Facebook friendship groups like the one in this study can be a very helpful platform to not only encourage interaction and promote cultural learning between citizens about their culture, history and states. They can also serve as a long-term cultural exchange where interactions can be observed over a longer period of time to gain useful data through discourse analysis while also serving as a forum to recruit participants to participate in interviews, which will provide a much deeper understanding of foreign publics' views on both state and non-state public diplomacy efforts.

Case studies of citizen diplomacy initiatives provide important insights into the value of things like cultural exchanges in promoting peaceful relations between states that previously have been in conflict. In 1987, the largest known citizen-led cultural diplomacy initiative happened between American and USSR citizens during the latter's glasnost and perestroika period. This event included a five-week walk between cities through Russia, a demonstration in Red Square against nuclear testing and even a meeting with political dissidents, which the Soviet government allowed to take place (Brigham, 2010). Prior to this event, Americans had very little freedom of travel or movement throughout the Soviet Union (Brigham, 2010, p. 597). It took a tremendous amount of time and planning to pull it off. The walk brought together 230 Americans and 200 Soviets citizens on a "ground breaking trip—walking, talking, and traveling together" for five weeks and 450 miles from Leningrad to Moscow and left a profound imprint on the participants' lives (Brigham, 2010, p. 595). The citizens practised citizen diplomacy on both a personal and political level (Brigham, 2010, p. 597).

The Soviet and American participants were foreign to each other on many levels. It was not easy for the participants to navigate the cultural differences.

As the participants walked, slept and ate meals together; interacted with citizens in the towns they visited; and planned and negotiated activities together, they had the opportunity to really learn about each other. 'Acts of spontaneous goodwill were innumerable' (Brigham, 2010, p. 605). One of the participants, Jessica Tracy, shared that 'the walk was about communication on a very basic level. That meant meeting their enemy face-to-face. "Peace" with a capital P was not often directly addressed, the simple fact that we were there together, talking about anything was what peace is all about' (Brigham, 2010, p. 605).

The American walkers arrived in Russia hoping to find similarities between their cultures, which they did at a very basic human level (Brigham, 2010, p. 615). However, they also encountered vast differences in culture, food, music, pace of life, traditions, governmental and economic systems and languages (Brigham, 2010, p. 615). There were cultural clashes, but the walkers developed friendships that deepened over the weeks and, for some, continued for many years after (Brigham, 2010, p. 622). 'The walks were a way to experience and celebrate the power of common citizens making a difference and changing the world' (Brigham, 2010, p. 615). These kinds of people-to-people initiatives have the power to be transformative to the people that participate in them.

Initiatives that are designed to focus on facilitating long-term cultural understanding are one of the most important and overlooked areas of public diplomacy efforts. As the case study has shown, citizens value these face-to-face interactions where they can spend time socialising with one another and developing friendships, and it is through this process of being with one another and navigating cultural clashes through dialogue that peace can begin to happen. Although not nearly as impactful, virtual cultural exchange initiatives, like online friendship groups, can also help to bridge the relational divide that exists between states that have a history of conflict.

2.8 New media

Media has always been a conduit for public diplomacy efforts. However, now it is also a medium for the more relational approaches to public diplomacy. This has been influenced by the shift from old public diplomacy to new public diplomacy and has been characterised by a shift in the type of media used in public diplomacy activities. The internet and the increasing role that social media plays in people's lives have had the most significant impact on how transnational communication and diplomacy are happening. Bollier (2003) even suggests that 'clicktivism' is replacing political activism. Arguably, it is not replacing political activism, but instead changing the way political activism looks. Some suggest that online communication is eroding diplomacy as it has historically been known. 'Diplomats remark increasingly, even plaintively, that advanced communications and other aspects of the information revolution are altering the nature of diplomatic time and space—they are quickening the tempo of diplomacy and forcing open its once largely closed processes' (Ronfeldt and Arquilla, 1999, p. 2). For example, Hain (2001) questions whether this marks the end of diplomacy as we know it. Factors such as globalisation have eroded traditional state boundaries, causing online communication to be the heart of the strategies, rather than an afterthought (Leonard and Alakeson, 2000, p. 4). As a result, both state and non-state actors alike are becoming co-creators of narratives and strategic influencers of one another in international relations.

The Center for Strategic and International Studies report on *Reinventing Diplomacy* describes the internet as the 'new central nervous system of diplomacy' (1998, p. 184). The emergence of social media platforms has changed the whole nature of what is considered media and how it is disseminated. This shift is causing a leveraging of the network approach to diplomacy, with a variety of online networks serving as hubs of information sharing and relationship building. The Aspen Institute expanded the network idea to call for a change in terminology from 'realpolitik' to 'netpolitik' (Bollier, 2003). This change suggests that online communication is now taking precedent over other forms of communication. However, there are dark sides to the internet and social media as well, as evidenced by misinformation campaigns and incivility, especially around political issues. The nature of social media provides a platform for not only message communication but also dialogue. It is up to the users to decide whether that dialogue is constructive or destructive. Online communication has expanded what it means to be networked and has important implications for public diplomacy and how it is done. However, although the online world allows information to be shared quickly and to vast numbers of people when compared with traditional forms of public diplomacy like cultural exchanges, there is still a question of whether the online methods are as impactful as face-to-face methods, which can and should inform policy decisions. As such, this research study specifically looks at the ways social media impacts the perspectives of citizens who participate in online diplomacy networks like Facebook friendship groups.

State and non-state actors alike are leveraging the power of social media in public diplomacy efforts to influence globally, which was not previously possible. However, scholars agree that the emergence of social media has had the greatest impact on the role of non-state actors in public diplomacy. In many ways social media has levelled the playing field between ordinary citizens and elites. This can be evidenced by the ability of ordinary people to 'trend' or get significant social exposure around the world, which can even translate into traditional media exposure.

Digital forums provide the ability for citizens to effect change on a large scale and mobilise people quickly to support a cause or even bring about policy change (Smith, 2017, p. 89). However, the nature of online forums and social media does require a change in approach including learning to communicate in short sentences and recognising that audiences have shorter attention spans. For example, Twitter only allows someone two hundred and eighty characters for a post. This requires arguments and comments to be framed differently. In addition, the way in which debate happens online is different. Much of the debate happens on social media platforms where people are commenting on one another's posts and comments. However, you do not always see the whole list of comments because certain comments get bumped to the top for viewing, so you are not always getting the whole picture of the debate happening when you scroll through social media feeds. Further, in order to be successful, Smith (2017) suggests that citizens need funding and the ability to track their digital influence, which is not always easy to do in this current environment. Nevertheless, social media provides opportunities to gather real time data and to recruit participants for interviews for deeper exploration.

The US government has a history of using technology in its public diplomacy. However, it was initially resistant to using emerging media until the terrorist attack of 9/11 (Cull, 2013). One of the US government's attempts to solicit dialogue online was through a no longer functioning website called Open Dialogue that it facilitated with the Council of American Muslim Understanding, which encouraged Muslims to share their thoughts on the US (Cull, 2013). During Karen Hughes' tenure as public diplomacy secretary, the State Department significantly expanded their e-diplomacy efforts. During Hillary Clinton's tenure as secretary of state, she expanded these efforts, including leveraging the power of citizen diplomacy, which included the use of Facebook and even 'virtual exchange' programmes (Cull, 2013). Further, the Center for Strategic Counterterrorism Communications also used digital public diplomacy to counter radicalisation (Cull, 2013). All of these efforts recognise that online modalities are the most beneficial way to reach large groups of people.

Social media has expanded the network approach to online communication and information dissemination. It is no longer possible for traditional media sources to wait for others to come to them; they, too, must become active in online networks such as Facebook, Twitter and even Instagram. Influence happens within these network loops, and using these various social networks is called 'total communication'. (Hall and Bach-Lombardo, 2017). These forums also allow users to build and maintain relationships around similar identities or goals (Boyd and Ellison, 2007, pp. 210-230). Shay (2013, p. 13) refers to this new approach as 'peer-to-peer', where civilians, by virtue of social media, are not only consumers of government information but also information producers, with the potential to bypass governmental bodies (2013, p. 13). Governments are collaborating with the public, 'so that citizens can obtain and produce information themselves'.

The use of Facebook friendship groups as a forum for public diplomacy fits under what some scholars refer to as the move toward Public Diplomacy 2.0 (Glassman, 2008; Van Noort, 2011; Cull, 2013; Iosifidis and Wheeler, 2016). Public diplomacy 2.0 is an approach, not a technology, but it is heavily dependent upon social networking technology and came about, in part, as an attempt to counter the efforts of terrorist groups' use of social networking to plan and recruit for their attacks (Glassman, 2008). There are three elements of this approach: facilitating the creation of relationships; dependence on user-generated content from blog comments, videos and pictures; and a focus on horizontally arranged networks of exchanging information (Cull, 2013, p. 125). One significant advantage of social media, which public diplomacy theorists have been calling for, is that it provides a forum for listening to the publics and the ability to track how particular words or ideas move across networks online (Cull, 2013, p. 126). Cull suggests this is both a form of advocacy by presenting the actor's point of view and a form of cultural diplomacy by transmitting culture (Cull, 2013, p. 126). This dual function of actors using the forums to share their perspectives and learn about one another's culture is consistent with what is happening in the Facebook friendship groups that this study is investigating.

Social media is not just about messaging but also about relationships. 'Building and maintaining meaningful connections or relationships with people around the world is at the heart of digital media-based public diplomacy efforts' (Seo, 2013, p. 157). Social media creates opportunities for virtual exchange where physical exchange is not possible. These 'mind-operating opportunities offered through an exchange experience' can contribute to the experience of others as well (Helland, 2017, p. 96). These virtual exchanges allow for the development of mutual understanding and respect and give a voice to those who may not have access to physical exchange programmes (Helland, 2017). A recent virtual exchange initiative called the Stevens Initiative, which was conducted by the Aspen Institute with funding by the US government found some promising results. This initiative, named after US Ambassador Chris Stevens, who was killed in the attack on the US Consulate in Benghazi, Libya, used technology to facilitate online learning activities between students in the US and twelve countries in the MENA region. The results showed increasing knowledge of the other country or culture, an increase in a desire to gain more knowledge and an increase in cross-cultural communication skills among participants (Aspen Institute, 2019). These kinds of virtual exchanges are valuable because they also provide access to underrepresented and marginalised people, and there are fewer religious, socioeconomic and demographic factors that influence participation (Helland, 2017, p. 97). The interesting thing about these forums is that they allow a different kind of dialogue, through words and images. Initial reports suggest that virtual exchanges are helpful. Helland (2017) notes that surveys of students from different cultures that have participated in virtual exchanges showed shifts in their attitudes and more openness and curiosity about other cultures. This shift in attitudes suggests that forums for virtual dialogues can be helpful forums for promoting understanding between cultures.

The emergence of new media has also expanded research into multicultural discourse including how language, identity, cross-cultural social relations and power play out in social media (Bouvier, 2015). The nature of social media is not only a media platform, but also a dialogic platform, which has a significant impact on how relationships happen. Social media provides both new opportunities and challenges in understanding discourse. Social media is now embedded into the fabric of everyday life, 'providing new opportunities for transnational communication and envisioning diverse cultural communities which draw upon diverse ideas, values and identities' (Shi-xu, 2014). As will be discussed further in the coming chapters, Facebook friendship groups provide a forum for individuals to bridge the geographic and cultural divide that exists between people from different countries.

The ability to use social media platforms to interact with people all over the world indicates that borders are no longer a constraining factor in relations between citizens and states. People armed with a keyboard or digital device can connect with other people all over the world through social media forums, allowing them to interact, learn from one another and even develop friendships. The advent of the internet has been a consequence and catalyst of globalisation at the same time. However, not all states are supportive of complete open access to the world through the internet, which is why states like China actively block websites like YouTube and Facebook, and actively police social media websites in the country. They recognise that the internet can have a dramatic impact on people's knowledge and views.

The global connectivity and the numbers of people on social media have created a new category of relationships known as cyber community. Some critics see these communities as providing togetherness without any responsibility to behave in a respectful way (Fernbeck, 2007). However, other theorists recognise that the way people relate is changing and argue for a new definition of world community that is rooted in symbolic interactionism. This approach calls for a shift from a place-focused view of community to a process-based view (Fernbeck, 2007). Jankowski sees the new emphasis on collectivity over geography (2002, p. 37). Arguably, it is necessary to understand both the spaces where people interact and the form community they find in these places. Not all communities will be the same, nor the depth of the relationships in these communities. However, they can still be valuable. In addition, it is also important to understand the way people interact within the different spaces they gather. This helps us understand that relationships and identities are socially constructed in a variety of forums and types of interaction, rather than based on the places people live. Fernbeck cites several studies that define online community as a 'significant social construct in terms of its culture, its structure and its political and economic character' (2007, p. 51). The nature of social community is 'both descriptive and prescriptive and based on shared interest, kinship or even space' (Fernbeck, 2007, p. 52). An extension of the idea of kinship is friendship, especially in modern society where not all people have strong familial relations. In that sense, they look for community in its variety of forums to fill those relational needs that they have.

Social media is a forum where competing narratives are created and shared through processes of messaging and interaction. In the same way that traditional media influences people's views, so does social media. This provides opportunities for people to use these social spaces to redefine narratives and reinforce more positive social norms. These more positive narratives can be controlled by individual people and reinforced through people sharing the information. In addition, 'algorithms themselves become realisers of discourse, of forms of social relations, signalling up what your user community values, and signalling what kinds of ideas and attitudes are common across the section of connectivity' (Bouvier, 2015, p. 153). For example, things that are 'liked' on social media have a higher ranking and therefore get more attention. Further, what is new with social media, which did not exist with traditional media, is that the things people like or view online are then fed back through ads and additional posts related to a subject (Bouvier, 2015). This creates a reflexive process that further influences online user thoughts, views and ideas. Of course, the nature of the algorithm does tend to reinforce a particular narrative and view. However, it does not always represent a person's whole view. For example, some people limit the kinds of things they post on social media for privacy or other reasons, or perhaps they prefer to avoid controversial or political issues because of the contentious nature of these things. It is also true that people sometimes say things on social media or other internet sites that they may not say in a face-to-face conversation because the online nature creates a level of distance or less fear of repercussions for what a person says. In fact, some even suggest that there is a difference between who someone is online and offline, which makes it difficult to understand the communicative processes and how they relate to people's values, ideas and identity (Bouvier, 2015). What this shows is that social media is a powerful medium for discourse and influence that can be used for positive reasons and negative ones. These messages and interactions reinforce behavioural norms. As such, it is important to have as many people as possible using social media to push for more positive and friendly narratives so these are the kinds of attitudes and actions that can be fostered between people and states.

Critics of social media suggest that it can distract from social engagement and public affairs because the dialogue is shallower (Bouvier, 2015). This has been described as the difference between weak ties and strong ties (Brown, 2011). Not all relationships are strong ties, but they both are important. Surface-level dialogue is common among people who are just getting to know one another, which is why it is sometimes called 'small talk'. However, dialogue must start somewhere and can potentially lead to deeper levels of dialogue should people pursue it. Nevertheless, even in those more shallow or superficial types of conversations, there is a level of influence that people are having over one another's attitudes and views. I would argue that every interaction and speech act matters and has the possibility of impacting someone's views positively or negatively. In addition, there are concerns with the increasing toxicity in social media; people will say things on social media that they might not say in everyday life, because social media provides a level of anonymity. It is because of the increasing toxicity of social media that more efforts need to be made to facilitate more constructive interactions, dialogues and narratives. Furthermore, Papacharissi (2002, p. 2) argues that, since offline and online interactions occur in a single social realm, the 'false/real dichotomy blunts the interpretive power of new media and research'. It could be argued that this dichotomy does not prevent interpretation but instead shows that identities are not fixed but instead continuously changing through interactions and discourse.

One of the biggest challenges of public diplomacy has been the ability to measure its effectiveness. As a result, social media has provided a platform to attempt to quantify and gain qualitative data on how public diplomacy messaging is received. For example, researchers look at comments on Facebook posts and likes as some of the main factors. Hayden (2013) argues, though, that it is difficult to draw a connection between Facebook likes and views on foreign policy. For example, Pakistan, which is viewed as having an anti-American sentiment, has the largest number of fans on the US Embassy of Pakistan's Facebook page (Hayden, 2013). Attempts were made to look at Embassy pages and note pro-America and pro-Obama words. Although this is not dialogue, Hayden (2013) argues that it does give some insights into deeper political thoughts. Further, the Embassy did try to make its Facebook page more interactive by occasionally posting pictures and answering questions (Hayden, 2013). Ultimately, only asking questions will give insights and understandings into what people really think about a state's foreign policy, its culture and its people.

In the current climate, social media provides an excellent forum for state and non-state actors alike to engage with foreign publics, build bridges of understanding and influence attitudes and narratives. People use social media forums to do research, to keep up to date on events and current affairs, to find out about opportunities and to learn about people and cultures. Social networking sites are places where conversations take place, and it is through these conversations that people influence one another's views, either positively or negatively. People comment on one another's post on social media, and through the process, people are actively engaged in sharing their competing narratives. When used constructively, it is also a place where individuals can counter negative images, stereotypes or narratives while promoting more peaceful and positive narratives. These narratives can and do impact people's views and are, therefore, a valuable resource for public diplomacy. Online social networking forums such as transnational Facebook friendship groups provide a kind of virtual exchange where participants can ask questions, share pictures and videos, and dialogue about themselves, their countries, and their cultures. For some, these forums will be the closest they ever get to meeting someone from that culture, for others, it will be the first step in the process of learning, which may eventually result in a face-to-face meeting with someone from that culture. In either case, not altogether different from other state-led public diplomacy activities, these friendship groups provide an excellent opportunity for citizens to help to build a bridge of understanding between their country and other countries and foster more peaceful relations in the world community.

2.9 Understanding the impact

Part of the rationale for doing this study is that, in recent years, public diplomacy has come under some criticism. However, the criticism has been largely attributed to the inability to appropriately measure the effectiveness of public diplomacy programmes rather than states having problems with the notion of public diplomacy in general. This is especially true when states are looking to public diplomacy as a tool to mitigate conflicts. If conflicts are continuing or even escalating, then arguably the public diplomacy efforts are not working. However, what this book suggests is that the issues can likely be attributed to the kinds of public diplomacy activities being conducted and a recognition that an activity can impact the views of citizens and culture without necessarily translating into improved views of a state's foreign policy or government.

Views and attitudes tend to be changing and are often contingent. Brown (2017) argues that relationships in the international arena are complicated and tend to change based on world events and the people in power. The effectiveness of some public diplomacy programmes is more measurable, such as economic benefits of programmes like the International Visitor Program and numbers of foreign exchange students attending US universities (Brown, 2017). However, this data does not tell states much about those exchange students' views on that state or that state's foreign policies. As such, both quantitative and qualitative research is needed. Brown suggests the Broadcasting Board of Governors, now called the US Agency for Global Media, as a possible source of research. This is an independent agency of the US government, which operates various media outlets like Voice of America, Alhurra and Radio Free Europe, to name a few. However, he argues for a clear determination of the target audience, outcomes and desired behaviour and content of messages; how the messages will be conveyed; and how the methods will be evaluated (Brown, 2017). Although measurements of impact are necessary, it still appears that Brown is focusing on a pure messaging-centric form of public diplomacy, leaving no discussion of evaluation of the more dialogic diplomacy, which is the new paradigm. There is a need for more understanding of the impact of both non-state and state-centric forms of public diplomacy. However, because the shift has taken place from messaging to dialogue and relationships, there is a special need to understand the impact of more relational approaches, which is what this book provides.

2.10 Conclusion

This chapter has shown that much of the scholarship on public diplomacy has described it as a purely state-centric messaging-centric activity. This is due in part to the fact that many of the scholars writing on public diplomacy are in the disciplines of International Communication and Public Affairs. However, a review of the literature shows that the term public diplomacy was first coined by an American diplomat who used that term to describe a variety of interactions between citizens designed to promote understanding between citizens of states. These efforts at promoting understanding were designed to improve views of foreign publics and which proponents believed would translate into more peaceful relations between states. This chapter has also shown that activities that are seen as more relational and foster two-way dialogue through citizen networks are preferred over one-directional messaging by both the US government and public diplomacy scholars because they recognise that understanding happens best through interactions and not just one-directional messaging, which is consistent with the earliest definitions of public diplomacy as developed by Gullion. As such, Facebook friendship groups can and do fit the definitions of public diplomacy when the purposes of these relations are to promote understanding and improve the views of one another's states and its citizens.

Chapter 3

Friend or Enemy?

3.1 Introduction

Throughout history, the concepts of friend and enemy have been considered central to political life. However, there are divergent perspectives on which comes first, friendship or enmity and which plays a constitutive role in politics. This has caused some theorists to focus on the politics of enmity and others to focus on the politics of friendship. Schmitt (1996) has come to be the strongest proponent of the politics of enmity.[1] In contrast, Aristotle is known for the politics of friendship. For Aristotle, politics of friendship means the ability for people of the same identity to transcend conflicts, which serves as the foundation for civic community (NE, 1994, IX, vi, 2). Alexander Wendt (1999) notes that perspectives of friend and enemy have also come to be viewed as constitutive of international relations and are based on a self and other dichotomy. Certainly, the history of wars and other international disputes does suggest that the nature of the international system being composed of individual nation-states, each with their own unique cultures, religion, ethnicities and politics can increase the likelihood of interstate conflict. However, central to this view is the belief that because people are different there will be conflicts. This premise assumes that difference means enmity is inevitable. According to Linklater, this view is rooted in the idea of patriotism, which Rousseau says, 'The patriotic spirit is an exclusive one, which makes us regard all men other than our co-citizens as strangers, almost as enemies' (quoted in Linklater, 1982, p. 17). However, Wendt (1999) suggests that these predetermined views of friend or enemy are socially constructed and not fixed. In addition, Wendt (1999) suggests that in International Relations scholarship, there has been an overemphasis on

---

[1] See Carl Schmitt. 2004. *Theory of the Partisan: A Commentary/Remark on the Concept of the Political*. Michigan State University Press. pp. 6 and 36 and Carl Schmitt. 1996. *The Concept of the Political*. University of Chicago Press. Schmitt argues that the politics of enmity and conflict are constitutive of human nature and that conflicts cannot be transcended (1996, pp. 58-68). In his view, the existence of conflict is what creates a person's identity and as a result the concept of political community relates to the distinction between friend and enemy (1996, p. 26). Schmitt's political enmity is based upon the view that people separating into collectives could result in war between the collectives. This causes Schmitt to draw a firm line between domestic and international relations by suggesting that enmity is inherent in international relations where a perceived threat exists among states.

the study of enmity while neglecting friendship. The move toward more constructivist approaches has caused a resurgence in scholarship on the concept of friendship in IR (Berenskoetter, 2014). This has caused theorists like Oelsner and Koschut (2014) to call for more conceptualising of the idea of friendship as meaningful relations among and between states and why it exists. In particular, scholars are calling for more non-western perspectives on the conceptualisation of friendship in international relations (Berenskoetter and Van Hoef, 2017, p. 20). The recent literature on friendship in IR explores friendship through both structural and normative lenses. However, the majority of the literature discusses friendship in the context of structural relations between states by analysing it through a security lens around things like security communities and special relationships between states (see Wendt 1999, Koschut and Oelsner, 2014). In contrast, the normative literature looks at friendship through a relational lens and draws upon some of the early political theorists' conceptualisations of friendship, which looks at friendships among citizens within a particular society. In the normative sense, friendship is seen as a virtue between good men (Aristotle, 1994). However, the emergence of theories of global citizenship begs for further exploration of how friendship impacts relations between citizens of different nation-states. This is especially important as it may help us better understand how friendship between people can promote more peaceful relations between states.

This book focuses on friendship as a relational concept. This book supports Wendt's argument that views of friend and enemy in international relations are socially constructed and that views of enmity can become a self-fulfilling prophecy where its beliefs generate actions that confirm those beliefs (Wendt, 1999, p. 263). The result is that these views of enmity reinforce enmity norms, which continue to escalate until full-blown conflicts erupt. Wendt argues that the problem is that the states are no longer even assessing other states as threats but instead treat them as enemies simply based on some existential threat (Wendt, 1999, p. 236). These collective views of actors within the system end up spreading like a virus of sorts, which can change the whole nature of relations within the system. Wendt suggests that actors start to think of enmity as central to the system rather than making assessments of individual actors, and as a result, feel compelled to represent all Others as enemies simply because they are part of the system (Wendt, 1999, p. 264). The result, according to Mead, is that these collective beliefs persist through time, often from generation to generation (Mead, 1934, pp. 154-156). This perspective suggests that the continued enmity views and behaviour is a result of peoples' role as actors in the collective rather than something participants actually know about the Other. If these views are socially constructed, then enmity should not be inevitable. The best way to end the cycle of enmity is for actors to decide to transform relations by choosing to behave differently, including changing the way they relate to one another in their interactions. People are at the heart of transforming relations. However, what Wendt fails to discuss is the role that people have in perpetuating these images nor does he discuss the ways that people can be involved in transforming relations.

This book extends Wendt's argument about the socially constructed nature of international relations. Taking a constructivist approach provides the opportunity for developing a new way of looking at the relations. The constructivist approach allows us to incorporate the role of identities, ideas and perceptions and observe how they are transformed through interaction (Oelsner, 2007, p. 272). However, this book diverges from Wendt's claim that the state is the main actor responsible for constructing this meaning. In limiting his discussion of relations to states, Wendt overlooks the important role that people have in facilitating peaceful relations within the international arena. If enmity can contribute to conflict, then friendship should be a conduit of peace. Berenskoetter (2014) agrees that friendship has much more to do with settling disputes peacefully. In seeing friendship this way, one can see that it can be a tool for facilitating peaceful relations within a variety of political contexts. However, there is almost no scholarly literature on the role of friendship in diplomacy and peacebuilding. This suggests that there is a need for researchers to study how friendship has been used in international relations through empirical case study research. This includes the exploration of the interpersonal bonds between political leaders and cooperation and trust-building activities at intergovernmental and civil society levels (Oelsner and Koschut, 2014, p. 6). This book extends the research on friendship into these areas while also taking their suggestion one step further by exploring friendship relations between citizens and how relations between citizens impact relations between states. As Oelsner (2007) notes, international peace is a relational concept, and it is necessary for states to have some sort of relationship or interactions to achieve peace. In this view, peace is a dynamic social process. Koschut and Oelsner (2014) assert that friendship should not be seen as limited to state-to-state relations, but seen as the composite of the total relations between both state and non-state actors. They also note that people-to-people friendships are likely even more important than the official acts of friendship (Koschut and Oelsner, 2014, p. 203). Therefore, the idea of international friendships recognises some level of bonds between actors. 'Interpersonal friendship implies that friendship among states exists both as interpersonal bonds (or interpersonal chains of friendship) and as collectively imagined experiences of friendship' (Koschut and Oelsner, 2014, p. 204). However, what will be shown in the empirical sections of this book, these bonds do not necessarily have to be deep for there to be some value to these international friendships.

This book also argues that since what friend means is socially constructed, it can and does mean different things in different contexts. This is consistent with the suggestion of Smith (2011) that there is no single universal definition of friendship and is therefore contextual. For example, Smith notes that in Western political thought, friendship has come to take on a variety of forms such as 'eros, philia, agape, amity, dynasty, citizenship, concord, loyalty, community, solidarity, neighbourliness, fraternity, compatriotism, and comradeship' (2011, p. 15). This is also consistent with Allan's view that friendship is a relational label rather than a categorical one (1979, p. 34). This view allows one to look at friendship as a 'family of related phenomena that highlight the affective side of friendship' (Smith, 2011, p. 25; Van Hoef and Oelsner, 2018, p. 115). By seeing friendship in this way, it can be an end, or a means to an end. In this book, friendship is seen as a relational process of facilitating more peaceful relations.

By looking at friendship as a relational process, it allows one to observe the many different ways it plays out in relations between people and states. Friendship has many different forms and political manifestations (Nordin and Smith, 2018a, p. 2). It can include personal and political attributes of friendship while at the same time creating a hybrid form of friendship. However, in international friendships, relations are based not on sameness but instead on difference. Nordin and Smith (2018a, p. 4) suggest that 'friendship starts from the premise that politics is built upon co-constitution of self and other, who inhabit a shared world and whose relations are dynamic'. So, rather than seeing friendship as something that is limited to people who are the same, this view recognises the value of fostering friendships between people that are different. The strength in viewing friendship this way is in what it seeks to achieve and its goal of bringing people together who share a world (Nordin and Smith, 2018a, p. 3). In this way, it can have transformative purposes which can serve as a conduit for peaceful relations between people around the world. As such, this book takes the position that international friendships are a dynamic social process of identity construction based not on sameness but on difference, which has the potential to transform relations in the international arena. These relations can be both personal and political in nature and are designed to allow people to bridge the difference that exists between people of different cultures. They are based on cosmopolitan views of a common humanity that binds people from all cultures together (Lu, 2000). So rather than just accepting that peace is only possible among people that have the same culture or are citizens of the same country, this book argues that international friendships can be a place where difference is explored between people as agents of states. It can be a place where understanding and respect can happen and where past views of enmity and conflict can be transformed through social interactions between people. It is a place where self and others no longer connotate friend and enemy.

This chapter sets out the theoretical literature on relational friendships between people and the framework that will be used to interpret the empirical data. However, because of the inductive nature of this research, it is left to the discussion chapter to reflect upon the interview data around the Facebook friendships and interpret the findings by drawing upon the theoretical literature on what friendship means in that context. In this way, the interviewees' words are used to understand what meaning participants give to Facebook friendships in the context of transnational Facebook friendship groups between Libyan and American citizens. In the discussion chapter, what becomes clear is that these Facebook friendships between Libyan and American citizens draw upon attributes of the Aristotelian types of friendship, forming a hybrid form of friendship.

This chapter starts out with a discussion of how friendship can serve as a tool for change within the international arena. There is then a discussion of how this study is positioned within the constructivist paradigm and takes the perspective that views of friend and enemy are a social construct and if these views are socially constructed, it is possible for actors to change the way they relate by choosing to relate as friends. There is a discussion of the Aristotelian framework for friendship and how that framework can be used to understand the friendships between Libyan and American citizens in this study. Finally, there is a brief discussion of how Aristotle's friendships have been drawn upon to understand social media friendships.

3.2 Friendship as a bridge to peace

This book takes the position that viewing friendship as a dynamic social process of identity construction provides the opportunity that it can be used as a catalyst for more stable peace in international relations. Rather than accepting enmity as inevitable in international relations, allowing the possibility of friendships sees transformation as possible. As Oelsner and Koschut (2014) assert, friendship can be an agent of change because the process of building and maintaining friendships actually transforms the international community by showing alternative ways of interacting. In this way, friendship is not a thing but instead a relational process. In seeing friendship this way, it serves as a form of positive peace (Van Hoef and Oelsner, 2018). Part of Galtung's discourse on positive peace was based on a recognition of the inherent sociability of humans and their desire to surround themselves with friendship and mutual aid through empathy, solidarity and norms of reciprocity and cooperation (1964, p. 1). Seeing friendship as a 'social practice "normalises" behaviour, attitudes, and gestures and helps to construct a positive culture of positive peace' (Van Hoef and Oelsner, 2018, p. 121). There are institutional components and speech acts that characterise these processes (Oelsner and Vion, 2011). They are a 'cumulative process of engaging a plurality of social spheres in strong commitments and promises, which are reinforced through mutual proofs, increasingly coordinated cooperation and the expression of a long-standing common destiny and common political goals' (Oelsner and Vion, 2011, p. 130). This process of relating with one another can result in a shift in public opinion (Viltard, 2009). Relationships and interactions can happen both face-to-face and online and can include joint initiatives like friendship groups. These types of friendships are productive because they help people learn about each other through shared experiences, which reduces anxiety and provides happiness and moral growth (Berenskoetter, 2014, p. 61). This process of creating connections and interdependence between people helps to reinforce cultural expectations and norms, which contributes to international order.

The process of building peace involves international actors developing a shared identity of friend despite existing cultural differences. International friendships are based on relational identity rather than some pre-existing identity like being a part of the same state. It becomes a way of identifying one's self and this can start with a conscious decision to be friends with people from another country, like participating in the Libyan and American Friendship Association. This book suggests that identity is conceptualised based on social relations rather than some fixed or pre-determined identity. Young (2000, p. 82) asserts that groups do not have identities, but instead, peoples' identities are constructed based on positioning in social groups. It is through interaction that people construct an identity of friend or enemy and the way people interact is an important factor on which view they develop. These views are formed through relationships with others through interaction and recognition (Smith, 2014). When entities involve friendship, it can raise very real expectations and norms and can have very powerful far-reaching effects' (Smith, 2014; Roshchin, 2006). In this way, friendship is focused on creating bonds between people or groups through shared values (Smith, 2014). The process of building bonds between people can have a transformative impact.

In viewing friendship as a relational process, citizens as agents have the capacity to 'alter the relationships among a particular set of states' (Koschut and Oelsner, 2014, p. 202). In this way, friendship can be seen as a relational process of identity formation that is constructed between actors. This view would suggest that people are not enemies or friends based merely on being members of a particular group, but instead they have the ability to construct an alternative identity through processes of interaction. By seeing the process of identity formation as a relational process between people, and not something that is assigned to a particular group, it allows actors to exercise their own agency in promoting peace and avoiding conflict. Actors can choose an identity of friends rather than living with a predetermined identity of enemies.

In international relations, friendships are based not on sameness of culture but on difference. Through the process of dialogue, communication and interaction, actors develop collective narratives. Through this process, friendship does what enmity cannot do. It compels actors to support each other in sustaining and developing narratives and a share understanding of international order (Berenskoetter, 2014). This social process of reframing identity narratives can be a catalyst to peace.

At the heart of friendship are efforts to build trust. This book argues that trust is a vital component of social relations and it is also a necessary component of peaceful relations. Furthermore, most would agree that when there has been a history of conflict, it is difficult to rebuild trust and requires intentionality among actors. Trust can be impacted by mutually held images that state and citizens have of each other, which affects their views on expected behaviour (Castanno et al., 2003). When states and citizens have a history of conflict, they must make gestures and engage in a variety of speech acts to build good faith and overcome suspicion among people.

The process of people talking and learning about each other helps to humanise one another. Psychologists call this interpersonal contact theory (Schroeder and Risen, 2014). For example, in a study of relations of Palestinian and Israeli youth that were part of the Seeds of Peace camp, researchers explored whether participation of the youth affected their attitudes toward the other youth. What they found was that those campers who were able to develop one close relationship with someone from another group were the ones to have the most positive attitudes toward the other group (Schroeder and Risen, 2014). It is through the process of dialogue and cooperation that a 'climate of confidence eventually results' (Oelsner, 2014, p. 150). This process involves an 'accumulation of speech acts, institutional facts, gestures, spoken and unspoken discourse, proofs of engagement and trust' (Oelsner, 2014, p. 159). Berenskoetter and Van Hoef assert that consistent use of friendship language in diplomacy 'discursively directs attention to all the acts that make such relationship meaningful—trust, honesty, solidarity, reciprocity, etc.; it mobilises these associations and raises expectations about corresponding practices' (2017, p. 7). In this process, actors construct a relational culture that both friends see as valuable and desire to advance, which in turn affects their behaviour (Hopf, 2013, p. 554). These types of friendships require some form of reciprocity. Trust can be built both personally between individuals and collectively between groups. The process of building trust generally starts out more superficially in friendships and then can build as intimacy grows.

Friendship can be a beneficial social process of people using behaviour and dialogue to construct a shared narrative. The process of cooperating together on shared initiatives can be a positive step in helping people to open up and learn from one another, which can foster norms of peace. Civil society and citizen diplomacy initiatives are essential to this process. Berenskoetter and Van Hoef recognise the important role that transnational civil society networks have in fostering peaceful relations between countries through cooperation and solidarity (2017, p. 756). This is consistent with cosmopolitan ideas of global citizenship and civic friendship (Woods, 2013). Schwarzenbach describes the process of solidarity and people caring for one another as the glue that holds society together (Schwarzenbach, 2009, p. 269). These networks can happen face-to-face and in online forums like the Facebook friendship groups that are studied in this book. As such, it is necessary to understand the meaning that people that participate in these networks give to friendship relations in international relations and provide helpful insights into how to facilitate more peaceful relations in the international arena. This will be explored in the empirical section of this book.

3.3 Friendships between people

This book is most concerned with the personal forms of friendship and how relations between people impact relations between states. Focusing on people instead of nations changes the very nature of interactions. Farrands argues that individuals matter and cannot be separated from the process of international relations (2001, p.155). Further, he attempts to suggest that by putting individuals at the centre of international relations it is possible to anticipate emancipation (Farrands, 2001, p.155). To some extent, the shift to a relational perspective on international relations has been influenced by Chinese thought. Western international relations are based on individuality, whereas the Chinese perspective is based on relationality (Qin, 2009). The Chinese perspective draws upon Confucian thought that emphasises the role of 'obligatory relations in providing harmony and stability in society' (Nordin and Smith, 2018b, p. 7). Nordin and Smith call for a shift from the positionality focus on friend and enemy because they believe this leads to anxiety (Nordin and Smith, 2018b). They draw upon the work of Zhao Tingyang, who claims that western ontology focuses on things while the Chinese tradition draws upon an ontology of relations that allows for 'peaceful transformation of enemies into friends' (Zhao, 2006, pp. 33-34). For example, Nordin and Smith draw upon the Chinese concept of 'guanxi' in exploring the concept of friendship. Rather than thinking about friendship as a personal or private relationship, they suggest that friendship is a 'way of thinking about the co-constitution of Self with Other' (Nordin and Smith, 2018b, p. 2). In their view, things are a result of relational processes rather than the other way around (Nordin and Smith, 2018b, p. 3). If friendship is a relational process, then it can have many different manifestations, and people can make a conscious decision to choose to relate differently

Most of the theoretical research literature defines friendship as a voluntary personal relationship (Paine, 1969). Smith characterises friendship in relationships as the bonds between people that are based on mutual ethical and affective concern (2011, p. 4). King (2007a) suggests that people-to-people types of friendship exist on a continuum from very close 'kin' type relationships to simple acts of friendliness. As such, being friendly can be a part of friendship. Friendliness can be simple gestures of kindness done unilaterally, or something reciprocal that is more intimate (King, 2007a, p. 135). Conversely, Burns (1953) even suggests that it is possible to be friendly with people you do not like. Walhof contends that friendliness can be offered to a stranger and where the actors do not know each other (2006, p. 576). King (2007a) sees this kind of friendship as rooted in morality. Some theorists have distinguished friend relations from other types of relations by claiming that friendships are private and personal in nature (Allan, 1979, p. 12). However, in the modern world, where many relations happen online, friendships could hardly be conceived of as merely being a private relationship. In addition, Allan (1979) questions the very nature of friendship between collectives or groups. Therefore, much of what is being defined as friendship today, especially online, would likely not pass muster with theorists like Allan. However, even Aristotle recognised friendship as a political relation that involved both personal and collective attributes which were seen as foundational to binding people together within a society. So, to suggest that friendship is only personal in nature is inconsistent with much of the early views of how friendship has been conceptualised in politics.

The foundations of the relational views of friendship in IR can also be supported by the early definitions of friendship set out by philosophers like Plato, Socrates and Aristotle, who explored the idea of friendship in their work. The early philosophers' views of friendship were relational while also political. Political friendships can be seen as existing on a spectrum where, on one end, you see Schmitt classifying friendship as a forced alliance between collective actors and on the other end, Aristotle viewing friendship as an affective relationship between people (Van der Zweerde, 2007). Harmony is sometimes seen as a generalised version of political friendship, which is extended to people within a political society as a whole (Brunhorst, 2005, p. 13; Aristotle, 1994). Harmony and friendship are both supposed to remove 'hostile discord' from the polis and from the soul of the individual (Aristotle, NE, 1994, p. 143; and Brunhorst, 2005, p. 13). Political friendship is analogous to personal friendship and is believed to be the force that holds cities together (Aristotle, 1994). However, it is seen as more of a utility friendship based on friendliness and civic virtue (Van der Zweerde, 2007). Aristotle's political friendships are based on peace and mutual accord, not on kinship or ideological ties (Lu, 2009). Aristotle's writing on friendship relations focused on relationships of 'trust, openness, honesty, acceptance, reciprocity, solidarity and loyalty' (Berenskoetter, 2014, p 51; Aristotle, 1994). The purpose of friendships is to create norms within society that foster concord and bring stability.

3.4 Aristotle's friendship typology

This book draws upon the friendship framework as set out by Aristotle to explore friendship in the context of Facebook friendship groups between Libyan and American citizens. However, it does this by adapting Aristotle's approach to apply to cross-cultural friendships between citizens in the international arena. To do so it requires a loosening of the ridged standards of sameness that Aristotle sets forth. Instead, I argue that the same kinds of friendships that he discusses can exist in both the same culture and cross-cultural relations. This book suggests that the value of international political friendship is in the process of people interacting and influencing one another both individually and collectively and the ways that these interactions allow people to develop trust and understanding, which are necessary to fostering more peaceful relations within the international arena. Figure 3 shows a visual depiction of how the Aristotelian friendship typology might look in the context of international friendships in this study.

Figure 3.1 International friendship as a social process.

International friendship as a social process

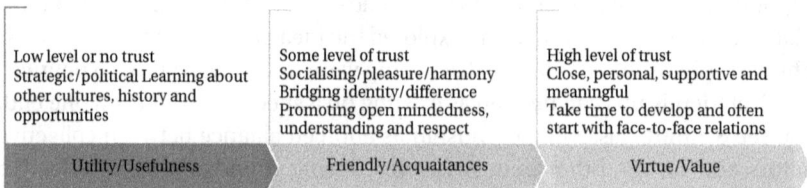

Low level or no trust Strategic/political Learning about other cultures, history and opportunities	Some level of trust Socialising/pleasure/harmony Bridging identity/difference Promoting open mindedness, understanding and respect	High level of trust Close, personal, supportive and meaningful Take time to develop and often start with face-to-face relations
Utility/Usefulness	Friendly/Acquaintances	Virtue/Value

Source: Author

For Aristotle, friendship was an inherently political concept and essential to living a good life within a political society. Aristotle characterises friendships as 'mutually recognized and reciprocated goodwill' (NE, 1994, Book VIII, 2 and 8). Friends are expected to help each other based on this reciprocal goodwill

(Aristotle, NE, 1994, Book VIII, 2 and 8). In his view, friendship was explicitly a relational concept which involved some type of shared activity or interaction. By Aristotle's definition, friendships were relations that people entered into for the value that these relationships provided to them. He sets out three types of friendships which are utility, pleasure and virtue (EE, 1996, 1236a, 35). The utility friendship is one where each party receives something in return. In these kinds of friendships, the value is primarily on the help or usefulness that they provide for the parties. By definition, these friendships are not permanent in nature. In addition, these friendships do not necessarily need to involve much interaction or emotion. The second kind of friendship he discusses is friendships of pleasure. In pleasure friendships there is more social interaction and a bit more emotions involved because people participate in them because they bring them some level of joy. However, they are lacking in depth and can be short-lived. In both utility and pleasure friendships, there are no or lower levels of trust present between the actors, and these friendships often lack much intimacy. In contrast, the highest form of friendship that Aristotle discusses is friendships of virtue, which are based on mutual appreciation for the virtues that others possess. These types of friendships are considered rare and are characterised by intimacy, affection and high levels of trust. In addition, these friendships also include the attributes of utility and pleasure friendships because the parties find them useful and enjoyable. However, virtue friendships tend to be more meaningful than the other types of friendships because of the emotional connections that the people share. Virtue friendships are deep friendships and often involve feelings of love and can be longer lasting in comparison to utility and pleasure friendships. These are an idealised form of friendship which takes time to cultivate. Aristotle says, 'a friend is not to be had without trial, and it is not a matter of a single day, but time is needed' (EE, 1996, 1238a). These virtuous friendships are sometimes called true friendships which suggests that it is the type of friendship by which all the other types of friendships are measured. In this way, the others are seen as substandard or less than.

The value of virtue friendships is in what they teach us about ourselves and how to live more authentic lives (Veltman, 2004, p. 225). However, the problem with this view is that according to Aristotle, the only way a friendship facilitates self-knowledge is if the person is like us (Veltman, 2004, p. 230). Cocking and Kennett (1998) argue against the requirement of too much similarity because people can have friendships with people who are different than them. Instead, the similarity has more to do with character, views and values, not cultural similarity. In that way, their character is said to mirror ours. However, even though friends of similar characters do not directly mirror one another, they still have elements of difference, all of which make us unique human beings. So, one could argue that interacting with people who are different from us can also provide a level of self-knowledge. Instead, as Friedman (1989 and 1993) suggests friendship relations involve people influencing one another's outlook through interaction. In fact, friendships of difference can also be very influential and help us understand 'the unique things about us when held up to those of others' (Veltman, 2004, p. 230). As such, friendships with people who are different can have a lot to teach people.

Immanuel Kant also discusses the more intimate forms of friendships in the *Lectures on Ethics* (1997) and *Metaphysical Principles of Virtue* (1996), where he describes these relations as being based on love and respect and which involve a process of people disclosing and revealing themselves. Kant holds similar views on the value of these deeper and more virtuous forms of friendship, which Aristotle sets forth. However, they differ on whether the value is in what these friendships provide for people or in the process of becoming friends. Kant sees the value in friendship as being known by another, whereas for Aristotle the value is in knowing another person (Veltman, 2004, p. 235). In both Aristotle and Kant's conceptualisations of friendship, trust is foundational, and the process of developing deep friendships involves building trust. Aristotle says 'trust and the feeling that he would never wrong me' is a part of friendship (Aristotle, NE, 1994, 1157a23-4; Aristotle, EE, 1996, 1244b25). Recognising the inherently reciprocal nature of friendship, the value is in both knowing and being known, and the interaction process cannot be one-sided if trust is to develop. Kant writes that the highest form of friendship enables friends of good character to rise above the resistance and anxiety that plagues most social interaction and to open themselves up to each other 'even without thereby aiming at anything' (Veltman, 2004, 231; Kant, 1996, 47, p. 138). These friendships, according to Kant, are where people are caring, self-less, loving and respectful, which can allow people to transcend the worry and distrust of most human interaction and reveal themselves completely to each other (Veltman, 2004, p. 231). Kant sees 'friendship is man's refuge in this world from his distrust of his fellows,' in which they can be transparent and honest about who they are (Kant, 1997 pp. 205-206). Since these types of friendships are cultivated by people of virtuous or good character, people are able to engage in honest self-disclosure with one another without fear of being hurt. Kant remarks that achieving these kinds of friendships is 'the whole end of man, through which he can enjoy his existence' (Kant, 1997, pp. 205-206). In this way, Kant suggests that the central goal of humankind is to know others and be known. However, despite espousing this idealised form of friendship, he notes that a trusted friend can one day turn into an enemy when they share one another's confidences (Kant, 1997, p. 28). As such, he cautions people to behave in such a way that they do not harm one another and thereby become an enemy. Therefore, like Aristotle, he recognises that building these types of deep friendships takes time and intentionality. As such, one might suggest that friendships are a relational process of self-disclosure characterised by people moving towards increasing levels of trust.

Since these virtuous types of friendships are rare, then that would seem to indicate that in daily life, utility and pleasure friendships are more common, and therefore, it would warrant more time being spent on investigating these kinds of friendships and how they play out in political life. Although virtuous friendship may be a normative aspiration to strive for, it would appear, based on the reading of Aristotle, that a level of goodness is a necessary precondition for all of the types of friendships he sets forth. It is a process of good people interacting with one another that is valuable and likely to produce concord. As such, even friendships of utility and pleasure can be valuable interactions that can impact the quality of relations within political society. This is why Aristotle says that the promotion of friendship is a special task of governments (EE, 1996, 1234b 1-2). The rationale for this statement is that treating people in a way that is good is an inherent characteristic of friendship which would mean that the more friendships within society, the more goodwill that is being shared between people. In this way, friendship in all its different forms is something valuable to cultivate within society.

By definition, friendships can be both political and personal. 'Friendship becomes political when it crosses the border between private and public spheres' (Van Der Zweerde, 2007, p. 159). Hannah Arendt saw that the public display of friendship does not in any way diminish it (1989, p. 51). In contrast to friendships of virtue, political friendships tend to fit within the utility and pleasure categories. Political friendships are the generalized forms of friendship of pleasure and utility which is a civil or civic virtue. It is possible to have a large number of less intimate or friendly relations with fellow citizens (Aristotle, NE, 1994, IX, x. 6; Van Der Zweerde, 2007, p. 160). Van Der Zweerde describes friendliness, or friendships of pleasure, as maintaining friendly relations within the whole of a given group of people in order to promote a positive atmosphere (2007, p. 151). It can also involve a group of actors working together to solve a practical problem (Van Der Zweerde, 2007, p. 159). It is the process of working together that helps people to become more virtuous and to get rid of discord. Van Der Zweerde argues that the idea of the idealised virtue of friendship is inappropriate for a public role, because it is seen as so special as to make it completely distant from public or political (2007, 160). As such, Van Der Zweerde suggests that friendships that are keeping a political community together are not friendships of virtuous men but, instead, a weakened and generalised form of friendship where virtuous citizens are capable of living with difference, including radical difference (2007, p. 161). I would argue that this collective virtue is one of being open-minded within the difference, because having an open-mind is necessary to develop relations with people who are different from you. Being able to bridge the difference involves a recognition that people can have a difference of opinion without letting this difference of opinion result in a friend-enemy opposition (Van Der Zweerde, 2007, p. 162). In this way, it is the process of striving for political friendships that are good and virtuous with other members of society, that brings value and peace within society. Therefore, in its political form, friendship is inherently a social process of becoming, not a thing.

Although partial to virtuous friendships, Aristotle recognises the importance of utility and pleasure friendships in political life. These friendships are described as civic friendships and are based on equality among citizens within a society and the needs people have to support one another (Aristotle, EE, 1996, 1242b, 15-16). However, because Aristotle was writing his work in ancient Greece in the context of the people of Athens, he sees these friendships as being based on sameness and limited to good citizens within society. His view specifically excluded people who are deemed to be a threat to cohesion (not good) or morally inferior including the majority of the population who were 'slaves, craftsman, tradesman, manual laborers and women' (MacIntyre, 1985; Lynch, 2002, p. 107). This also includes 'barbarians' which were essentially non-Greeks who are seen as not sharing the same moral values as the Greeks within the city. He says, 'a friend is another self' and to perceive and to know a friend is in a manner to know oneself (Aristotle, 1994, NE, IX, iv, 5). This view has caused some theorists to suggest that being from the same culture was a necessary precondition of a shared identity and consequently, friendship. However, if Aristotle puts so much emphasis on the idea of being good and virtuous, then it is more likely that being good has less to do with being a part of the same culture and more to do with the idea of shared beliefs, values and goals. Aristotle's contention is that having those things in common translates into concord and the avoidance of conflict within society. The idea is that if citizens share a common view of the value of being good and virtuous that it will result in them treating one another with goodness and respect because the 'virtuous man have a general disposition to philia, or brotherly love' (Hutter, 1978, p. 116). Telfer (1970) suggests that friendship promotes the general good in society 'by providing a degree and kind of consideration for others welfare which cannot exist outside it'. This creates a sense of duty among friends to aid and support one another, which becomes constitutive in friendship relations (Annis, 1987). Since these normative expectations become rooted in these friendships, Aristotle denied the possibility of conflict within the city based on different views of what is good. Instead, in his view, harmony with each other based on good character results in harmony being reproduced within the society (Aristotle NE, 1994). In Aristotle's view, friendship holds the city together and is more valuable than justice because the very essence of friendship eliminates the idea of enemy. In this way, friendship becomes a moral code of conduct expected of citizens within a society and includes normative expectations that create the foundation for peaceful relations within the city. These same kinds of normative expectations can be observed in international friendships and will be talked about in the discussion chapter.

3.5 The value of international friendships

Since the value of friendship is in what they teach people, this would suggest that all friendships, including international friendships, have the potential to be beneficial. In addition, utility, pleasure and virtue friendships are all possible and valuable in international relations. Yet, these variants of friendship are valuable for different reasons. Some of these relations, like utility and pleasure friendships, start out shallow, and others can move on to becoming more intimate. The value is in the process of people becoming friends. Arendt suggests that the process of developing friendship consists of people 'talking about something friends have in common' (Arendt, 1990, p. 82), I would argue that the value of friendships is learning about the things we share in common and the ways we are different. One of the critiques of Aristotle's views of friendship is it was based on his view of Greek citizens within ancient Athens and this resulted in a limited view of friendship based on people of the same culture. However, I would submit that both same-culture and cross-cultural friendships involve learning about ways that people are both similar and different. The world and people are much more diverse and relationships much more varied than in the limited views espoused by Aristotle. However, rather than discounting all the ideas put forth by Aristotle, it is possible to adjust his typology of friendships to suggest that the value in friendships is the social process and what it teaches people and the ways that it helps people understand themselves and others. This process of interacting, learning and understanding has both personal and political implications. We learn about people individually and collectively. By seeing friendships this way, we can see that knowing and being known is a foundational principle that can help to produce concord within all of society, whether domestic or international. When you get to know people, whether individually or collectively, you start to see them as human beings, just like yourself and although maybe from a different culture, ultimately, at their core still very much like you. If you are open-minded you are able to see them as a person worthy of value, respect and relationship. In viewing friendships this way, one can see that political friendships can exist between people from different cultures when they share the common values of promoting understanding, building bridges of respect and goodwill. These are good and virtuous qualities to hold. The value in these kinds of friendships is not in people sharing the exact same views, but instead people finding common ground between one another within their different views. Goodness and goodwill can serve as a conduit of social cohesion within international relations, which is why gestures of good will are foundational to diplomatic practice. Gestures of good will help to foster trust, trust fosters friendship, and friendship facilitates peace.

It is the interactions and dialogue that happen within friendships that make them valuable. Dolan suggests that dialogue among friends reveals the truth in their opinion, which constitutes a common world (Dolan, 2000, p. 266-268). Finding this common world requires intentionality of learning, understanding, empathising and supporting one another which helps to draw people together and bring stability within society. The value of these interactions relates directly to the friendships that are being explored in the empirical section of this study. I have seen this kind of good and virtuous communication and behaviour being exhibited in the context of Facebook friendship groups between Libyans and Americans. In these groups, the participants share about themselves and their culture in order that they might promote understanding and respect between the people of Libya and the US. One recent example where I observed this happening was when a Libyan in the Libyans and Americans United for Friendship and Peace group said they had seen the movie *13 Hours,* which is a fictionalized account of the attack on the US Consulate in Benghazi, Libya. This person shared how they were offended by that movie because of how it portrayed the people of Benghazi and what they perceived as a mischaracterisation of the events that happened on that day. Part of this person's concern was that they thought this movie reflected the sentiment of the American people. Soon after this post, many people in this group, including myself, posted responses encouraging the Libyan that most Americans recognise that Hollywood movies use creative licence to exaggerate things for affect. In addition, several Americans shared how they know Libyans personally and some have visited Libya, and they do not perceive all Libyans as being in support of the attack on the consulate. In addition, there was a discussion of previous posts in this same Facebook group on the day the attack happened and how many Libyans had protested against the attack. The overall thread of comments on this post was focused on validating the concerns, dispelling wrong perceptions and being encouraging. This is the kind of interaction that dispels misunderstandings and promotes trust which can help to improve relations within the international community. If the Americans in this group had not responded to this person's concerns, this person might have assumed that all Americans shared the views that were portrayed in this movie. As such, the dialogue around these concerns was valuable to both the Libyans and Americans in this group by helping to dispel myths and facilitate more openness and trust among members of the friendship group.

The value of international friendships is in what individuals teach one another about who they are personally and also about their culture, history, values and religion. When people learn about people from other cultures, it helps to humanise them, and this is essential to dispelling stereotypes and narratives that have contributed to conflicts. A very practical example of a stereotype is the suggestion that all Muslims support terrorism, which was raised as a concern in this study. This characterisation leads to Islamophobia and distrust of all Muslim people. If a person holds this view, they are bound to believe that all Muslims are an enemy and, as a result, a threat. The only way to confound this narrative is to dispel it. Muslim people are the ones most equipped to dispel the myth and help people understand what they do believe.

Just as in domestic affairs, friendship in international relations can be a conduit of peace and a tool to avoid conflicts. However, in order for it to work as such, it is necessary for actors to recognise that friendship is not limited to people within the same culture or society and that it is possible to foster friendship between people from different cultures. This requires open-mindedness. Rather than pushing people to all be the same, there should be a recognition that even within difference there is much that binds people together and a great deal people can offer one another. However, in order for this to happen, there must be a respect for one another within the difference that exists among people from different cultures and identities. Unlike Aristotle's suggestion that virtue is connected to being from the same community or culture, I would argue that this virtue has more to do with a person's character, willingness to learn, interact with people from other cultures and ultimately respect others. Just as in Aristotle's views of friendships, these kinds of relations can foster trust between people, which is an important factor in maintaining concord or peace within the global society. In this way, the like-mindedness that the actors share is one of open-mindedness and respect for others. As Aristotle and Kant both discussed, there is value in both knowing and being known, and people have much to teach one another if they are willing to take the time to engage in constructive dialogues. As such, the value of international friendships is in the social process of interaction which brings value to people personally and to society politically. In international friendships, people are teaching one another not just about themselves personally but also about their culture, history, religion, politics, etc. Learning about the ways people are similar and different helps people to understand one another, and understanding is what leads to trust. Just as in domestic relations, trust is an essential component of strong and stable relations. As such, there is a tremendous value in building trust in international relations, which is a necessary factor in peaceful relations between people. In international relations, the shared values and beliefs that are necessary are ones of good will, respect, and open-mindedness. These are virtuous qualities that are essential to fostering civic community within the international society and transcending conflicts that may arise.

In the coming empirical sections of this book the Aristotelian framework of friendship will be used to explore how Libyan and American citizens use Facebook friendship groups to learn, promote understanding and facilitate positive relations between Libya and the UA and its people.

3.6 Social media's impact on international friendships

In modern times, social media networks can be a place where friendships and the Aristotelian view of a shared life can happen. Friendship networks are becoming popular, especially among citizens, with the increasing role of social media in people's lives. Social media has now opened the door for more diverse transnational friendship networks. In these forums, people talk about both personal and political subjects but the language and behaviour exhibited in these platforms are not always positive and can even rise to the level of toxic at times. As such, having a virtuous posture of being open-minded and promoting good relations is also foundational to promoting a good life through social media discourse. Nonetheless, the very nature of these forums in providing participants with the ability to share their views and broach all kinds of subjects can be useful if they are done in a way that is open-minded and respectful. These networks have a role in influencing society to behave with more respect, rationality and affection (King, 2007b). The process of people sharing information about themselves and learning about people from other cultures can promote understanding and is a necessary first step in building peaceful relations.

Globalisation and the intentional move toward multilateral organisations have had an impact on the expansion of international friendships. With this move came more cosmopolitan views of global citizenship and support for norms that treat all people as belonging to the community of humanity and deserving to enjoy equal moral status as citizens of the world (Lu, 2000; Smith 2017). Norms of citizenship include civility and respect for all people (Digesar, 2016). Cosmopolitanism and constructivism can be integrated to characterise efforts to facilitate a friendly international environment and a global peaceful community where the international common good is a priority (Kaldor 2003). On a citizen level, social networks are the most accessible environment to facilitate these shared norms and friendly relations.

Early views on friendship relations and network studies looked at social distance as a factor in understanding friendship relations. However, the nature of geographical distance has changed with the advent of online communication mediums. No communication medium has had as much impact on facilitating global friendships as the internet and social media. In a 2005 Oxford survey of internet use, Digennaro and Dutton (2007) found that the internet is reconfiguring how friendships and social relationships happen. That study found that 20% of internet users have met new friends online, and about half of those individuals go on to meet one or more virtual friends in person. 'These findings suggest that the internet plays an important role in reconfiguring the social networks of many users' (Digennaro and Dutton, 2007, p. 591).

Considering the amount of time spent on social media, it could be argued that these forums have become their own online world. I would argue that we are no longer living in a world that was envisioned by the Westphalian system of states. The internet transcends borders, allowing people who were previously foreign to each other now to be friends and have daily communication if they wish. 'If the world has changed, social scientists must be prepared to understand it' (Tarrow, 2005, p. xii).

Social forums bring together a variety of citizens to build friendships, influence social movements and foster more peaceful relations. These online forums provide spaces for dialogue and exchange that transcend national borders. An example of such a group is the World Social Forum project, which focuses on friendships between people, ideals of social justice and recognising diversity and solidarity (Patsias and Patsias, 2014, p. 164). Patsias and Patsias (2014) assert that the forum goes beyond just sharing values and interests and attempts to foster relationship building. These forums require participants to treat each other as equals and are founded on the principle that understanding your identity is linked to social cohesion in relations with others (Patsias and Patsias, 2014). The way the group members react helps to define norms. The thing that is unique about social networks is that the very nature of these networks results in friendships. However, how friendship is defined in an online environment is quite different from how it has previously been defined in friendship relations in day-to-day life.

It is possible to view social media friendships through the Aristotelian lens, and several information technologies scholars used Aristotle's theory of friendship as the preferred framework for exploring online friendships in a special issue of *Ethics and Information Technology* from September 2012. However, most of the scholars seemed to question whether online friendships reach the level of a shared life which Aristotle discusses (Kaliarnta, 2016, p. 66). Their concern was whether the opportunity for moral reflection of self and others can easily transfer through an online medium (McFall, 2012; Sharp, 2012). However, Elder argues for an Aristotelian view of social media friendships. From his perspective, online relations meet the definition of a 'shared life', which Aristotle argues is imperative to friendships (Elder, 2014). Today, friendships are not governed by positionality or living together but instead are often activity-based. In an online environment, people have conversations, share ideas and pictures and play games. It is certainly a kind of socialising. In addition, just like in face-to-face relations, people will debate, argue and sadly even abuse people. So, in many ways, social media is just changing how people communicate, not the way they communicate. The 'interaction between two individuals online can become frequent and intense, with exchange of personal details and stories, as well as a heightened sense of connection and understanding' (Kaliarnta, 2016, p. 66; Henderson and Gilding, 2004).

One concern that has been raised about social media is the deceptiveness of people. Cocking et al. (2012, p. 183) suggest that this ability to present a false image of yourself hinders the ability for mutual understanding and appreciation of another's virtues. However, Elder (2014) contends that in online forums you can take time to get to know if someone is trustworthy by looking for consistency of behaviour (Elder, 2014; Kaliarnta, 2016). In addition, the advantage of internet is that everyone has an equal opportunity to share their views. Furthermore, Chang and Cheng (2004) found in their comparison study of online and offline friendships that typical misunderstandings and cultural differences that exist in offline settings are actually less pronounced, making online friendships easier to develop (Kaliarnta, 2016, p. 70; Chan and Cheng, 2004). He concludes with the statement that 'rather than fear social media as a threat to genuine friendship, we should consider how it can be used to foster an important good, by considering it in the context of the shared life characteristic of the best friendships' (Elder, 2014, p. 296).

It is important to note that in these articles, they were not discussing the political attributes of friendship which Aristotle is most clearly dealing with. So much of their critique centres around whether social media friendships ever advance to the level of friendships of virtue in a purely online medium. This view is consistent with our findings in the empirical section of this book, where face-to-face interactions for a period are seen as a necessary precondition to reach the deeper levels of friendship of virtue. However, most agree that friendships of utility and pleasure can and do happen online. In addition, the political purposes of friendships of utility and pleasure can also happen on a social media platform.

Online friendships are causing a reconceptualisation of not only what friendship means, but also what relationships and dialogue mean. Influence is happening differently than it happened in the past, and online friendships create natural forums for influencing attitudes and promoting understanding between different cultures. Online friendships are also challenging the boundaries of what has historically been perceived as friendships in international relations by positioning relational friendships at the centre of processes designed to foster more positive and peaceful relations in the international system.

3.7 Conclusion

The preceding analysis shows the value of personal forms of friendship in creating peace within international society. With the recent re-emergence of interest in friendship comes a desire for further exploration of the more normative and relational aspects of friendship in IR. The area most in need of additional research is that of exploring friendship as a social process between people. In addition, rather than just focusing on relations between political elites, there is a need to understand how friendships between citizens impact relations between states. This chapter has shown that friendship can be a social process of identity construction where citizens from different cultures engage in processes of dialogue and interaction to find common ground, promote understanding and build trust and respect. There was a discussion of the Aristotelian typology of friendship and how this framework can be used to understand the purposes of Facebook friendships between Libyan and American citizens. There was also a brief discussion of how the empirical data will show that these transnational friendship groups can be a place where utility and pleasure friendships happen, which allow people to negotiate differences that exist between people of diverse cultures. Finally, there was a discussion of how Facebook friendships meet the definition of a shared life which Aristotle discusses.

The next chapter explores the methodological approach used in this book to understand how Libyan citizens construct meaning around friendships between Libyans and Americans in the context of Facebook friendships.

Chapter 4
Historical Context

4.1 Introduction

Libya is an interesting case study to explore the impact of public diplomacy efforts, because there is an increasing call among scholars for more research into the global south. Libya is especially interesting because they have been a neglected demographic in conflict research in general, and we know almost nothing about citizens' views about relations with the US, which is especially problematic considering they were subject to US sanctions and a 23-year travel ban during Gaddafi's time in power and then subject to a travel ban again during Trump's time in office. These kinds of factors and the ongoing conflict within the country of Libya all provide the need to understand the unique history. This is especially important because many of the answers given by the participants in this study discuss historical issues both within the country of Libya and between the US and Libya.

This chapter provides a description of the history of conflict between Libya and the US and the rationale for this study, and why more efforts need to be made into promoting peaceful relations between Libya and the US There is also a discussion of the current security situation in Libya and how the ongoing conflict has implications for other states. Since many of US public diplomacy efforts since 9/11 have been focused on promoting positive images and combating extremism, the US has a vested interest in combating the propaganda and the influence of terrorist groups which have made inroads in Libya since the Libyan revolution. As will be discussed in further detail in the findings chapter, the Libyan people in this study noted that they value exchange opportunities between Americans and Libyans that foster open-mindedness, trust and understanding between the people of these countries. However, their views of America are also connected to their views of US foreign policy, which is seen as partly responsible for the years of conflict and strained relations between the US and Libya. Efforts that had been made to restore relations and improve Libyan views of America that started after the Libyan revolution have been stalled since the US withdrew its embassy and staff, ceased many of the civil society and capacity-building programmes and banned Libyans from travel to the US. The US government supported the Libyan revolution and overthrow of Muammar Gaddafi, and there was an expectation by Libyans in this study that the US would do more to help Libya transition to democracy and rebuild following the revolution. The limited support by the US has left the Libyan people in this study feeling abandoned by the US, and their views of the US are largely influenced by the extent to which the US is actively trying to help Libya rebuild following the revolution. There is also a recognition by participants that bringing stability to Libya is vital to providing stability in the region, and countering extremist activities in Libya and improving relations between Libyan and American citizens are necessary to counter extremist narratives that have infiltrated parts of Libyan society. As such, the US has a vested interest in doing more to bring stability, assisting with conflict resolution and reconciliation programmes, assisting in capacity-building projects and engaging in more proactive diplomatic initiatives that counter negative narratives that have existed between the US and Libya for many years.

The country of Libya has historically held an important place in US foreign policy. Its strategic location in North Africa has provided an ideal place for US military bases in the past. This, coupled with its rich oil reserves, has kept the US interested in and engaged in the region. However, relations between Libya and the US have been marred for many years by conflict and divergent foreign policy priorities. Many had hoped that the overthrow of Muammar Gaddafi would change things in Libya for the better and improve relations between Libya and the US, but unfortunately, change has been slow in coming and the US needs to do more to improve relations with Libya.

The following is an overview of this chapter. First, this chapter starts with a discussion of the historical significance of Libya to the US government and how relations with Libya declined during Gaddafi's time in power. Second, there is a discussion of the challenges for democratic transition in Libya and how ongoing conflicts in Libya continue to create instability in the region and abroad by creating a breeding ground for terror cells like ISIS to gain a foothold. These ongoing conflicts resulted in the death of US Ambassador Chris Stevens and several other Americans. There is also a discussion of the ongoing conflict between militias and leaders in the east and the west of Libya over issues of oil and power. Third, there is a discussion of the US ban on the travel of Libyans to the US and how this ban has had a negative impact on relations between Libya and the US and caused the Libyans in this study to have negative views of the US government. Fourth, there is a discussion of the current US government's public diplomacy efforts toward Libya. Finally, this chapter includes a brief summary of the topics discussed and a conclusion that the historical conflict and ongoing conflict within Libya both necessitate more efforts by the US to foster improved relations.

4.2 Historical significance

To understand the current state of relations between America and Libya, it is necessary to understand past relations. This book is most concerned with relations between Libya and the US from the end of the reign of King Idris in 1969 to the contemporary period. The modern country of Libya is composed of three historically distinct regions: northwestern Tripolitania, northeastern Cyrenaica or Barqa and the more remote southwestern region of Fezzan. Ninety per cent of the population lives along the Mediterranean Coast with the interior of the country being underpopulated (CIA, 2019). Libya is the fourth largest country in Africa in terms of land area, but the population is just over seven million people. It has a tribal culture, with Arabic as the official language. In addition, there are several distinct ethnic groups that speak their own languages. The major ethnic groups are Arabs, Amazigh, Tuareg and Teda. The official religion is Islam, with 96% of Libyans identifying as Sunni Muslims (CIA, 2019).

During the nineteenth century, the Ottoman Empire controlled much of Libya. In 1911, Italy invaded under the auspices of freeing the Libyans from Ottoman control. However, what followed were decades of colonial abuses, with Libya constantly engaged in anticolonial insurgencies (Blanchard, 2018, p. 33). On 24 December 1951, Libya gained independence. After independence, the UN helped create a federal system of government with the central authority vested in King Idris Al Senussi, while legislative authority was held by the prime minister, a Council of Ministers and a bicameral legislature (Blanchard, 2018, p. 33). During this time, King Idris was faced with a nation of extreme poverty and high illiteracy (Greavette, 2005). This caused Libya to rely heavily on foreign aid from the United States, United Kingdom and France.

During the 1950s and 1960s, the US operated an airbase at Wheelus Field outside of Tripoli, which was an important airbase and intelligence centre and, at one point, the largest US military facility outside of the US (Boyne, 2008). In 1959, oil was discovered in Libya which brought greater economic independence and growth for Libya in the 1960s. However, the weak national institutions and the gravitation of Libyan elites toward the socialist and pan-Arabist ideology of Egyptian leader Gamal Abdel Nasser caused a marginalisation of the monarchy (Kawczynski, 2011). With this move came increasing criticism of US and UK military bases in Libya, especially following Israel's defeat of Arab forces in the 1967 Six-Day War (Vandewalle, 2012). In mid-1969, King Idris left the country for medical reasons and in September 1969, a young army captain named Muammar Gaddafi led a military coup in Libya.

The US government did not actively oppose the coup because initially, Gaddafi presented a more reformist agenda and claimed to be anti-Soviet (Blanchard,

2018, p. 33). However, soon after coming to power, Gaddafi called for the immediate and full withdrawal of US and British forces from Libya, which was completed by the mid-1970s. During the early 1970s, Gaddafi started to become more supportive of the Soviet Union and began supporting revolutionary, anti-Israel and anti-western movements throughout Africa, Europe, Asia and the Middle East (CIA, 1975). These activities, coupled with Gaddafi's involvement in state-sponsored terrorism, caused US and Libya relations to deteriorate.

The first terrorist activity that catalysed a deterioration in relations was the Labelle disco bombing. The 5 April 1986 bombing of the Labelle Berlin disco resulted in the death of two US servicemen and one Turkish woman and the injury of 229 additional people, 79 of whom were Americans. President Ronald Regan blamed Libya for this attack after intelligence messages were intercepted between Libya and East Berlin. Ten days later, US Air Force fighters retaliated against Libya by bombing strategic locations in Tripoli and Benghazi. It is believed that 40 people were killed, many of them soldiers (Malinarich, 2011). In 1996, after many years of investigation, Libyan Musbah Eter, a Libyan intelligence agent who worked for the Libyan Embassy in East Berlin, was arrested for the Labelle disco bombing with four other suspects. He was summarily convicted in 2001 and sentenced to twelve years in prison.

On 21 December 1988, there was a terrorist bombing of Pan Am flight 103. This bombing resulted in the death of 270 people, including 190 American citizens, when the plane en route from London Heathrow Airport to New York exploded over Lockerbie, Scotland. This tragedy was the single worst terrorist attack against American citizens before 9/11. The investigation was carried out by the British and later Scottish government with the assistance of the FBI. Several years into the investigation, the evidence led the Scottish government and other agencies assisting with the investigation to Libya. Abdel Basset al Megrahi, a Libyan intelligence agent, and Al Amin Khalifah Fhimah, director of Libya Airlines' office in Malta, were charged in 1991 (BBC, 2015). In 1992, the UN imposed sanctions on Libya for the Lockerbie bombing. However, it was not until 1999 that Gaddafi turned over the accused for trial at Camp Zeist in the Netherlands. In January 2001, the court acquitted Fhimah and convicted Megrahi by unanimous vote and sentenced him to life in prison (BBC, 2015).

After the conviction and sentencing, the Libyan government started to take steps toward altering the direction of its foreign policy. Libya's efforts were rewarded with progressive steps toward a normalising of relations. One of the first steps was the unanimous decision by the UN, in September 2003, to lift sanctions against Libya after the Libyan government agreed that it would accept responsibility for the Lockerbie attack. In December 2003, the Libyan government also agreed to cease production of weapons of mass destruction and agreed to international inspectors. On 1 May 2003, the Libyan government formally accepted responsibility for the Lockerbie bombing by merely accepting responsibility for the actions of its agents (Sipress and Mintz, 2003). However, until his last days, Gaddafi continued to deny Libya's involvement.

On 17 February 2011, Libya joined the wave of revolutions in North Africa and the Middle East in the Arab Spring by revolting against Gaddafi first through demonstrations and then armed conflicts when Gaddafi attempted to suppress the demonstrations. Libya's Arab Spring was unique in terms of the role that external actors such as NATO played in response to UN Security Council and Arab League resolutions. The UN Security Council invoked the doctrine of the Responsibility to Protect, or R2P, by a unanimous vote in favour of punitive sanctions against Gaddafi's regime less than two weeks after the street protests broke out in Libya (Esselmont, 2016; Boduszynski, 2015). Following that decision, the Arab League called for a no-fly zone over Libya, which was the first time in its sixty-five-year history that the group supported non-Arab intervention in an Arab state (Northern and Pack, 2013, p. 116). By mid-March, the UN passed resolution 1973, which authorised the use of all means necessary to protect Libyan civilians threatened by Gaddafi's regime (UN, 2011). Gaddafi was killed by the Libyan people in the Battle of Sirte on 20 October 2011.

By most accounts, the Libyan people were grateful for the help in being liberated from forty-two years of Gaddafi's 'brutal and erratic' rule (Boduszynski, 2015, p. 736). I facilitated development programmes in Benghazi during the Libyan revolution and conflict resolution and leadership training programmes twice in 2012 and early 2013. On all those occasions, leaders of education, health and other government sectors and emerging capacity-building programmes which I encountered were all asking for the US to come to Libya to help them develop. Despite this, western governments such as the US's took what has been described as a 'light footprint' approach (Sanger, 2012). This was influenced by a perception that the Libyan people did not want the help of other countries. However, most Libyan people I met tended to look more favourably on capacity-building, education and development programmes while cautioning against outside involvement in state-building. This can likely be attributed to their brutal experience with Italian colonialism and the history of self-interested western policies after independence from Italy, compounded by forty-two years of being indoctrinated into Gaddafi's anti-western and anti imperialist propaganda (Boduszynski, 2015). However, despite opposing outsiders' direct involvement in nation-building programmes, the people tended to view western nations quite favourably and supported developing new economic ties and external security assistance (NDI, 2013).

Western embassies, including that of the US, returned to Libya soon after Gaddafi's fall, but their policies emphasised that the western role should be small and focus on supporting the Libyan-led transition (Chorin, 2012, p. 235 and p. 303; Martin, 2015, p. 129). As a result, western countries did the bare minimum to help, which led to a struggle for influence among the tribes, towns and militias. The United States' light footprint approach in Libya can also be attributed to a lack of political will at home, after years of fighting wars in Iraq and Afghanistan. It was also impacted by economic recession in the USA and Europe and an optimistic belief that Libya had the economic means and resources to conduct its state-building (Boduszynski, 2015). President Barack Obama called this approach 'leading from behind'. This was influenced, in part, by the National Transitional Council's rejection of boots on the ground out of fear of backlash from militias (Martin, 2015, p. 120).

Blanchard suggests that Libya's post-Gaddafi developments are characterised by three phases. The first immediate post-Gaddafi period took place from October 2011 to July 2012 and focused primarily on identifying interim leaders and facilitating recovery from the 2011 conflict (Blanchard, 2018, p. 5). The second period was a time of contested transition that took place from July 2012 to May 2014 and was focused on a process of ensuring the legitimacy and viability of interim institutions. The third period has taken place from May 2014 to the present and has been characterised by instability and violence among 'political-military coalitions' and Islamic extremist groups, but also by increased efforts by parties to promote reconciliation (Blanchard, 2018, p. 5).

Unlike other countries that participated in the Arab Spring, Libya did not have the knowledge or structures in place to make any formidable steps toward democracy on their own. This was attributed, in part, to decades of suffering from isolation brought on by sanctions and being subjected to Gaddafi's xenophobic ideology (Boduszynski, 2015). 'This deprived both the political elite and ordinary Libyans of the potential democratic knowledge that results from various kinds of ties to the west' (Boduszynski, 2015, p. 737). Unlike other post-conflict transition situations, such as Afghanistan and the Balkans, the international community did not send peacekeeping troops or implement efforts of reconstruction or the disarmament of militias. Instead, the international institutions often hired the militias for security, and this exacerbated state fragmentation (Miller and Truitte, 2017).

Following the revolution, Libya experienced a complete disintegration of the security sector with the fall of the regime (Bodyszynski, 2015, p. 742). Local militias continue to provide security in much of the country, increasing challenges to efforts by the national government to gain control. Some of these militias are engaging in criminal enterprises such as trafficking, terrorism, sabotage, extortion, blackmail and sexual assaults, and taking over the oil pipelines (HRW, 2014). In addition, extremist Islamist militias have destroyed historical sites, like the World War II cemetery in Benghazi.

4.3 Challenges to democratic transition

The path of transition to democracy has been particularly difficult for Libya because Gaddafi's form of authoritarianism suppressed not only free expression and autonomous social activity but also the development of the state and civil society (Vandewalle, 2012). The absence of a centralised governmental system has hindered the provision of security and public goods and has prevented the development of democratic institutions (Boduszynski, 2015, p. 736). In 2012 and 2014, a constitutional drafting assembly was held, as well as elections for legislative bodies. Blanchard (2018) notes that the election process was administered transparently but was hindered by threats to candidates and voters, declining rates of participation and 'zero-sum' political competition. As a result, efforts to transition Libya to a democracy have failed, and instead, multiple internal skirmishes and civil conflicts between rival militias have ensued.

A 2013 survey conducted by the National Democratic Institute indicated that the majority of Libyans support democracy, with 85% of respondents indicating that they believe that democracy is the best form of government (NDI, 2013). However, there was a 10% decline in optimism for Libya's state of affairs from May 2013 to September 2013. At the time of writing this book, Libya has gone through another civil war and has made very little progress in transitioning to a democracy. I have personally seen an increase in Libyans on Facebook talking about a desire to return to the days of a dictatorship because, during that time, there was at least security. The 2013 survey showed 41% of respondents believed Libya was worse off since the 2011 revolution but predicted things would improve in three years (NDI, 2013). Unfortunately, most would agree that this has not been the case. This could likely be attributed to the failure of the government to effectively promote conflict resolution programmes between citizens. With 92% of respondents supporting the need for conflict resolution programmes, it should be one of the highest priorities.

The western countries' post-revolution support has primarily been civil society and elections support. In 2011, the US provided $90 million in humanitarian assistance to Libya. In 2016 and 2017, the amount totalled $28.3 million, some of which went to support UN humanitarian efforts (Blanchard, 2018, p. 29). However, the lack of efforts to disarm militias and build reconciliation while neglecting sufficient security, has been more than an oversight. 'Libya's rich indigenous tradition of mediation and reconciliation could not be effective in the face of massively armed groups' (Boduszynski, 2015, p. 743). The US and UK did offer help with weapons recovery initiatives, but they were limited in scope and were cancelled when the security conditions deteriorated (Boduszynski, 2015, p. 743). Similarly, efforts to train police failed for lack of a unified command structure and were cancelled when the US training programme for Special

Forces was overrun and had equipment stolen (Turse, 2015). However, it was the attack on the US Consulate in Benghazi by Islamists and the murder of US Ambassador Chris Stevens and three other American citizens that caused the US to significantly reduce its engagement in Libya even further, especially as the attack became a political bargaining chip for Republicans to attack the Obama administration for allegedly failing to provide sufficient security. There was ultimately a trial and conviction of Abu Khattala for conspiracy and providing material support to terrorists for the attack on the US Consulate, and he received a sentence of twenty-two years in prison (Hsu, 2018).

Blanchard has argued, 'The attacks on U.S. personnel and facilities in Benghazi had a chilling effect on international efforts to support Libya's transition, as did subsequent incidents in which militia groups demonstrated their willingness and ability to disrupt the workings of the national government in order to preserve their interests' (2018, p. 6). As a result, many US diplomats were evacuated from Libya while US efforts shifted to finding the perpetrators of the attack (Sengupta, 2012). The security conditions in Libya continued to decline in 2013 and 2014. By the summer of 2014, skirmishes took place near the US Embassy in Tripoli. In July, the US Embassy, as well as other missions, departed Libya and set up remote operations in Tunis or other locations.

By 2014, the transition process had stalled as the security situation deteriorated further. The June 2014 election of the new House of Representatives to replace the General National Congress (GNC) was contested, causing another year of 'stalemate and failed attempts at mediation' (Blanchard, 2018, p. 6). The eastern part of Libya aligned with the Tobruk-based House of Representatives and militia forces from Benghazi, calling itself the Libyan National Army (LNA). This group was led by retired General Khalifa Haftar, a former military officer under Gaddafi who later became an exile in America, only returning to Libya during the revolution. This alliance targeted a range of Islamist forces and other militias (Gomati, 2014). While in the western part of Libya the remnants of the GNC in Tripoli aligned with a militia called Libya Dawn to contest the House of Representatives and LNA's legitimacy (BBC, 2016). As the violence escalated, the remaining US diplomats were evacuated.

The struggle for power within Libya is ongoing and escalated when the Libyan National Army and ISIL, led by Haftar, began to launch attacks on Tripoli and forces loyal to the UN-backed Government of National Accord (Aljazeera, 2017). It is believed that, according to World Health Organization figures, approximately 1,100 people have been killed, more than 5,750 wounded, and 100,000 displaced since the Tripoli offensive began (Aljazeera, 2019). Attacks have occurred against health workers and facilities, which have been strongly condemned by Ghassan Salame, UN Envoy to Libya, who has stated that 'we will not stand idly by and watch doctors and paramedics targeted daily while risking their lives to save others. We will spare no efforts to ensure that those responsible will face justice' (New Arab, 2019).

The situation has been exacerbated by the involvement of foreign states. Turkey and Qatar have been the main supporters of the UN-backed GNA government, while Egypt, Saudi Arabia, Jordan and the United Arab Emirates are backing Hafter (Aljazeera, 2019). In July 2019, France, Britain, Egypt, the UAE, Italy and the United States called for an ending to the hostilities, suggesting that terrorist groups were trying to exploit the security vacuum (Aljazeera, 2019). However, the US continues to send mixed messages because Trump's phone call with Haftar in June 2019 expressing his support for Haftar's efforts to combat terrorism has been construed as undermining support for the internationally recognised government (Wayne, 2019). Acting Defense Secretary Patrick Shanahan said that a military solution is not what Libya needs and instead urged Haftar to pursue democratic stabilising efforts in Libya (Wayne, 2019).

The US government has engaged in periodic military strikes against ISIS targets and other terrorists in Libya. In particular, the US supported Libyan forces in Operation Odyssey Lightning, a 2016 campaign to eliminate and expel thousands of ISIS supporters from the coastal city of Sirte (Blanchard, 2018). The US government believes that the threats posed by ISIS members and Al Qaeda have decreased, but recognises that these groups have not been completely eradicated and that conditions could deteriorate in the future (Blanchard, 2018). In July 2017, the US announced that ISIS is 'no longer in control of the territory of Libya although it continues to be active within the country' (UN, 2017). Further, ISIS attacked a court complex in Misrata in October 2017, and the US engaged in airstrikes against ISIS targets in November 2017. In March 2018, US AFRICOM Commander General Thomas Waldhauser described ISIS forces in Libya as 'dispersed and disorganized and likely capable of little more than localized attacks' while also noting continued US military support for anti-ISIS fighters, but encouraging political reconciliation as necessary for lasting security (Waldhauser, 2018).

The ongoing conflicts in Libya are not only a security issue but also a foreign policy and diplomacy issue, and international organisations like the UN and other states have been actively working with Libya to try and broker a peace agreement that can allow the country to stabilise and move toward one unified government. As the security situation in Libya has deteriorated and rival militias and terror networks fight for control over the country, international states have also gotten involved in trying to advance their own interest. The terror networks, the radicalisation of citizens and the trafficking of migrants from Libya all present serious issues that states like the US must be concerned with and engaged in combating. Since 2014, US officials and other international actors have attempted to convince rival Libyan groups that inclusive, representative government and negotiations are preferable to attempting to achieve dominance through militias and arms (Blanchard, 2018). In addition, the UN Security Council has authorised financial and travel sanctions on individuals or groups that are attempting to threaten the completion of political transition or are threats to the peace, stability and security of Libya (Blanchard, 2018).

Following a year of bitter conflict compounded by the rise of threats from Islamic State supporters and other extremists, in December 2015, some of Libya's leaders signed on to a reconciliation proposal facilitated by the UN. The UN also helped to negotiate an agreement to create the Government of National Accord (GNA), which was charged with overseeing the completion of the transition (UNSC, 2015). This agreement called for a nine-member GNA Presidency Council composed of members of Libya's key factions and regions, and which would hold national security and economic decision-making power, with the House of Representatives as the legislative power in consultation with the new High Council of State made up of former GNC members (UN, 2015). However, not all Libyan leaders have supported this effort. Fayez al-Sarraj was designated as the Prime Minister and worked with members of the Presidency Council to implement the agreement. However, these efforts have been opposed by rival political factions, including Field Marshal Khalifa Haftar's Libyan National Army. The plan was launched in 2017 with the hope that it would be finished by the end of 2017. The hope was for elections to take place in early 2019, but at the time of this writing, elections still have not been held.

The US government has supported multilateral efforts in Libya but at times has also acted unilaterally (Blanchard, 2018). However, Blanchard notes that various Libyans have accused the UN and other third parties of unwarranted interference in Libya's domestic affairs, 'particularly when they perceive outside interventions to undercut their interests or serve those of their rivals' (Blanchard, 2018, p. 13). Blanchard (2018) notes that for the US, the key issues in Libya are 'transnational terrorist and criminal threats emanating from Libya; [and] the security and continued export of Libyan oil and natural gas'. Libya has the tenth largest oil resources in the world and the largest in Africa. Blanchard suggests that 'conflict and stability in Libya have taken a severe toll on the country's economy and weakened its fiscal and reserve positions (2018, p. 14). The US is also concerned that Libya is a transit country for Europe-bound refugees and migrants. This has become even more concerning, given recent reports of slave auctions and human trafficking in Libya. In addition, the security of weapons stockpiles and unconventional weapons materials is also a significant concern (Zakaria and Stewart, 2011). However, undoubtedly, one of the key US interests developed when the Islamic State opened up a branch in Libya after foreign fighters arrived from Syria in 2014. In fact, by early 2016, senior US officials estimated the group's strength had grown to 6,000 members across the country among a larger community of Salafi jihadists (Brennan, 2016).

Some suggest that it was the revolution that resulted in the radicalisation of Libyans. During the revolution, many Libyans returned from exile to help out. Some were fighters, but others returned to help in media, medical and humanitarian areas. One of those exiles was Ramadan Abedi, a member of the Libyan Islamic Fighting Group, which is associated with Al Qaeda (Hasan, 2018). His 22-year-old son Salman also returned with him. Friends of Salman said he returned to Britain from Libya a changed person (Hasan, 2018). After the people overthrew Gaddafi, Salman joined the Islamic State and went back to the UK as an angry young man (Hasan, 2018). On 22 May 2017, Salman blew himself up at a concert in Manchester, UK, killing twenty-two people and injuring 112. Islamic State took responsibility for the attack in Manchester. Shortly after the terror attack, Hashem Abedi, Salman's brother, was arrested in Libya. On 15 November 2018, the Head of the Presidential Council, Fayez al-Sarraj announced that they had finalised the extradition of Hashem Abedi to the UK and that he would be sent to the UK at the end of 2018 (Assad, 2018).

The US government also sees the Al Qaeda Islamic Maghreb as an ongoing security threat. This group is believed to be active in Libya's more remote areas. A June 2015 US airstrike in eastern Libya targeted prominent Al Murabitoun jihadi figure Mokhtar Belmokhtar, who was the leader of the group that attacked a natural gas facility located in Amenas, Algeria, in 2013, which killed three Americans (Blanchard, 2018, p. 19).

The preceding has shown that the history of conflict with Libya and the ongoing terror attacks and conflicts involving Libyans, including the attack on the US Consulate, indicates there is a need for the US to do more to counter extremist narratives and to foster more peaceful relations within Libya and between Libyans and Americans.

4.4 Travel ban

The Trump travel ban has had an impact on Libyan views of the US government and impacted relations between those states. In March 2017, Trump signed Executive Order 13780 banning travel into the US from certain Muslim-majority countries for 120 days and indefinitely from Syria. This order included individuals from Libya. In September 2017, this so-called 'Muslim ban' was downgraded to certain restrictions on countries that the administration perceived as doing too little to protect against terrorists coming into the US. The September 2017 guidance provided restricted entry for Libyan nationals as immigrants and non-immigrants in business (B-1) and tourist (B-2) visa classes (White House, 2017). According to the administration, the justification was that the government of Libya faces significant challenges in sharing public safety and terrorism-related information, has significant problems with identity management protocols and has not been fully cooperative in repatriating Libyan nationals removed from the US (White House, 2017). In September 2017, the government in eastern Libya announced that it would engage in a reciprocal arrangement against Americans, calling the US decision a 'dangerous escalation, which puts Libyan citizens in one basket with the terrorists the army fights [and which] will force the Interim Government to adopt only one option—the principle of reciprocity' (Libya Observer, 2017).

Ongoing terror attacks in Europe and other parts of the world only served to bolster the rationale for the proposed travel ban among Trump and his supporters. Trump tweeted that change was coming after a bomb exploded in the London Underground (Shear and Nixon, 2017). Trump used the Manchester bombing and London Underground bombing as an opportunity to tweet about the travel ban, which stirred up more fear and anti-immigrant views, especially among his supporters.

4.5 US Embassy public diplomacy efforts

With ongoing tensions in Libya, the US Embassy in Libya has started to engage citizen diplomats in their public diplomacy efforts. On 25 September 2018, the US Embassy in Libya launched the USA Café group on Facebook. The group description says, 'A space where you can interact with Americans, discuss different topics and get to know America and the American culture'. This group currently has over 4,000 members. US student interns and embassy staff use this forum to hold Facebook Live talks on topics like American history and culture, holidays, sports and business, and to share about exchange opportunities. Most of the talks are done in English by student interns at US universities, but on occasion, there are talks in Arabic.

As I have argued elsewhere, 'the value of this initiative is that it shows the power of social media to be a conduit of education and diplomatic bridge-building. Participants regularly ask questions and provide feedback to the speakers' (Gibson, 2019). The members of the group sometimes post pictures of different parts of Libya, showing a desire for dialogue beyond one-way messaging. However, the comments and feedback are not always positive and sometimes appear to reflect the ongoing turmoil in the country. The information shared about exchange opportunities and education programmes in the US seems to be the most popular among Libyans, with many eagerly seeking information on how they can go to the US (Gibson, 2019). Having this Facebook group while having a travel ban for Libyans sends mixed messages. At times, I have seen Libyans ask questions about why the US is not doing more to help in Libya with its ongoing security and development issues. In addition, it seems that the Libyan participants are interested in more interaction, as is supported by their asking questions. For example, one participant shared about being accepted into a US university programme and expressed concerns about the visa interview process and how to navigate it. Unfortunately, there was no reply to these questions. Instead, it appears that the US Embassy in Libya still sees public diplomacy as a one-directional messaging activity focused on cultural understanding, with little concern for bi-directional dialogue. In addition, they also seem to ignore the role that US foreign policy has in ongoing tensions with Libya.

4.6 Conclusion

In conclusion, this chapter has shown that the history of relations between Libya and America has been marred by conflict. Libya has remained an important state for the US government because of its rich oil reserves and its strategic location in North Africa. However, US interests should not stop there. The US government's commitment to promoting democracy and fighting terrorism should incentivize them to do a better job of restoring positive relations with the Libyan people. Libya's ongoing insecurity and its proximity as a hub for human trafficking are equally problematic. In addition, it is important for the US government to be concerned with efforts by religious extremists and terror networks to radicalise the Libyan people. Security and military efforts are insufficient in combating these extremists. Instead, there must also be proactive public diplomacy efforts and conflict prevention programmes. These programmes must not only focus on promoting positive views of America and its culture but also instil trust among Libyans by engaging with them as friends instead of enemies and focusing on capacity-building programmes that will not only help Libya transition to democracy but also develop as a stable country.

The history of conflict with Libya, the ongoing conflict within Libya and the travel ban on Libya are all significant issues in terms of Libyans' views of US and its foreign policy. As is shown in the findings chapter that follows, the Libyan citizens who participated in the focus group interviews spoke a great deal about these issues and how they inform their views of the country and its people. They also discuss ways that they think more peaceful relations can be fostered including relational approaches between citizens, capacity-building among civil society organisations and changes to US foreign policy like the travel ban.

In the following chapter, the empirical results are presented of both the pilot face-to-face and Facebook focus group interviews with Libyan citizens on their views about Facebook friendships between Libyan and American citizens.

Chapter 5

Findings from Focus Group Interviews

5.1 Introduction

This chapter provides the empirical results of this book, which included both face-to-face and Facebook focus group interviews with Libyan citizens. The purpose of this study was to explore what effect transnational friendships between Americans and Libyans have on Libyans' views of Americans and US foreign policy. The researcher believed that a better understanding of what meaning Libyans give to Facebook friendships with Americans and whether these relations impact their views of Americans and US foreign policy would better inform the kinds of public diplomacy policy decisions that are made. This study involved exploring what friendship means, perceptions of friendships with Americans, the best way to promote more peaceful relations and whether and how friendships with Americans impact Libyans' views of US foreign policy. The empirical part of this research involved collecting focus group data from one pilot face-to-face focus group with Libyans in Denver, Colorado, USA and an additional Facebook focus group of Libyans located in Libya. There was a great deal of overlap between the topics that were discussed in both the face-to-face focus group and the online Facebook group. As such, the results of the focus group interviews have been combined and organised around overarching themes. The participants' responses have been anonymised. For clarity's sake, the participants in the face-to-face focus group are designated by SP for 'speaker' and a number. Participants in the Facebook focus group are designated by FB and a number. The chapter presents the findings obtained through focus group interviews with thirty-eight participants.

The data is structured under the following themes: the meaning of friendship; differences between same culture and cross-cultural friendships; open-mindedness and respect; online versus face-to-face friendships; the impact of media on views; cultural exchange promotes understanding; trust-building and inclusive communication; capacity-building and education programmes; civil society programmes have more impact than government; US foreign policy is the problem. The overarching theme of the findings is that Facebook friendships between Libyans and Americans promote understanding, which can improve relations between these states, but these friendship groups do not improve Libyans' views of US foreign policy.

5.2 Meaning of friendship

The participants uniformly saw friendship as a strong relationship between two or more people that could happen in a variety of settings, including life, work and studies. It was seen as one of the special relations in society. It was described as 'the best quality humans can have in life' (FB6). These relationships bring joy and happiness. One participant described this as 'friendship is almost one mind in two bodies' (FB3). Friendship is seen as a basic human need. For example, SP3 said, 'We are human beings. I mean, we have to socialize. It's part of our sociology'. This definition is consistent with the early theoretical literature's account of friendship and will be discussed further in the discussion chapter.

Friendship is viewed as a normal part of social life and starts when there is a level of personal comfort between people. It is seen as especially important to have friends when you are outside your comfort zone, and you do not have your family around. SP2 said, 'So you don't have your family, your related people, so you are trying to find friendship to go on, and then it could grow more and more'. This view sees friendship as a support system, which is especially beneficial when you do not have your family around.

Central to the concept of friendship is trust and the ability to be honest with each other, no matter what the cost. One participant noted that 'friendship is a trustful alliance, mutual cooperation and standing for each another against the life issues' (FB18). Friendships are also about support and having people who make you a better person. This involves 'having someone accept you exactly the way you are, supports you when you struggle, and helps you to do the right things while doing the best to make you happy' (FB22). This is consistent with Aristotle's early definitions of friendship of virtue and will be fleshed out more in the discussion chapter.

The participants indicated that friendships can fall into a variety of different categories, like friendships with benefit and those without benefit. SP3 said, 'I prefer friendship without benefit'. Friendship without benefit is not an instrumental type of friendship but is having a friendship with someone simply because you like being with them. SP1 described friendship without benefit as a friendship 'without any obligation, without needing anything from him; just for the sake of friendship. Not for people's money or...' These friendships were seen as real friendships and are therefore more valuable because the person is not seen as using you for their own benefit, but instead just likes being with you. Participant SP3 said, 'and your friend, he'd be like yours, not be fake man, you know what I mean? Don't pretending someone else. That's friendship'. The different types of friendship that were discussed are consistent with the different types of friendship put forth by early political theorists like Aristotle and will be explored more in the discussion chapter.

The participants noted that making friends can be difficult. They start casually as acquaintances, where you are starting to get to know people, and then can move toward a deep friendship. It is difficult to move from being acquaintances to deep friendships and is usually dependent on feeling a deep connection with a person. Unfortunately, having different opinions with people seems to be a strong indicator of whether someone moves from being an acquaintance to a strong friend or not.

The challenge of moving from being an acquaintance to a relationship characterised by deep friendship was described as particularly difficult these days. SP3 noted, 'it is very difficult to get someone nowadays; not easy'. In addition, this participant maintained that keeping friends can also be very difficult. SP3 noted, 'I don't know…because for the last few years' experience, I've been shocked with my friends. I lost a friend just for my opinion. Yes… That was very, very hurting'.

Friendships are seen as a valuable and necessary part of life, and the participants recognise that there are different kinds of friendships, ranging from acquaintances to deep, meaningful friendships, and each having their own value and purpose. These discussions on the different kinds of friendships are consistent with the theoretical literature, which indicates that what friendship means is contested and will be explained more fully in the discussion chapter.

5.3 Differences between same-culture and cross-cultural friendships

The participants discussed the fact that they generally have specific reasons for making friendships. In both same-culture and cross-cultural friendships, you must have something in common. Being from different cultures does not make deep friendships impossible. However, there are some differences between same-culture friendships and cross-culture friendships. Same-culture friendships are among people from the same nationality and are based on personal knowledge of a person and the commonalities shared in life and culture. Same-cultural friendships are entered into for personal reasons, whereas cross-cultural friendships are between people from different cultures or nationalities and can be entered into for personal reasons and cultural reasons. 'Who we friend outside the country can convey to us his/her culture and change your view towards people in that country' (FB1).

Some participants noted that religious and cultural differences can make friendships between Americans and Libyans more challenging. However, it was maintained that it does not have to be a barrier. SP3 said, 'we have a lot in common'. What is key is the ability to understand and respect the differences between cultures. One participant said about one of their American friends that 'we exchange ideas, support each other . . . you learn different new things from them, it's healthy to see the world from different angles' (FB7). Differences in language and religion were considered more of a factor than cultural differences. SP1 noted, 'I still think the main reason is religion-driven and language-driven'. However, the religious challenges centred more on the fact that Libyans, being Muslim, tend not to go to bars or drink alcohol. Although it was noted that some Libyans do drink alcohol, it is generally not consistent with the Muslim lifestyle. This difference has more impact on where they socialise rather than whether they socialise. For example, SP3 said:

> My American friend when they invite me to dinner, they don't drink because they know I can't sit at a table with drinks. So, it is harder to go to restaurants together, but we can go to houses together. That's one of the things, that they have to make adjustments when they want to go out with us.

The participants also discussed the fact that, in many ways, there are even differences between friendships with people from other parts of Libya. They may eat different food or have some different cultural norms from the part of Libya they are from, but sharing those similarities and differences is what makes those friendships 'amazing'. In friendships, you are always learning new things. But SP2 noted, 'So yeah, I can let go more with a Libyan girl than with an American one'.

Although religious differences can be a barrier to relations between Libyans and Americans, the participants discussed the fact that there are a lot of connecting points between Christianity and Islam which can be helpful in bringing Americans and Libyans together. SP3 said, 'The best American friends I experienced, even here or in West Virginia, are Christian people. They are very supportive, they are very understanding. I think we are alike...' SP1 noted, meanwhile, that it is easier developing friendships with Americans who are older and have more exposure to multiple cultures. SP1 mentioned that 'we are religion-based cultures, so we follow our religion to our life. It, therefore, helps to have a friend who understands how Muslims pray and what are the forbidden things to do'. SP5 said, 'Actually, I have a lot of friends, American and different religions too, but when I'm meeting them, we talk just like humans, not focus about religions and different cultures'. The view that the Muslim religion does not have to be a barrier to relations with Americans is influenced in part by their religious beliefs, which require them to respect all religions and all people.

The view of the extent to which religion serves as a barrier to relations tends to be influenced in part by perspectives on the type of behaviour and lifestyle choices that people engage in. Libya is a Muslim-majority country and, as such, tends to follow more conservative views. Islamic law governs not only what is legal, in many situations, but also what is perceived as appropriate cultural practices. This has very important implications for social interactions with people from non-Muslim majority countries. The extent to which religion is seen as a significant barrier is likely influenced by how significant a role religion plays in each individual person's life. FB9 states:

> Religious differences play the major part in the prevention of making friendships with Americans. This is due to the fact that we, as Muslims, are advised to avoid any contact with whatever that may in any way, lead us towards the path of committing a sin, and having a friendship with someone who is not Muslim is included in that. Communication with strange men and women by the opposite gender is prohibited in Islam, and this is especially the case for females, for females are forbidden from getting married to men whom are not Muslims. Other reasons may include that partying, drinking alcohol and eating at restaurants serving pork, which are very common in America and are completely forbidden in Islam.

Despite the significant barriers that religion seems to provide for people from different cultures and religions, FB9 went on to say that friendships between Americans and Libyans are still possible so long as Americans respect Islam's rules. He said, 'As the world advances, Islam is finally respected by foreigners, and having a friendship with a foreigner, within the limits of Islam, is not really a bad thing to seek' (FB9). This explanation goes against many of the early views of friendship in Politics and International Relations, which suggests that friendships between people of other cultures are problematic because of the self/other distinction and will be fleshed out more in the discussion chapter.

There was a recognition among participants in this study that religion can be used for good or evil, as has been shown throughout history. Unfortunately, the participants noted that media tends to emphasize the bad side of religion while neglecting the good. SP3 talked about the time when there was a snowstorm in downtown Denver, and his mosque opened the doors to provide food and shelter to people. He emphasised that this is the true side of Islam, and unfortunately, the media only shows the violence and terrorism being perpetrated in the name of Islam. According to another participant, 'the media works hard on that they create Islamic phobia' (FB29).

Although there are challenges in developing friendships with people of other cultures, the participants overwhelmingly recognised that cross-cultural friendships are worth it. 'The cross-cultural friendships were helping me a lot to fill the gaps between race, colour and religion' (FB2). It was also discussed that cross-cultural friendships provided an added dimension from purely same-culture friendship. That component involves cultural learning. In cross-cultural friendships, you are learning as much about the culture as you are about the individual. These relationships also involve expanding your worldview. One participant shared a story about his first trip to visit the US and a meeting with an airport security official that developed into a friendship after the security official learned that he was from Libya and asked to take a photo together. They bonded over a discussion of connections between the history of Boston and the city of Derna in Libya. The key to developing cross-cultural friendships is to find common ground with people and work to build upon that. Ultimately, the participants in this study value cross-cultural friendships because they provide opportunities for people to learn from one another.

5.4 Open-mindedness and respect are key

Open-mindedness, curiosity and respect were discussed as the most important factors in building cross-cultural friendships. The participants overwhelmingly supported the idea that honesty and mutual respect remove any barrier that exists between people of different cultures. Having cross-cultural friendships can also influence people's views of another person's culture. SP2 said, 'I think it's amazing to understand more people, people that have a different view'. Having an open mind was related to the idea of global citizenship. Deep within this concept is the recognition of the commonalities that all humans share and a desire to build upon these commonalities. SP6 noted that his grandfather only had an elementary education, but he learned to speak Italian, German and Arabic. He was seen as an open-minded person because he was willing to know and respect others. This kind of quest for learning is seen as very important in bridging the divide between cultures. Finding common ground requires effort and curiosity. The participants noted that a willingness to learn about people of other cultures can start online. With the internet, the world is truly at people's doorsteps. 'I think distance isn't a big issue as long as you have some common thoughts with the international friends' (FB31). SP2 said you can learn 'what Libyan culture is and what Libyan people are, it's easy to have friendship online and yes, it depends on the other side of the computer'. It starts with being open-minded and having a desire to know and understand humanity.

With open-mindedness and curiosity being seen as the most important characteristic of people who desire to build relationships with people of other cultures, it is conversely seen that closed-mindedness is the biggest barrier. If people are not willing to learn about other people, then they are not willing to be friends. It is a willingness to do research and try to learn about people's culture that indicates whether someone is open-minded. According to SP4, online, 'you can just get a lot of information'. SP2 said of closed-minded people, 'They're gonna fake it for sure. So you can have thousands on Facebook of people, but just ten friends'. This distinction is important because it shows that participants make a clear distinction between real friends and simple Facebook connections.

Close-mindedness was mentioned as a significant factor in hindering cross-cultural relations. FB3 noted that 'closed minds cannot see the overview'. SP2 said, 'I think that's one of our Libyan problems. We have a restricted view, you just look at life from one very, very key thing'. The participants noted that some people are just naturally more interested in learning about other cultures than others, based on their innate curiosity or because they are diplomatic and they have some political reason to enhance relations. However, there was a recognition that open-mindedness can be learned, but people have to care enough to want to learn. Part of that comes from having one foreign friend that you love, who 'motivate[s] them to learn these friends' cultures' (FB38).

Being subject to the indoctrination of Muammar Gaddafi's anti-western views and his intentional censorship and control of media, as well as being subjected to years of UN and US sanctions, has had a historical impact on the views of the Libyans in this study. FB9 gave an example of how historic relations between America and Libya have hindered the open-mindedness of Libyans:

> Making friendships with foreigners in general, and with Americans in particular, have not been very welcomed in our Libyan society. This is due to some religious and cultural differences between the societies... growing up, I remember being told that English songs were made to curse and humiliate us: Arabs in general. This might be because we fear what we don't understand, and may also be a result of the previously unfriendly relationships between the two countries. Moreover, the Libyan society is a conservative one, with almost no communication with anyone who cannot speak Arabic, therefore, the idea of just communicating with foreigners rather than having friendships with them is usually never thought of by Libyan people.

Another cultural challenge to building friendships with Americans was the perception that Americans would not find Arabs as interesting because of the geographical location and because of the current security situation. However, there was a recognition that 'Adversity is the nature of our life. Neither religion nor culture will be a barrier to developing friendships with Americans' (FB22). Willingness to bridge the cultural divide was seen as most important in building relations between Americans and Libyans.

Open-mindedness was considered the most important factor in developing cross-cultural friendships. In addition, cross-cultural friendships help to create open-mindedness among people. In that sense, they are mutually constitutive of one another and will be explained further in the discussion chapter.

5.5 Online versus face-to-face friendships

The participants recognised that as technology changes the way that people communicate, it also impacts the ways that people make friends. One obvious difference is 'online you use your fingers while meeting people you use your mouth' (FB6). Since the introduction of Facebook, people can now make 'friends' with people all over the world. However, the question remains among some whether these virtual friendships are truly friendships in a normative sense. Others might suggest that social media is changing not only the way we relate with other people but also how we socialise and interact. Considering the amount of time people spend on social media, it could be argued that social media friendships are the new normal way of making friendships. However, others might suggest that these relations are rather shallow and lacking in the depth of intimacy that is present in traditional friendships.

The participants in this focus group spent a significant amount of time discussing how online friendships differ from face-to-face friendships. Some of the participants did not consider Facebook friendships to be real friendships but instead considered them to be more of an acquaintance. For example, FB9 said, 'We know each other maybe! Maybe if we got to know each other over Facebook then to meet somewhere will make us friends, otherwise no!' Others took a similar stance by distinguishing from Facebook connections and Facebook friendships. Most people who are members of Facebook would likely agree with this sentiment because many 'friends' on Facebook are people whom they have never even met before and even rarely, if ever, enjoyed any real communication with. So, in that sense, calling these people friends does not necessarily translate into those people being actual friends in a meaningful way.

Social media was described as valuable, because it bridges the divide between people from different countries. SP3 said, 'Due to the new technology the distance does not affect the ability to make friendships with Americans'. Before the creation of the internet and social media, you would have difficulty in connecting with a person from another country. For people who have never met before, Facebook serves as a type of virtual introduction, where you can research and learn about someone and explore whether you might want to pursue a real friendship with them. SP6 said, 'You're gonna find all the data, all the information. For example, I want to know these guys, how they drink, how they eat so I'm gonna search on social media before connecting with them so I'm gonna get the information before I start to connect with them. It's the best way to do it'.

Another advantage of social media that participants suggested was that it allows you to bridge the communication divide that also exists between people of different languages. Translation software has come a long way since it was first introduced and is now integrated into social media platforms. So, even when people post things in a foreign language, you can translate the posts and understand what they are saying. It is becoming increasingly common on Facebook to see posts with comments in multiple languages. SP3 said, 'I think social media helped me a lot. I got a lot of American friends; we do a lot of work publishing articles, editing stuff... .we never met face-to-face'.

Those participants who live in the US also noted that when they moved to the US, they found the different accents throughout the US to be difficult to understand. It is especially problematic with people from the southern part of America. SP3 said, 'On social media, you don't find it so, you're gonna learn, you're gonna get what they say'. The participants' responses on the value of social media are consistent with the theoretical literature on the importance of new media in building bridges and promoting understanding and will be explained in the discussion chapter.

Meaningful friendships had the most impact on the participants' views. Face-to-face friendships are perceived as much more meaningful than Facebook friendships. FB3 said, 'Face-to-face friendships are absolutely different from online friendships'. Emotions have a strong impact on friendships and the depth of emotional connection is more prevalent with people you spend in-person time with. FB30 said, 'If you want to be a strong friendship, you have to start with a direct face-to-face for a period of time'. FB31 said, 'To have a strong online friendship you must stay long time talking and trying to know each other more while face-to-face friendships are always faster and more transparent as you can't hide your quick thinking by slow thinking before answering in a chat'. The participants maintained that simply being with people in day-to-day activities allows you to 'share dialogues, food, visits... etc. So we have understood the nature of each. Whereas online friendships are friends in a default world we can't feel' (FB1).

In addition, there are limits on what a person can learn about people on social media. This is especially true when people limit what they share about themselves or, as is sometimes discussed, that people have a different online persona than a real-life persona. Whether this is actually true, it is most certainly correct that you only get a partial picture of someone online. SP6 said, 'There are things you cannot find in social media but face-to-face, you can learn a lot'. However, other participants noted that in face-to-face conversations, people are more willing to say what they think you want to hear and that social media gives a truer picture of who people are. SP6 said, 'Some people, they're gonna lie in front of you but social media, you're gonna get more than 80% of people who are gonna say the truth'. SP1 agreed with this perspective and noted, 'Social media is kind of law-free environment, so you can see what many people think.

Face-to-face, they can't say it because they're afraid. They can't tell you the truth. They can fake it'.

The participants were part of either Facebook friendship groups designed to foster cross-cultural friendships between America and Libya, or members of other Facebook groups organised around a variety of interests, such as hobbies, family and career. They joined these groups to learn and socialise with people with common interests. FB2 said, 'I was joining Facebook friendship group since 2012. The name of the group is Libyans and Americans United for Friendship and Peace. I would say Facebook friendships affect positively between people in both countries. They are helping to understand each other'. These Facebook groups help to promote understanding between people of different countries. FB29 said the reason he participated in Facebook friendship groups was 'to learn about and from others, exchange experiences and ideas and be part of the international community and understand what's going on and to try to help my country'.

The participants indicated that most of the American people they considered as friends on Facebook were people they had met previously. As such, they saw the Facebook relationship as a continuation of a friendship that started face-to-face. In that situation, Facebook served as a helpful forum to keep in touch. FB29 said, 'it's free and easy to contact friends, send photos and stay in touch all day'.

Online relationships through social media are increasingly becoming the new normal way of interaction, especially in terms of facilitating cross-cultural relations with people who live in other nations. They are different from face-to-face friendships, and Facebook profiles and forums are often used more to learn and gather information rather than to interact in meaningful ways. In that way, Facebook is used both as a social platform for interaction and a media platform for learning.

5.6 Impact of media on views

The participants in these interviews recognised that both traditional media and social media are having an impact on people's views both negatively and positively. Consistent with the views of many people, the participants noted that mainstream media tends to focus on showing only the bad things and not the good things. For example, there was concern that the media focuses heavily on Muslims involved in terrorist attacks but gives little attention to Muslims involved in doing positive things. There was also a recognition that news sources tend to frame the story through their ideological perspective. SP4 said, 'Then they have news, what they need to show people. They will not sometimes show the truth. This is the way to give the people like, opposite ideas about countries and this stuff'. This same participant went so far as to suggest that both mainstream and social media even include non-truth to manipulate the hearts and minds of people. One participant shared that the media has had a significant impact on the way Muslims, in general, are viewed. FB29 noted, 'Media works hard on that, they create Islamic phobia, as we noticed clearly on the last election in US. In politics this is an attempt to alienate and isolate'. However, media could also be used to raise awareness and 'create sensitivity between countries' (FB29).

The participants also noted that both traditional and social media have had an impact on their views of America. In many ways, Libyans' exposure to diverse media perspectives on global events is recent, because during Gaddafi's time as leader, media was strongly state-controlled and censored. However, with the internet came more freedom and opportunities to learn about other places and perspectives, and it gave Libyans the ability to begin to make their own decisions about what they believe.

The internet and social media have had the biggest impact on helping people learn about other cultures. SP2 said, 'The internet, social media opens new doors. You just take the name of a country, you can see the pictures and this is amazing'. Although Facebook is a social network, the participants shared that they more frequently use Facebook as a forum to find out about issues that are in the news. However, there were varying views on whether media, including social media, has more of a negative or positive impact. FB2 maintained that 'media plays a key role in forming and shaping opinions and deepening already existing cultural misunderstandings between cultures and religions'. Another participant said,

> Media Media Media! It's responsible for making bad reputation about other countries and it's really good at picturing them as retarded and barbarian...now if the media succeeded making this picture...this will indeed make the Americans scared of that country without even meeting them or getting to know them personally and this might lead to conflict with support and agreement of the population (FB18).

The positive ways that media impacted the participants' views included seeing media clips of the USA intervening to help people around the world, including Libya. However, the participants also noted that their views were also positively impacted by seeing Americans engaging in demonstrations against their own country on human rights issues such as Trump's travel ban and the treatment of minority groups. This was especially important to illustrate to Libyans that not all Americans support their government's policies.

Some of the participants shared that the media had given them negative and distorted views, which ended up changing when they met Americans. For example, FB28 said, 'Yes indeed what I use to know or to hear is that USA citizens do not like Arab people, they ignore them and they look snobby but it was not like this. My best friendship is from USA'. FB1 said of media, 'it had an impact before having American friends, like all American seemed to be as their policy: unfair, tyrant and aggressive'. It was only through meeting Americans face-to-face that they 'see the true picture of Americans' (FB1).

There was also a recognition of the fact that governments now increasingly use social media as part of their public diplomacy efforts to target the Arab world. However, the participants did not perceive this as a bad thing. FB2 said, 'These countries are using more media outlets than ever to connect with the Arab people, and they are relying also on both website and social media platforms in the Arabic-language for broadcast news and current affairs programming in the MENA region'.

There was agreement among participants that although social media platforms such as Facebook do help to bridge the divide by providing some opportunity to learn about people from other cultures, they do not necessarily change Libyans' views of Americans. FB2 said, 'To be clear, Facebook is not changing my views of Americans. Facebook has changed the way we communicate'. However, there was a caveat to this participant's statement, because he had lived in the US for almost four years. So, in no way was Facebook changing his views because he already knows the American people from living among them. FB2 said, 'I know the American people in person. They are (generally) very nice, welcoming and friendly people. Facebook has helped us to be close to each other'. These nuanced distinctions are important, because they show that participants are influenced to some extent by both by face-to-face relationships and social media relationships, and when they have personal relationships with Americans they perceive those relationships with Americans as more impactful than online friendships.

The value of Facebook for people who already have American friends is in the ability to stay in touch and nurture existing relationships. FB20 said, 'If it supports realistic communication, it's more influential on issues, or it will be easy come, easy go'. It also helps people to network and learn. FB1 said, 'It make the whole world as a small village we can tour via the internet in just a few hours. So when we like to know anything about any country, just post your question and after seconds we can get the answer. This can allow people to create an international cooperation between countries'.

The participants had different perspectives on whether they used Facebook to search out American friends. In particular, there was a difference in answers between Libyans who live in the US and those in Libya. Where a Libyan in the US is more likely to use Facebook to research more about a person they had already met, the Libyan participants in Libya do not actively use Facebook to try to make friends with Americans. FB1 said, 'I don't use social media to learn about any country'. FB3 said, 'I don't use Facebook to learn about Americans'. Others had very strong views on whether friendships should even be made online. FB8 said, 'I am not a fan of making friendships via social media. I use Facebook to communicate with people that I know'. FB31 said, 'I can't imagine myself surfing the web and my goal is to make friendship with Americans or to get to know them more, but this can happen accidentally if you have interests in common'. An example that FB31 included was 'I made some American friends on Facebook because I met them in a group for watercolour artists and most of them were Americans although it's a global group'.

The area where the participants tended to have the strongest views was on whether Facebook friendships improve their views of Americans. They maintained that Facebook does not change their views of Americans, but face-to-face does impact their views. Instead, Facebook friendship groups provide opportunities to learn about Americans on a more superficial level and provide a level of understanding between cultures that did not exist before. FB3 said of Facebook friendships, 'I don't think it has much impact'. FB8 said, 'I believe that FB helped in widening the communication between people from different backgrounds and perspectives but at a superficial level. The time wasted is more negative effect from my point of view compared to the benefits'. In addition, FB8 noted, 'I don't generalise and judge a whole population from Facebook posts'.

Face-to-face was seen as the best way to learn about people and their culture and to dispel myths. FB3 said, 'A real contact changes views'. SP4 said, 'If you wanted to know about any countries or any people in those countries, I think face-to-face, it makes you more clear. Because, like when we see Facebook or this stuff, sometimes I cannot imagine if this is truth or not'.

The participants' comments about the good and bad of media and how positive media messaging is necessary for people and governments to promote more positive images, are consistent with the theoretical literature on the importance of public diplomacy and will be talked about in the discussion chapter.

5.7 Cultural exchange promotes understanding

The focus group participants maintained that cultural exchange programmes are the most helpful way to improve relations between Americans and Libyans. Strained relations between America and Libya during Gaddafi's time in power and years of sanctions had left Libyans with very little exposure to American people and culture. However, after relations began to be normalised between the two countries, the US State Department began to implement some limited cultural exchange programmes. Unfortunately, after the assassination of Ambassador Chris Stevens, most of these programmes stopped. FB2 said,

> I think that the role of the US Embassy and State Department in promoting good relations between American and Libya is limited. There are no active participation of citizens and open discussion between America and Libya. Such as these activities are important in promoting good and close relations with the United States. It is very important that discussion also takes place elsewhere.

Most of the participants were aware of different projects the US had been involved with. When asked about whether the US Embassy does a good job of promoting good relationships between Americans and Libyans, SP2 said, 'No, I worked for the Italian Embassy for five years in Libya, before the revolution and three after. The job that the Italian Embassy did in Benghazi, it's more social'. However, SP4 disagreed with SP2 and discussed the fact that he had met with the late Ambassador Chris Stevens to discuss opening a culture office. SP4 said, 'Since 2012 they started opening scholarships for the first time, started an exchange program. I have consulted to choose people to travel to the states. But that's happening since September 2013 and he was killed, everything changed'.

The participants discussed the fact that there is a need for the Libyan Foreign Ministry and Libyan Embassy to be involved in fostering good relations between Americans and Libyans as well. However, the participants did not know about any cultural exchange programmes being facilitated by the Libyan Embassy or Foreign Ministry.

Programmes like scholarships for Libyans, student exchanges and even a virtual hub were mentioned as possible ways to foster understanding. FB31 said, 'For me internet activities are not really effective the way the real activities are'. The participants favour programmes that involve mutual exchange and learning between countries. They recognise that both Americans and Libyans need to learn about one another. FB7 said, 'Joint programs in art, sport, education, etc. show the Americans the real Libyans who hate war and violence, who wants to live in peace and share their culture with the rest of the world'.

The participants noted that cultural exchange and friendship groups are, to some extent, a kind of citizen diplomacy. This is consistent with the theory literature and will be more fully interpreted in the discussion chapter. They recognised that citizens do play a vital role in building good relations between Americans and Libyans. There were diverse answers. These included FB5, who said, 'Yes, I think that'. FB30 said, 'somewhat'. FB31 said, 'Yes, if it is well controlled and does not lose the aim of the group after sometime'. While FB1 said, 'It depends on each group's activity' and FB30 indicated that 'Trust and alternate benefits' were necessary. FB3 said, 'Word of mouth can promote good relationship. The citizens are acting as ambassadors of their countries'. FB31 said:

> It depends on the activities promoted by "the other culture" through their embassies and consulates. If they share their activities and get involved in Libyan activities in different ways, this will make their culture reaching a lot more citizens and these citizens of course will attract much more citizens who will be interested to see more of the other culture.

This perspective reflects the fact that cultural exchanges can have a compounding effect because participants in cultural exchanges share about experiences with other people. FB1 said, 'They play an important role in changing the negative views of same country citizens as well when they participate in activities with different cultural people can understand how they think towards their country and try to convey the true picture of their country'.

During the focus group interviews, the participants also discussed the fact that cultural exchange programmes need to do a better job of reaching the average citizen and being focused on cultural learning between cultures. Too many programmes were seen as being focused on the educated or more elite members of Libyan society. FB31 said, 'A lot of these citizens have no idea that they can actually reach the embassy or if their voices can be heard if they try to reach the embassy, besides the embassy and the consulate are so far by distance from here and this indeed will make it harder to build bridges'. SP2 said, 'The problem, what I have concern about is the normal Libyan woman and man. That's what I'm concerned about, not us. We can have resources even without the embassy and consulate'.

For those participants who had experience participating in cultural exchange programmes, they noted some interesting things that they had learned and the positive impact it had on them. FB7 shared their experience participating in the International Visitor Program in the US. On the trip, she/he visited the US for three weeks. She/he visited Washington, DC, San Francisco, Missouri and Florida, and had meetings with USAID, the State Department, the Libyan ambassador, politicians, lawyers, NGO advocates, schools and universities. She/he said, 'The American people were very kind and friendly and I was surprised by different things'.

The participants also recognised the value of non-state actors' involvement in cultural projects. NGOs have also received funding to do some cultural projects in Libya. SP3 noted, 'Also we do forget the Department of State has funded a lot of NGOs who've done a lot of projects in Libya. I've been following this. You talk about millions spent on Libya in NGO groups'.

These findings support the theoretical literature that discusses the importance of non-state actors in diplomatic strategies that promote cross-cultural understanding and will be discussed further in the discussion chapter.

5.8 Trust building and inclusive communication

Central to the idea of improving understanding between cultures was the topic of trust-building between countries. In particular, the Libyans who participated in the Facebook focus group discussed concerns about the lack of what they considered 'inclusive communication' by US State Department officials with people in all the regions of Libya. This discussion included a need for Americans to understand the role that national identity and regional identity play in people's lives. Historically Libya has been divided into three regions: Tripolitania, Cyrenaica and Fezzan. During Gaddafi's rule, the people in Cyrenaica suffered more at his hands than the people of Tripolitania. In addition, the people of Cyrenaica, and Benghazi in particular, were much more vocally outspoken against Gaddafi's policies, which caused him to treat them more poorly. Furthermore, Benghazi, the largest city in Cyrenaica, was where the Libyan revolution began. In addition, because the oil resources are located in Cyrenaica, the people of that region are adamant about ensuring that the people of Cyrenaica are not put in the same position as they were in the past, which is one of the main reasons for the ongoing fighting. Interestingly, several participants from the Barqah area in Cyrenaica posted photos of the landscapes in their local area and pictures of their local flag and an oil rig, showing a strong regional identity. FB19 noted, 'Barqah/Cyrenaica has its own regional national identity from culture, heritage, customs and traditions, history accents and dialects, political views, etc'.

This regional identity is especially important at this time, when leaders are still negotiating the type of governmental structure Libya will have. In addition, because Libya has continued to be plagued with internal fighting, this has caused a great deal of uncertainty among the people about the potential for Libya to be structured in a similar way as it has been in the past. Much of the internal conflict centres around oil rights. FB4 said, 'Most of the Libyan internal fighting is about the resources and especially oil revenues'. He noted that with the amount of oil that Libya has, every Libyan should share equally in the oil and have a good life, but that for '50 years this wealth has been controlled by very few people and the rest of Libya is living below poverty formula, this has to change'. As foreign governments consult with Libya about its plans for democratic transition and the establishment of a government, there is still a great deal of controversy over what that government should look like.

Participants in Cyrenaica noted a great deal of concern for what they perceived as a lack of inclusive communication by members of the US government. FB20 suggested that one way to improve trust in Libya was for the US government to 'communicate with the three regions of Libyan in an intensive and fair manner'. For this to happen, there need to be more consistent efforts, which have been lacking since the US Consulate in Benghazi was destroyed and the US Embassy in Libya moved to Tunisia. FB4 said, 'Have an open mind and stay'.

One participant noted a concern about the US government's consultation with Islamists and members of the Muslim Brotherhood. This behaviour is causing suspicion among some of the Libyan people. In addition, FB4 discussed the importance of a strong US presence in the east of Libya because of the 'old and good relationship the US had from the early 50's till the late 60's'. He also noted, 'A lot could be done their starting with a US Consulate and a culture centre and also help rebuild the destruction of the war'.

A lack of trust was also seen as a factor in perceptions about the efforts by the US Embassy to promote good relations. FB1 said, 'I think there is a notable effort. However, what spoils these efforts is mistrust'. Biases and lack of transparency are perceived as a contributing factor to mistrust. FB6 said, 'Without facilitating trust the future between Libyan and American people will take long time even if the politician come to agreement. I know a trust is a vital factor'. In comparison with the theoretical literature on the importance of public diplomacy, building trust between countries was highlighted as an important feature and will be explained more fully in the discussion chapter.

5.9 Capacity-building and education programmes

The participants in these focus group interviews made a strong connection between the US helping to rebuild Libya and improving its image in Libya. Capacity-building and education programmes are seen as a paramount concern for the Libyan people in improving stability in the country. Since the US has held a historic role as a leader in the world community, it is also seen as the most important country in providing developmental assistance. Therefore, the Libyans tended to connect the provision of capacity-building and educational assistance with improving relations between the US and Libya. Conversely, the failure of the US government to provide ongoing assistance with rebuilding is in some ways perceived as a lack of concern for the country of Libya.

There was a recognition of the fact that the US government has already provided a great deal of capacity-building assistance through the US Embassy and NGOs, and this has had some impact on changing Libyans' views of

America. FB1 said, 'I think America has already begun changing Libyans' views of America through the programmes from the embassy and volunteers who come to help us. However, we're looking forward to getting more help'. In particular, there was a desire for more training programmes for military, police, government and business leaders that can assist in 'standardization of institutions' (FB5). FB4 wants to 'invite Americans to come to Libya and demand US involvement in Libya's economy and infrastructure and support US policies in the region'.

In addition to the cultural exchange programmes discussed previously, there is also a desire for knowledge exchange programmes. FB6 noted the need for training in business innovation, trading and tourism projects. FB28 recognised the need for cultural exchange projects in Libya that are connected to culture and not political views. The participants have put a lot of weight on the ability of the US to reform and rebuild Libya while improving relations. For example, FB4 said, 'The US and Libya can have the best relationship, the US can invest in Libya's economy, and rebuilding the infrastructure. Training the army and police force is the most important. Help distribute oil revenues equally and disarm the militias and gangs'.

Some of the other participants wholeheartedly discussed support for capacity-building and training programmes but drew the line with the US meddling in domestic politics. However, they also desired for other countries to stay out of domestic politics as well. SP2 said, 'Everyone, even Turkey even Emirates, even Saudi Arabia. Everyone has to stay away. Just Libyans sit down like our grandfathers did and figure it out'. For example, SP2 said, 'Stay away from politics. Yes, I agree'. While SP1 said, 'Stay away from our country, we'll be fine'. So, there was a lack of consensus on whether the US should be involved in disarming militias and gangs and distributing oil, which appears to be more of a domestic affair. For example, FB16 said, 'But we don't want interference with the army and the police'.

There was a recognition by participants that Libya needs significant infrastructure assistance as well as training. FB4 said, 'Libya is in need of everything from A to Z'. As such, they are looking for a long-term partnership with the US, not just short-term one-off projects. For this to happen, it requires business investment. To start with, they need education support. FB5 said, 'Can help Libya in all things, economy, army, police, education, health, also improve cultural relation'. FB5 agreed, 'I think these solution to Libya, so to improve relation between US and Libya'.

The participants in this study saw the US government as a leader in the world community materially, ideationally and militarily and, as such, they support the view that the US has the capacity to do more to help Libya rebuild than other states. They also desire for the US to prevent other foreign states from meddling in Libya, which is due to the perception of the US government as taking on the role of the world's policeman. There was also a discussion of the importance of continued cooperation between Libya and the US. FB4 maintained that it is important to continue the legacy of Ambassador Stevens who is known as someone who loved the city of Benghazi and its people. FB4 said, 'He was working on all these projects in Benghazi and we have to honour his wishes by continuing his work and show the world Libya and the US are partners working together to fight terrorism and promote peace'.

Cooperation between Libya and America is directly linked with improving relations between these states. By partnering together on long-term projects, it shows commitment and a desire to have long-term relations. Long-term commitment is important to building trust and improving the image of the people of these states. For example, FB1 suggests 'build[ing] a real cooperation with America in different fields [and] through this Americans can perceive Libyans-two countries are getting more closer'.

5.10 Civil society programmes have more impact than government

The participants uniformly had much more positive views of civil society actors than government actors. As a result, they tended to discuss the need for more partnerships and projects led by civil society and educational institutions rather than government. The participants see the US as a role model in the area of education and industry. However, FB1 noted that this was not necessarily the case in the area of government and religion. Part of the participants more favourable views of civil society organisations is influenced by what is seen as a natural altruistic motive of these groups. Having lived under the rule of a dictator for many years and having no real civil society organisations to speak of during that time, they tend to distrust governmental leaders as a whole, not just the American government.

The participants wanted to see more civil society programmes, because these programmes are seen as very effective in improving relations between states. When discussing her participation in the International Visitor Program in the US, FB7 said, 'These kinds of programs are very useful, interesting and promotes good relationships between the two countries', FB1 said, 'Sometimes, individual initiatives are more effective in changing the negative views between countries than what governments can do, especially when people get benefits from these projects such as a work of scholarship'.

Educational programmes were overwhelmingly cited as the most beneficial way to improve relations between countries. FB1 said, 'It is very effective to get the views much closer'. This was also seen as very important in targeting religious intolerance. FB6 said, 'We fight it by education and exchanging learning.

Don't forget that Muslims believe in Christianity and believe in Virgin Mary is one of the 4 women who's placed in heaven by God'. Although there was a discussion of formalised educational programmes, there was also a recognition that just meeting together and dialoguing is a form of knowledge exchange. Education was also seen as a good place to focus efforts, because as FB1 noted, there is 'mutual comfort, though [not] trust yet'. Those educational programmes facilitated by civil society and universities were seen more favourably than governmental programmes. For example, FB5 said, 'If it is direct between people and university and only supported by politics'.

During the Facebook focus group interview, I showed the participants a video about an online collaborative learning initiative between US and Libyan students facilitated by the Aspen Institute called the Stevens Initiative, which is named after the late Ambassador Chris Stevens. The participants all saw this initiative as an effective programme and a very good project. SP3 shared a personal example of being invited by a university in the US to present on the political and security situation in Libya and how this impacted views. This person said,

> I remember it was an amazing day. So, I've been talking about Libya. It was 2015. I've been honest. I showed them what's really happening since 1969 to 2016 in like, one hour. I think like me, start to have a small group like political science professors. I remember one told me, 'Your experience in the last few years is more than my experience 20 years in political science'. He said, 'You lived something I wish I can live'.

After the Libyan revolution, the doors started to open for more opportunities for Libyans to learn from the US and improve relations between the states. This was the main motivation for SP3 to participate in civil society projects with the US. SP3 noted, 'For me it was the revolution in Libya. If we want to succeed, follow United States better. Have good relationship with the United States'. This same motivation to improve relations between Libya and the US was behind SP3's decision to start the Libyan and American Friendship Association group on Facebook. SP3 saw this forum as an opportunity to connect many different types of people: 'political people, business, culture and education'. Other participants who are members of groups like this noted that groups serve more than one function. SP2 said, 'I do it for two reasons, because I'm social and I like to know people and understand. Even because I live here I want to know how they think about me'. However, SP2 went on to discuss that she/he joins other Facebook groups that do not have Libyans in them, specifically related to issues that she/he cares about. As someone who currently resides in the US, this person sees these groups as a way to form community, even when there are not any other Libyans in the group. SP2 continued, 'you do it because you live here. You want to be part of a community, of a society, you want to be yourself, show them that you're not an alien and at the same time, know them because you live here'.

This section of findings indicates that there are a variety of reasons people participate in exchanges and civil society projects. These reasons include that they might have something concrete they want to learn, they have a desire to connect with others, to socialise, and to show people that they have more commonalities than differences. These findings are consistent with the theoretical literature and will be discussed more in the upcoming chapters.

5.11 US foreign policy is the problem

Much of the rationale for the US government's efforts to increase its public diplomacy efforts in Muslim-majority countries following 9/11 was based on then-President George W. Bush's belief that America had an image problem. Bush believed that the poor image of the US was related to a perception of differing values between Americans and citizens of Muslim-majority countries, in particular Arab countries. As such, since 9/11, many US public diplomacy efforts were focused on educating foreign publics about American culture, history and people. Although these projects are helpful, the participants in the Libyan focus groups made it very clear that they see US foreign policy as the reason for conflicts and not the American people or American values. They all noted US foreign policy as the reason for strained relations between the US and Libya. FB9 said, 'I found that government have to do with this more than religious and cultural differences'.

FB6 said, 'US foreign policy is the biggest factor causing conflict between countries'. The participants' discussion of US foreign policy went back in time and showed the impact of historical memory on views as well. For example, FB30 viewed America as wanting to colonise Libya and cited US Navy activity off the coast of Libya during the Tripolitan War in 1801-1805. However, for most participants, negative views of US foreign policy were more recent. In particular, several mentioned the American air raid on Tripoli and Benghazi in 1986 and the blockade for ten years that came about after it was found that Gaddafi had engaged in acts of state-sponsored terrorism. There was also some mention of the terrorist attack on Pan Am 103 over Lockerbie and how the resulting sanctions impacted the country of Libya. This tragedy continues to hang over the heads of Libyan people with many still questioning whether Libya was really responsible for that attack, which can even be seen in the way they frame the tragedy. FB8 discussed the resulting effects of the international community's response to the Lockerbie attack on the Libyan people:

> The implemented sanctions on Libya after Lockerbie accident. Normal
> Libyans were suffering and not the leaders. Also it was not based on

sound evidence. There are other suspects like Iran and extreme Palestinian organization. Even if Libya was responsible; they left Gaddafi ruling. Libya continued to export the oil because the west needed it and we were punished twice; by the sanctions and by continued to be ruled by Gaddafi.

Despite some lingering questions about Gaddafi's responsibility for the Lockerbie attack, the participants noted that the Libyan people also suffered deeply at the hands of Gaddafi and do not perceive him as a victim or a saint. Instead, there seems to be a residual recognition that, in the end, it has been the Libyan people that have suffered the most during the years of sanctions and they have been treated as if they were all terrorists simply because they are from the country of Libya. FB3 said, 'The past government used to cause conflicts with America that caused bad reputation to all Libyans'. Others recognised that both countries' policies have impacted relations between Libya and America. FB6 said, 'The bad policy between Libya and USA is bad politics'.

Some of the participants shared that their concerns with US foreign policy were related more to current issues. There were concerns about the US government's infringement on oil and gas companies (FB16). Others saw the US government as crossing the line and intervening in local issues (FB3). In addition, a few of the participants noted that they perceive America as engaging in terrorism around the world and questioned what they perceive as unjust US involvement in wars in Iraq (FB3 and FB16). However, consistently, the US support of Israel was raised as an issue that affects Libyans' views toward America (SP3).

The US travel ban was described by all participants as a significant factor contributing to their negative views of the US government. Libya was designated as one of the seven countries subject to Trump's travel ban. The participants suggested that Libyans are being unfairly singled out for this ban. SP2 said, 'One Libyan makes something wrong, are we all judged?' FB28 described this as 'guilty until proven innocent.' FB7 said, 'Libyan people felt that's unfair to allow countries that export terrorism to travel to the US and ban us who are suffering from terrorism'. While FB3 described it as 'a new type of racism'. FB1 said, 'It's undoubtedly unfair and this makes the American policy disgusting and can't gain other cultural people's trust'. One participant did not see the impact of the travel ban as being as strong as the policy back in the '80s and '90s (FB6), which referred to the UN and US sanctions against Libya.

The Libyan participants residing in the US perceived the travel ban as having adversely affected their ability to travel back to Libya. SP4 shared a story about how his sister passed away and he was unable to travel back to Libya for the funeral out of fear that he would not be able to return and finish his studies.

SP1 said, 'We cannot go to visit our family. Do you think this is the freedom?' SP2 added, 'If you came here as a student visa, it's a one entry. If you go back you have to do the visa again. The ban is that you are on a list for no visa. That's the point'. However, others disagreed with this statement. For example, SP3 said, 'Not a chance, if you have one visa it will not affect you'. SP1 added, 'Right now but at the beginning it was different. You're not allowed even to apply. It's changed'. SP2 further stated, 'But it changed. What happened is that my dad passed away and I couldn't go'.

Since the travel ban is seen as a significant issue impacting the Libyan participants" current views of US foreign policy, the participants hold the view that doing away with the travel ban is an important step in improving the way the US government is viewed by Libyans. FB3 said, 'Lift the travel ban and ease immigration rules'. FB3 said, 'Treat Libyan with human rights perspective' and FB1 added, 'Surely, yes stop the arbitrary policy toward Libyans such as travel ban'. While FB28 maintained, 'I hope American State department gives visa to Libyans to travel there and the reverse for its citizens because this decision has a big impact on our relation'.

Despite the participants' clear problems with US foreign policy, the participants overwhelmingly agreed that they separate their views of the American people from US foreign policy. FB1 noted the US policy is unfair and ironhanded, and before the meeting Americans thought the people were like their government. This was influenced a great deal by the anti-American rhetoric that they were fed by Gaddafi. However, that is no longer the case. As people learn more, their views change and they are able to separate their views. This is especially true because the Libyan people do not see their views as being the same as the views of Gaddafi, so they give the same level of deference to citizens of other countries that they want people to give to them. FB1 said, 'Exactly as I think as my American friends did of Ghadafi's policy'. FB28 shared a story about going to Malta in 2002 to apply for a US visa and for six days being afraid to go to the US Embassy. This participant noted that she finally got up the courage to go inside and asked to meet with the consul. FB28 indicated that he was very polite when asked about travelling to America on holiday. FB28 shared with him that she was afraid that he would refuse to issue a visa because she was an Arab Muslim wearing a head scarf. FB28 stated that he was nice and reassured her that he would not deny her a visa for that reason and this experience affected her views of the US government. FB28 added, 'I think for me as a citizen the past has no effect but what is happening now matters a lot like the travel ban'.

Programmes designed to improve Libyans' views of the American people and culture have almost no impact on the Libyan participants' views toward the American government. FB3 said, 'The American people are naïve, innocent, very nice and you can use all other kind words. We know them very well. But

American politics is something different'. FB20 posted a picture of a man wearing a shirt that said, 'Saying all Muslims are terrorists is like saying all Americans are like Trump'. FB3 added, 'When someone do a mistake, we should not generalise and say all Americans are same as Trump'. As such, the travel ban does not impact the Libyans' views of the American people, only their views of US foreign policy. SP22 said, 'It doesn't affect. I think both nations share the same human values regardless of political issues'. However, FB16 said, 'Difference between government and people. But American people are often in the hands of the government'.

The only exception to the general consensus that participants separate their views about society and government policy was made by a participant who lives in the US. SP2 noted that although she generally separates her views of the government and the people, since the election of President Trump she has started to question who the people are that voted for Trump. In addition, she also noted feelings of increased racial discrimination since the election of Trump. SB2 shared an example of being harassed by a man at the supermarket because of her conservative Muslim dress. However, she was quick to qualify that statement by also mentioning that two American women at the store came to her defence and told the man to leave her alone.

Views of the US government have also been influenced in part by the lack of US involvement in helping to rebuild Libya after the revolution. FB2 said, 'Libyan people were hoping that the US government will continue its support to Libya and help rebuild the country after the revolution but the negativity of the White House disappointed the Libyans when they were looking highly at US government'.

Generally, the participants held very favourable views of the American people. FB8 said, 'I differentiate between American people and American policy. Firstly, I can not judge a whole population. I have dear American friends who helped us, listened and were very friendly. I am against American's government in other countries all over the world'. When asked about anti-American sentiment in Libya, SP1 attributed that to a perception that 'they are supporting our enemies. They are not supporting our friends'. He continued, 'too many issues; Israel is one of them. But on the government basis. I'm not talking about the American people'. However, when asked about the murder of American citizens in Libya, SP1 did concede that in regard to the extremists who have killed American citizens, that they are angry with both the American people and the American government. SP1 noted, 'If they catch an American citizen in Libya they will kill him. Just to get revenge. They don't care; if he's American. They don't appreciate like us'. However, SP2 interjected, 'I respect this opinion but we're still talking about a percentage of people. Because when the ambassador in Benghazi got killed, I was in the second rally against that and there was a lot of Benghazi people protesting about what happened because this is not us'. These statements reflect the fact that anti-American and extremist rhetoric is a problem in Libya and this is one reason that efforts to promote understanding were needed.

In the end, the Libyan participants see the history of conflict between America and Libya as being a government problem and not a problem between citizens. FB32 said, 'I think as a Libyan citizen that the friendship between the two peoples existed from the fifties during the reign of King Senusi. After the Qadhafi coup, the relationship took on another direction because of Qadhafi's policies and because of the US government in general'. FB32 added that although he does not have American friends on Facebook, he blames the US government for messing up relations. This is based on his perception of US interference in domestic affairs of countries in the Middle East. This participant urged the American people to 'press their government to change its policy in the Middle East, in particular in the Palestinian issue and stop its support of the terrorist Muslim Brotherhood'.

This section has shown that the participants in this study separate their views of the American people from their views of US foreign policy. In addition, they perceive American foreign policy as being the most significant factor in the conflict between the US and Libya rather than issues of values. This will be explained in more detail in the discussion chapter.

5.12 Conclusion

This chapter has presented the findings of the focus group interviews with Libyans on friendship with Americans. Friendships were seen as very important to the Libyans who participated in these focus groups. However, they recognised that finding 'real' or true friendships can often be difficult. They also recognised that cross-cultural friendships are, in general, more difficult, but they valued them and believe that friendships between Americans and Libyans are possible and beneficial. Although participants saw the value that social media has had in connecting people who live all over the world, they also recognised the limitations. Facebook was described as a valuable forum for learning more about issues and doing research on topics and people, but not as good a forum for actually forming friendships. In this way, Facebook friendship groups promoted some general cross cultural understanding, but the friends in these groups were not seen as true friends but more as acquaintances. Instead, face-to-face relations between Americans and Libyans were described as the most valuable way to improve understanding between cultures and promote long-term peaceful relations. As such, the participants highly supported cross-cultural exchange programmes between the people of Libya and America. They noted that capacity-building and civil society programmes are valuable as well, because they promote knowledge and cultural exchange. Therefore, from their perspective the best way to promote peaceful relations between America and Libya is for America to do more to educate the Libyan people, help the country develop and inclusively communicate and support Libya's democratic transition.

Although the participants described the US as a valuable partner in capacity-building programmes, they showed a general distrust for the US government, which was influenced exclusively by US foreign policy decisions. US foreign policy was seen as the biggest reason for historical conflict between the countries, however the participants also recognised Gaddafi's role in the countries' past conflicts. The Libyan participants in this study had hoped the Libyan revolution would result in improvements in conditions in the country of Libya and foster better relations with the world community after years of isolation. However, the current Trump travel ban on Libyan citizens has tainted their view of US foreign policy further.

In the end, the participants support fostering friendships and peaceful relations between the people of Libya and America. Programmes that promote exchange and understanding between countries do have some impact on their views of the American people, and there is a recognition of a need for more cultural programmes that target 'normal' rather than highly educated people. However, they separated their views of the American people from US foreign policy. As a result, friendships with Americans and cultural understanding about America have little impact on their views of American foreign policy and the American government. The only way to improve the participants' views of the US government is for the US government to engage in more fair foreign policy toward Libya.

Chapter 6

Discussion

6.1 Introduction

In this chapter, the findings will be interpreted, discussed and synthesised with the theoretical literature, which has been covered in earlier chapters. While the findings chapter included a report of the various findings organised around the themes that were identified, this chapter is written in a narrative format under the respective research questions rather than being structured around themes as was done in the previous chapter. The first section provides an overview of how the findings connect to the overall theme of the book. Then, the discussion of the findings is organised under each of the three research questions, providing the reader with an explanation and deeper level of interpretation of the findings while answering the research questions by drawing upon the theoretical literature. The final section is a concise conclusion, which sums up what the findings show about each of the research questions.

6.2 Overview

This book explores the role of citizens in using Facebook friendship groups to reframe identity narratives. This book supports the view of the socially constructed nature of relations and how social relations impact whether actors view one another as friend or enemy. It also recognises that the language and behaviour used in relations can become a self-fulfilling prophecy, where the way actors relate reinforce views which in turn reinforce behaviour. The action of viewing another actor as an enemy will result in conflict if the actors do not find a way to change the way they relate. However, this book also takes the position that transformation of relations is possible if actors begin to engage with one another as friends. To observe how this plays out practically in international relations, this study explores friendship as a personal relationship between citizens, which is designed to build trust and understanding and foster more peaceful relations between states and citizens of states. Much of the literature on friendship in international relations has been limited to structural relations between states. What is lacking from existing literature is the social component of friendship involving people as agents. In this book, I argue that if views of enemy and friend are socially constructed, it is possible to reconstruct relations around friendship to observe whether constructs of friendship result in improved relations between states and citizens of states. People are central to reconstructing relations around friendship. The best way to explore this is through studying constructs of friendship between people from states that have historically been in conflict. To do this, I chose to study the social constructs of friendship between Libyan and American citizens on Facebook. These Facebook friendship groups serve as a kind of citizen-led public diplomacy where participants use these online forums to promote understanding and improve views, with the intention of promoting more peaceful and positive relations between Libya and America. These activities serve as a kind of virtual cultural exchange. These everyday activities, like socialising in Facebook friendship groups and sharing about one another, are part of the way people learn about other cultures, which in turn helps them to reframe identity narratives that people have about people from other states. This study takes a bottom-up approach by looking at how friendships between citizens can foster better relations between states that have a history of conflict. To do this, this book draws upon the Aristotelian framework on political friendships to explore how these friendships play out in the context of citizens within international society. Through conversations with one another, people start to discover the ways that they are similar and different, which also helps to dispel stereotypes, humanise other people, build trust and promote peaceful relations. It is through the process of socialising and humanising one another that citizens start to see one another differently than they previously had and recognise they are not tied to the identity narratives that have been imposed on them by their states or media. Instead, the actors have agency to transform relations and take on a collective identity of friends with the other members of the friendship group. Through this process it can foster more peaceful relations between their states.

If part of the rationale for expanding US public diplomacy efforts following the terrorist attacks on 9/11 was because President George W. Bush (2001) believed that the terrorists attacked civilian targets because they believed American values were incongruent with their values, then countering negative views of who Americans are, what Americans believe and the things they value should decrease the likelihood that people will want to attack America. This is why citizen diplomats have been encouraged to be involved in this process because relations between people are being directly linked to relations between states. Terrorists did not attack the US government on 9/11, they intentionally attacked the World Trade Center, a civilian target. Attacking the World Trade Center and other civilian targets is seen as an attack on America, its people and its culture, not just the government. As a result, the US government recognises the need to improve the way America, its people and its government are perceived. The US government sees them all as being linked together. This is why public diplomacy efforts are heavily focused on promoting cultural understanding. Public diplomacy is not just about improving an image for its own sake. Instead, promoting a positive image is connected to promoting more peaceful relations between states and citizens of states. As the argument could go, if they like us, they are less likely to want to harm us. If they are attacking us, they must not understand us, so to keep them from attacking us, we need to help improve the way they see us.

The earliest literature on friendship involved Aristotle and even Plato talking about the different kinds of friendships among citizens in a society. This research builds upon the existing literature and develops the idea of the social side of friendship in the context of global citizenship, which is consistent with the cosmopolitan shifts within International Relations. In Plato's Republic and Aristotle's works, friendship was essential in developing and maintaining a harmonious polity (Plato, 1987; Smith, 2011, p. 19). The same could be said of efforts to establish a harmonious global polity.

There are two main streams of theoretical literature that I have drawn upon to inform this book. The first is the literature that deals with the shift from 'old' to 'new' public diplomacy and the role of citizen diplomats in fostering peaceful relations. The second is the theoretical literature which discusses how friendships between people help to create concord or peace in political society. Current IR scholarship draws upon early Politics literature, which defines friend in an affective and normative way and deals specifically with relations between people. Most of this literature limits its discussion of friendships to relations among people in the same society. However, in recent years theorists like Oelsner and Koschut (2014) and Berenskoetter and Van Hoef (2017) have been calling for more empirical case study research into the role that interpersonal bonds play in relations between states.

In this book, I argue that states are collectives of their citizens and, as moral agents, citizens have a vital role to play in fostering positive and peaceful relations between citizens and states. If views of others as friends or enemies are a social construction, then arguably, constructing relations around friendship would have a more positive impact on relations between states. It is also true that treating others as enemies can result in reciprocal enmity. For example, the very act of enacting a travel ban against people or subjecting a country to international sanctions communicates a message that they are seen as a threat, an enemy. These actions can foster feelings of reciprocal enmity which has been the case with relations between Libya and the US. Years of strained relations left the Libyan and American people with no opportunity to interact or learn much about one another. This left some Libyans with questions about whether the American people shared the same views of the US government. As such, following the Libyan revolution and Gaddafi's death, many Libyan citizens made a decision to join Facebook friendship groups with Americans and use this forum as a way to promote understanding, trust and respect between their countries with the goal of fostering peaceful relations.

The research has shown that the participants in these focus group interviews recognise the value of friendships between Libyans and Americans and do not believe that cultural difference prevents the ability for them to be friends. In addition, they see Facebook friendships as having a dual purpose of fostering understanding and trust both individually and collectively. These activities are helpful in promoting trusting relations between the people of Libya and America and dispelling stereotypes and misinformation that they have been exposed to throughout the years. As such, the participants noted that they do not hold bad feelings or views toward the American people because of the US government's foreign policy decisions. They hold separate views of the American people and the American government and its policy. However, they do have negative views of Trump and the US government for its foreign policy decisions, including the travel ban and years of sanctions, which impact Libyan citizens. They see this travel ban policy as unfairly singling Libyans out while allowing people from countries that they perceive as exporting terrorism, like Saudi Arabia, to travel to the US. In this way, they see themselves as being unfairly treated as enemies, simply because they are from the country of Libya. This treatment has a negative effect on how they view the US government.

6.3 Analysis of findings

The findings suggest that citizen-led Facebook friendships between Libyans and Americans serve as a kind of citizen-led public diplomacy that helps to promote understanding and respect between people, which is important for states that have a history of strained relations. However, the findings also indicate that participation in Facebook friendship groups does not have an impact on the Libyan citizens' views of American foreign policy. These findings were reached by looking at three research questions. The first research question that this study explores is:

(i) What meaning do Libyans give to Facebook friendships?

The Libyan participants' perspectives on friendship are consistent with Aristotle's views that there are different kinds of friendships. Just as Aristotle discussed friendships of utility, pleasure and virtue, the participants in this study noted that friendships can be utilitarian in nature or exist mainly because you like someone and find the friendship enjoyable. The participants recognised that friendships are essential to human life and are relationships that people strive for. They discussed that friendships can start out more superficial and then grow deeper. SP2 said, 'so you are trying to find friendship to go on, and then it could grow more and more'. The Libyan participants also agreed that friendships of pleasure are better than friendships of utility. SB1 said, 'I prefer friendship without benefit'. Friendship without benefit is a friendship 'without any obligation, without needing anything from him; just for the sake of friendship. Not for people's money or.... ' (SP1).

The participants also discussed the deeper forms of friendship, which Aristotle would characterise as virtue friendships. One participant characterised friendship as 'almost one mind in two bodies' (FB3). This characterisation is similar to Aristotle's description of virtue friendships as being based on some level of similarity or sameness. However, the participants also discussed the fact that cross-cultural friendships are possible, so this sameness is not necessarily based on people being from the same place or having the same culture. Instead, it has more to do with the kind of interests, values and character a person has. These deeper friendships are seen as more meaningful than the other types of friendships. FB6 described these special relations as 'the best quality humans can have'. This characterisation is consistent with Kant's (1997) view that enjoying these friendships is the whole goal of humankind. For example, FB22 noted friendships involve 'having someone accept you exactly the way you are, supports you when you struggle, and helps you do the right things while doing the best to make you happy'. This characterisation is consistent with Aristotle's view that friendships involve people influencing one another and helping them becoming better people. Generally, the participants in these interviews recognised friendship as a relationship that brings joy, happiness and support. This mutuality is also consistent with Aristotle and Kant's characterisation of friendships where the building of trust between people happens through reciprocal processes of knowing others and allowing others to know you. Aristotle characterised friendship as affective relationships of reciprocated goodwill (1994, p. 115b30-5). This process of giving and taking and helping and encouraging one another is part of showing that you care about someone and desire the best for them. Veltman (2004) characterised these friendships as a process of helping one another to live more authentic lives. The collective value of friendships is in the way that these relations challenged people to become better human beings which was thought to result in concord, or peaceful relations within society. Aristotle considered good and virtuous people as peaceful people.

Aristotle noted that friendships of virtue are seen as an ideal friendship, but also recognised that these kinds of friendship take time to cultivate. Friendships can start as acquaintances where people are getting to know one another and develop into deeper friendships. The participants in this study shared the view that moving from more surface-level friendships toward deeper-level friendships is not always easy. For example, SP3 noted that it is difficult developing deeper friendships and also difficult keeping them, especially when the friends hold different opinions. This is similar to Aristotle's suggestion that 'a friend is not to be had without trial and it is not a matter of a single day, but time is needed' (EE, 1996, 1238a).

The process of developing these deeper levels of friendship requires people to cultivate high levels of trust and the ability for people to be honest with one another. Kant (1997) describes these kinds of friendships as being based on love and respect and involve people revealing and disclosing things about themselves to others. Similarly, FB18 said, 'Friendship is a trustful alliance, mutual cooperation and standing for each other against the life issues'. Aristotle says that 'trust and the feeling that he would never wrong me' is part of friendship (NE, 1994, 1157a 23-24).

Although people are called friends on Facebook, the participants in this study do not see Facebook friendships as true friendships. Instead, they fit within the utility and pleasure categories of friendships. The participants suggest that to reach the true friendship category, some level of face-to-face interaction is necessary. True friendships are more akin to friendships of virtue, which Aristotle discusses. This is consistent with Aristotle's (1994) views of friendship, which suggests virtuous friendships tend to be very intimate. True friendships are characterised by higher levels of trust between people. FB22 said friendship involves 'having someone accept you exactly the way you are, supports you when you struggle and helps you to do the right things while doing the best to make you happy'. FB30 noted that developing strong friendships requires face-to-face interactions for a period of time. Instead, the factor that most influences whether the participants see a friendship with an American as an authentic friendship is whether they have met the person and got to know them personally in a face-to-face manner. FB1 maintained that being with people in day-to-day activities allows you to 'share dialogues, food, visits... etc. So we have understood the nature of each.

In the same way that Aristotle puts a higher value on virtue, the participants see these deeper or true friendships as more meaningful and having the most impact on their views of Americans. Face-to-face friendships allow for stronger emotional connection to happen. FB30 said, 'If you want to be strong friendship, you have to start with a direct face-to-face for a period of time'. Similarly, FB31 said, 'To have a strong online friendship you must stay long time talking and trying to get to know each other more while face-to-face friendships are always faster and more transparent as you can't hide your quick thinking by slow thinking before answering in a chat'. The process of building friendships involves time asking and answering questions and being increasingly transparent with one another which builds trust and intimacy. When people have trusting relationships with people, they allow them to speak into and influence their lives and views more.

The findings suggest that the decision to participate in Facebook friendship groups with Americans is primarily influenced by a desire to learn about Americans, to socialise and to promote understanding between cultures. The value in Facebook friendships is in learning and relating to one another. These processes of interactions help to humanise people to one another and build respect and trust collectively more than individually. In seeing friendship this way, one can see that they are not just personal relations but also political relations. In international relations, diplomacy is the political tool which is used to promote understanding and foster trust within the international community. Friendships can be a form of diplomacy because they are a place where relationships are developed and fostered and where understanding between people, as agents of states can happen. This is consistent with Fitzpatrick's argument that for public diplomacy to be truly relational it must achieve mutual understanding (2013, p. 30).

The characterisations of Facebook friendships by the participants in this study are most similar to the utility and pleasure categories of friendship that Aristotle discusses. They are valued for their usefulness in providing information and allowing people to socialise with one another and begin to build understanding and trust between Libyans and Americans. In seeing friendship this way, one can see that friendship is a process of becoming. The value in these friendships is the social process of identity construction where actors can choose to relate as friends. By seeing friendships this way, one can see how these friendships can have the transformative purposes of facilitating peaceful relations between people from different countries.

The participants recognise and value the various ways that friendship plays out in the context of Facebook relations, however, they also recognise the limits to the utility and pleasure functions of friendships in building long-term trusting relations between Libyans and Americans. In the end, the participants see the more virtuous or true types of friendships as the most influential. Developing virtuous friendships requires some face-to-face interaction for a period of time (SP6 and FB1). This is because face-to-face interaction is seen as important to building trust, and as Aristotle and Kant note, trust is foundational to deep, virtuous friendships.

The participants' discussion of friendship is consistent with King's (2007a) scholarship which sees friendship existing on a continuum from very close relations to acts of simple friendliness. On this continuum, participation in Facebook friendship groups starts closer to the friendliness end of the continuum. In this way, FB9 said, 'We know each other maybe! Maybe if we got to know each other over Facebook then to meet somewhere will make us friends, otherwise no'. In comparison with Aristotle's (1999) discussion of the types of friendships, Facebook friendships in the context of this study fit within the utility and pleasure categories, with the primary purpose being political. It moves into the political because the purpose is to foster improved views between the citizens of Libya and America.

The participants noted that cross-cultural friendships can be entered into for personal or cultural reasons. Cultural reasons would involve participants promoting cultural understanding between the countries in order to improve relations, which is a political purpose. FB1 said, 'Who we friend outside the country can convey us his/her culture and change your view toward people in that country'. It becomes useful when participants educate one another about their countries, and share information about scholarships, exchanges or other useful information. FB7 said, 'We exchange ideas, support each other... you learn different new things from them, it's healthy to see the world from different angle'. Facebook friendships are also pleasure friendships because those Facebook groups allow for socialising, which people enjoy doing because it is part of what it means to be human. However, rarely do activities in the Facebook groups rise to the level of the deeper friendships of virtue, which Aristotle idealised. Instead, the characterisation is most consistent with Van Der Zweerde's discussion that friendships that are capable of keeping the international political community together are a weakened and generalised form of friendship where virtuous citizens are capable of living with difference (2007, p. 161). This ability to live with difference involves acceptance and respect.

The participants in this study value cross-cultural friendships because they help people bridge the gap between race, colour and religion. The process of interaction with one another allows people to construct an identity of friend with one another as they navigate areas of difference. In cross cultural friendships, you are learning as much about the culture as the individual. Success in cross-cultural friendships depends on the people, their character and how willing they are to be open-minded and respectful of differences while adapting their behaviour where appropriate. This view is consistent with Van Hoef and Oelsner's (2018) argument that friendship is a social practice that evolves through time and normalises behaviour, attitudes and gestures that construct a peaceful culture. It is also consistent with the argument by Koschut and Oelsner (2014) that stable peace is created through multiple ties of friendship. It is a dynamic social process of identity construction. FB1 said, 'Who friend outside the country can convey us his/her culture and change your view towards people in that country'. Although the participants recognised the differences that do exist between Libyan and American culture and religion, they also recognised 'we have a lot in common'(SP3). One participant said of her friendship with one American friend 'we exchange ideas, support each other . . . you learn different new things from them, it's healthy to see the world from different angles' (FB7). It is through this process of interaction with one another that people develop an identity of friend. The value in these friendships is in the process of becoming friends and what these relations teach people about themselves and others both individually and collectively.

The participants in this study agreed that cross-cultural and international friendships are not only possible, but valuable. In addition, they disagree with the contention that differences in things such as religion and culture have to keep people from being friends. Instead, the participants see a value in fostering friendships between people who are different because these friendships also have much to teach people. By allowing for friendships within difference, it seeks to achieve the goal of bringing people together who share a world (Nordin and Smith, 2018a, p. 3). This view is consistent with the perspective of Cocking and Kennett (1998) and their suggestion that too much similarity is not necessary in friendships. Instead, in order for cross-cultural friendships to develop and flourish, the people involved must share some common values, such as open-mindedness and respect for humankind.

The participants noted that although there are differences in culture and religion between America and Libya, what they have found is that friendship is possible even within the difference. It was the process of dialoguing and interacting with one another that they have learned about similarities in religion. For example, SP3 said, 'The best American friends I experienced even here or in West Virginia are Christian people. They are very supportive, they are understanding. I think we are alike . . .' The key seemed to be the willingness for the parties to understand some of the religious expectations and what is allowed and forbidden and the willingness to adapt their behaviour accordingly. SP1 mentioned that Libya is a religion-based culture, and therefore, religion impacts all areas of their life. As such, it is helpful to find a friend who understands their religion and the things they are required and forbidden to do. I would argue that these are good and virtuous qualities to have within diverse societies. The participants recognise differences in things like culture can lead to misunderstandings. However, conflict is more likely when people are unwilling to respect others. The key to building friendships with people who are different from you is having open-mindedness, curiosity and respect. In this view, instead of the society envisioned by Aristotle where friendship was limited to fellow Greeks, friendship can also be a process where differences are bridged between people of different cultures.

Difference is an inherent part of living in a diverse world, but it should not be something to be feared. These views are consistent with the arguments made by Nordin and Smith (2018a) that friendship is a mobile network of relationships between persons that are based on both identity and difference. Difference does not have to lead to conflict. This perspective suggests that conflict involves severing a relationship rather than people having a difference of opinions. The key to developing cross-cultural friendships is very similar to developing the same cultural friendship, finding common ground with people and working to build upon that. The participants related being open-minded to the idea of global citizenship, which Lu (2000) discusses and the recognition of the commonalities that all humans share and desire to build upon them. The desire to learn about other cultures was seen as a necessary first step in building cross-cultural relations. This idea recognises that people cannot be forced to want to build relations, but instead, there are some inherent virtues that exist in people who desire to build cross-cultural relations. SP2 exhibited this kind of virtue when they said 'I think it's amazing to understand more people, people that have a different view'. Similarly, SP6 shared a story about his grandfather who, although only having an elementary education, was seen as an open-minded person because he had a yearning to learn several different languages, build relationships with people from other cultures and respect those people. This desire and open-mindedness toward people from different cultures is a necessary character trait for cross-cultural relations to be developed.

When people are close-minded, they will find it difficult to bridge the cultural divide with people from other cultures. FB3 described this as 'close minds cannot see the overview'. The participants noted this has been seen as a problem with Libyan people, who tend to have a restricted view of the world, which is primarily focused on religion. However, the participants noted that although being open-minded and curious is, at times, a character trait that people are born with, it can also be learned, but people have to want to learn. It tends to begin with having one foreign friend that you love, who 'motivate[s] them to learn these friends' cultures (FB38). This process of building friendships requires time and interactions which Aristotle discusses. Unfortunately, during Gaddafi's time in power developing friends between Libyans and Americans was not welcomed. This is due to the years of sanctions against Libya and the people being subjected to state-controlled media, which were filled with anti-American sentiment, which left many Libyans believing that difference in cultural and religious views would be an obstacle to relations. FB9 noted she/he grew up being told that English songs were made to 'curse and humiliate us: Arabs in general'. However, she/he noted that this might be 'because we fear what we don't understand, and may also be a result of the previously unfriendly relationships between the countries'. This statement shows that unfriendly relations can actually contribute to the continuation of unfriendly relations, because when relations are strained, people do not interact with one another. If people do not interact, then they are left to speculate about how others view them. The only thing they have to go on in developing their views is how they are treated. So, if you are treated as an enemy by another, the natural response is to internalise that view and respond to the other as an enemy as well.

The participants in this study recognise is that the best way to move beyond the fear and enmity of another is to take a step and try to bridge the divide. The internet has provided a safe forum to do that, where participants could begin the process of learning about Americans, its culture, religion and history. Facebook took this opportunity one step further by allowing Libyans the opportunity to learn about Americans collectively in friendship groups by allowing them to read posts specifically designed to educate Libyans about America. Using Facebook friendships this way is consistent with Aristotle's (1996) utility friendship because it allowed the participants to learn and begin to understand more about the American people and its culture, without much interaction. This stage is an important place for the Libyans to start, especially if they are a bit wary about America and its people after years of conflict. SP6 noted that the value of Facebook is allowing someone to research and find all the data about them. In the Facebook friendship groups, the participants are learning about the country more collectively. However, participants shared that they also use Facebook to research about people individually to decide whether they want to take the friendship to the next level and interact with people more personally by friending them. SP6 said 'I want to know these guys, how they drink, how they eat so I'm gonna search on social media before connecting with them so I'm gonna get the information before I start to connect with them. It's the best way to do it'. One might suggest that part of what these people are trying to assess from doing this research is whether the person on the other end of the computer is a good or virtuous person that they want to interact with more personally. For people who have never met before, Facebook serves as a virtual introduction, where a person can research and learn about someone and explore whether they might want to pursue a personal friendship with them.

The participants recognised that technology is changing the way people communicate and interact. The most obvious difference is 'online you use your fingers while meeting people you use your mouth' (FB6). Although, much of what happens on Facebook fits within the utility category of friendship, these friendships also move to the level of pleasure friendships. People want to know others and be known, just as Aristotle and Kant discuss. SP3 said, 'We are human beings. I mean, we have to socialise. It's part of our sociology'. It is this desire to be sociable with people that catalyses people to reach out and try to build a bridge or participate in a transnational friendship group. Part of the reason people congregate on Facebook is to socialise and interact with other people around shared activities and discussions. In the context of Facebook, people can socialise and interact with one another and they participate in these groups because they find them enjoyable. However, the participants described these friendships as more of acquaintances. For example, FB9 said, 'We know each other maybe! Maybe if we get to know each other over Facebook then meet somewhere we will make us friends, otherwise no! The participants noted that the nature of these friendship forums like LAFA and LAUFP are not seen as altogether different from other Facebook groups organised around a variety of interests and hobbies. They join these groups to interact with like-minded people. This is consistent with Elder's (2014) argument that social media friendships can meet Aristotle's definition of a shared life supports this view. Part of a shared life involves dialogue about a variety of topics including ourselves and politics. This is consistent with Aristotle's view that friendship deals directly with being political beings within a society. The main difference is that the purpose of these Facebook friendship groups is to promote good relations, so to do that participants focus on promoting positive images of their countries and helping others understand things about their country and culture.

The participants see friendship groups between Americans and Libyans as being more of a virtual cultural exchange that allows them to learn generalities about each other's countries, history and cultures. It also provides a pleasure function by allowing people to interact with one another's posts and socialise by discussing topics, posting on one another's posts, sharing nonverbal gestures like emojis, sharing videos, and pictures about themselves and allowing others to respond to those. FB2 said, 'I would say Facebook friendships affect positively between people in both countries. They are helping to understand each other'. All of these activities are part of the process of people seeking to know others and be known an important process in trust building. So, one could characterise these interactions as a virtual cultural exchange experience. In cultural exchanges, people interact with one another on more superficial levels, but those interactions have the purpose of promoting understanding and improving relations between people and states. This social process is an important first step in getting to know people of other cultures collectively and requires time and intentionality. As Helland (2017) suggests, these virtual exchanges allow for the development of mutual understanding and respect. This is consistent with Zaharna's (2012) contention that culture plays an important role in relational public diplomacy and in accounting for the reciprocal agency of the targets of public diplomacy. Efforts to build understanding around culture in the context of Facebook friendship groups between Libyan and Americans start out as a collective understanding. In viewing friendships this way, they primarily are political friendships. However, the focus group participants noted that if they are curious about someone, they can learn more about a person individually by reading their Facebook profile and deciding whether they might want to 'friend' them on Facebook. This means that the participants are open to developing deeper, more intimate friendships if the opportunity for face-to-face interaction arises. In this way, Facebook connections are similar to face-to-face friendships, which start out more as acquaintances and can advance to deeper virtue friendships with time and intentionality. Having these acquaintances is seen as a necessary first step in building relations between Libya and America. As Cowan and Arsenault discussed, the relationships that are formed serve as building blocks for broader dialogue between countries (2008, p. 17). The value of these friendships is in the social process of dialogue and interacting with one another. However, the relations often start with a decision to be friends by participating in friendship groups, and it is through interacting with one another with increasing levels of intentionality and vulnerability that the participants can move towards deeper levels of true friendships. It is in true or virtuous friendships, as Aristotle (1994) discusses, that the most influence happens. However, there is also a level of influence that happens at the utility and pleasure levels that is politically valuable and necessary in fostering peaceful international relations between states, especially when there has been a history of conflict.

(ii) How and through what modes of reasoning/narratives do transnational citizen-led Facebook friendship groups between Libyans and Americans affect Libyans' views of Americans?

The primary reason that participants in this study are involved in Facebook friendship groups with Americans is to promote understanding and respect and to dispel negative stereotypes they see portrayed in the media. The participants spent a significant amount of time discussing the ways that they believe traditional media contributes to negative views and enmity toward Libyans and Muslims more broadly and the need to dispel those narratives. For example, there were concerns that the media spends too much time talking about Muslims being involved in terrorist attacks and not enough time on Muslims doing positive things. There was a recognition that news media often portrays stories through their ideological lens and shares incorrect ideas about a country (SP4). This participant also went so far as to suggest that mainstream and social media include a lot of non-truth to manipulate the hearts and minds of people. Similarly, FB2 maintained that 'media plays a key role in forming and shaping opinions and deepening already existing cultural misunderstandings between cultures and religions'. FB2 also noted that the media is responsible for promoting negative image of other countries like they are 'retarded and barbarian' which will make people scared of them without people getting to know one another personally, which can lead to conflict. It is interesting that this person used the word 'barbarian', because it is consistent with Aristotle's (1994) characterisation of non-Greeks, which he saw as not virtuous and a threat to social cohesion. What this statement suggests is that the way people are characterised impacts the way they are treated and whether people even believe it is possible to relate to them in friendly or peaceful ways. A characterisation of someone as a 'barbarian' results in them being automatically excluded from the possibility of friend rather than being assessed individually based on their individual character, and this is the problem that Wendt (1999) was concerned with. These views become a self-fulfilling prophecy. If a whole country of people is collectively seen as barbarians, they are perceived as a threat and, therefore an enemy. These views are further exacerbated by the media portraying images of all Muslims as people to be feared. So, it is not just that all Libyans are being seen as barbarians, but also all Muslims. As such, these people are prejudged as enemy based on their religious and national identity. FB29 suggested that "Media works hard to create Islamic phobia". However, this same person also recognised media can be a force for good or evil. FB29 said that media can also be used to 'create sensitivity between countries'. As such, the participants recognised that both Libyans' and Americans' views are heavily influenced by media portrayals. The participants discussed that they do not have control over the stories the media shares, but they can be involved in dispelling false narratives through interactions between people. The only way to effectively combat these negative depictions and stereotypes is to learn from the people directly. This characterisation is consistent with the discussion of relational public diplomacy in the literature where former US State Department Under Secretary for Public Diplomacy and Public Affairs Judith McHale says 'I think that the more we can have people having direct conversations with each other—and through those conversations and initiatives, through history of cultures we can learn about each other and if we do that, at the people-to-people level, that will provide us with a path to a more peaceful and prosperous future' (Brown, 2010). The participants in this study recognise they have an opportunity to be a part of reframing the narrative about who they are and what relations between Libya and America will look like. They do not have to be content with being portrayed as enemies, instead, they have the agency to choose to relate as friends.

The Libyans in this study exhibited a sense of pride in their country and culture and struggle with the fact that their image has been marred for many years by Gaddafi and other Libyans' involvement in terrorism. FB3 said, 'The past government used to cause conflicts with America that caused bad reputation to all Libyans'. They want people to know that most Libyans desire peace. In this way, the participants recognise that this social media forum is a place where citizens of both countries can reform identity narratives by changing the way they see one another and choosing the way they relate. This starts with the participants relating as friends. Cowan and Arsenault's (2008, p. 19) perspective is that understanding and relationships should supersede changing opinions. These interviews suggest that the participants also recognise that understanding comes before changing opinions. If Libyans and Americans understand more about one another, than they will not have as much to fear because people often fear what they do not understand.

Although these participants do recognise their own unique cultural identity and take pride in what it means to be Libyan and Muslim, they also recognise that we are all humans and that is a powerful thing that should be celebrated rather than focusing too much on difference. There is more that binds people together in humanity than what separates people. What is most important to the participants is being open-minded and willing to consider other perspectives. In that posture, people are able to build a bridge and facilitate more peaceful relations between people of different societies. FB22 said, 'Neither religion nor culture will be a barrier in developing friendships with Americans'. The participants recognised that citizens have a role in this process, an idea that is central to democratic thought. This is especially interesting, considering that Libyans have spent most of their lives living in an undemocratic society ruled by a dictator. Nevertheless, they recognise that building friendships between states involves people, which is consistent with the views of Oelsner and Koschut (2014).

The Libyans who participated in this study show that they have a desire for peaceful relations between Americans and Libyans, and recognise that they, as citizens, have a very important role to play in promoting good relations. The participants suggested that there are a variety of citizen initiatives that can be used to improve the way people view one another and foster more peaceful relations. These can include a variety of everyday initiatives that bring people together and allow for interaction. This is consistent with Gullion's earliest conceptualisation of public diplomacy, which focused on people influencing one another through interactions (Brown, 2010). The value is in what people seek to achieve. Critical peace theorists recognise the need for everyday interactions between people and, therefore, rather than limiting peace-building initiatives to states, they recognise that citizens are vital to long-term successful peace processes (Richmond, 2008b). In international relations, diplomacy is one of the main tools used to foster peaceful relations. Using citizen diplomacy initiatives that foster peaceable sociability between citizens of different states helps to foster views of a common humanity, which helps to break down barriers and build bridges between people in those states. In this way, there is a recognition of the agency of people as conduits of peaceful relations in international relations.

The participants in this study do not see fostering peaceful relations as merely a state function but also a societal function. FB3 said, 'Word of mouth can promote good relationships. The citizens are acting as ambassadors of their countries'. Central to society-centric diplomacy are citizens (Fulda, 2018). Participating in Facebook friendships serves as a kind of bridge-building activity between citizens, where they can learn about one another's country and facilitate positive relations. The participants in this study recognise that the very act of joining a Facebook friendship group with Americans suggests that the participants are interested in promoting peaceful and positive relations with Americans, but also in combating negative stereotypes that exist about one another.

These citizen-led Facebook forums provide an opportunity for the two-directional promotion of positive images rather than only one-directional messaging, which is more typical of state-centric public diplomacy efforts. Nye described effective public diplomacy as 'a two-way street that involves listening as well as talking' (2004, p. 111). FB29 said the reason she/he participated in Facebook friendship groups was 'to learn about and from others, exchange experiences and ideas and be part of the international community and understand what's going on and try to help my country'. This is consistent with the discussion by Melissen (2005) about the shift to dialogic forms of public diplomacy involving non-state actors. Dialogues about events, history, culture and religion all serve as important components of getting to know one another. It is through these relationships that understanding of values happens (Melissen, 2005). These dialogues are a deliberative process where citizens can create new ways of relating to one another and what Habermas (1990) would refer to as normative expectations of a good life'. The citizens in these Facebook friendship groups are reconstructing relations between their countries by engaging as friends instead of enemies. In this way, knowledge is seen as power because it allows participants to make informed decisions about one another's countries and people, and as Arendt (1970) discusses, it allows actors to act in concert with each other. This is consistent with the perspective of Kirkpatrick (2011) about the devolution of power from state to non-state actors. It is also consistent with Fisher's (2011) argument that public diplomacy involves engaging or empowering the community. The participants in this study recognise that they have an important role to play in improving relations between their states. By choosing the way they will relate to one another, they can foster more peaceful relations.

Facebook is seen as both a media and social dialogue platform, where people can learn about each other, and socialise at a superficial level. It is also a transnational network which Zaharna (2009) argues is important to overcoming cultural differences, fostering credibility and controlling narratives. Berenskoetter and Van Hoef (2017) assert that these transnational networks are important in fostering positive relations between countries through cooperation and solidarity. Facebook bridges the divide between cultures that is caused by geographical distance and provides a forum where the world is truly at people's doorsteps. SP3 said, 'Due to the new technology the distance does not affect the ability to make friends with Americans'. There are both negative and positive things on Facebook, so it does not result in improving Libyans' views of Americans exclusively. Instead, it changes the way people communicate. This is consistent with the discussion by Boyd and Ellison (2007) that these forums allow users to build and maintain relationships around similar identities and goals.

The participants in this study see Facebook friendships as having a useful purpose of promoting understanding and countering stereotypes and negative narratives that the media communicates. For example, FB28 said, 'Yes indeed what I use to know or to hear is that USA citizens do not like Arab people, they ignore them and they look snobby but it was not like this. My best friend is an American'. This shows that the process of interaction and friendships with Americans has an impact on the way the participants in this study see Americans collectively.

The participants also recognise that social media can serve as a form of diplomacy. For example, FB2 recognised that 'countries are using more media outlets than ever to connect with the Arab people'. Since the purpose of public diplomacy is to promote a positive image of a state, its culture and its people through promoting understanding between people, then efforts that are focused on dispelling stereotypes and helping people gain a more accurate picture of another's culture and its policies are important. As such, context and history are important and one cannot take a one-size-fits-all approach to public diplomacy efforts (Seo, 2013). It is only through learning about one another's culture that participants can gain an accurate picture which helps to avoid generalisations about a whole group of people. This was indicated as a particular issue for Libyan participants in this study during Gaddafi's time in power when they were subjected to censored media. During that time, they did not know whether the information they were given by Gaddafi about America was accurate. FB1 said, 'before having American friends, like all American seemed to be as their policy: unfair, tyrant and aggressive'. It was only through meeting Americans face-to-face that they 'see the true picture of Americans'. This is consistent with Cowan and Arsenault's argument that dialogue as a form of public diplomacy is a mechanism to dispel stereotypes and forge relationships across social boundaries (Cowan and Arsenault, 2008, p. 20). In that way, these groups are often educating Libyans for the first time about who the American people are and about their culture, and dispelling some myths like the belief that Americans all support their government's policies.

The participants discussed that the value of Facebook friendships was in allowing them to begin to learn about the US and the American people, which was not possible before. FB8 noted that Facebook 'helped in widening the communication between people from different backgrounds and perspectives but at a superficial level'. The value of Facebook is bridging the divide that has existed between America and Libya both geographically and politically by bringing them closer to each other (FB2). FB1 said, 'They play an important role in changing the negative views of same country citizens as well when they participate in activities with different cultural people can understand how they think towards their country and try to convey the true picture of their country'. Similarly, FB1 described the value the internet has in making the whole world like a small village, which could facilitate international cooperation between countries. However, the participants were hesitant to put too much weight on Facebook posts because it was difficult to know if what was posted was even true nor to generalise about a whole population from Facebook posts (FB8). As such, Facebook has more to do with changing the way people communicate and allowing Libyans to learn about the US and interact with Americans on a more superficial level. Facebook is most valuable when it supports realistic communication and tends to be more influential on issues (FB20). Instead, the participants put more value on face-to-face relations. FB31 said, 'For me internet activities are not really effective the way the real activities are'. There is something about seeing someone face-to-face and spending time with them that helps you develop a personal bond and make informed decisions about whether you perceive them as trustworthy. The participants recognise that there are limits to what you can learn about people on social media. This can be attributed in part to the belief that people have different online and offline personas. Friendships between Libyans and Americans that move to the face-to-face level or involve a level of personal interaction that is more intimate are more likely to impact their views.

Therefore, the participants strongly suggested that social media friendships are friendships in the default when face-to-face is not possible. It is like a virtual introduction where they can learn a bit and socialise with Americans while discussing topics. However, it does not have much impact on their views because the relations tend to be shallow. So it is just a starting place for dialogue. Instead, the participants suggested that face-to-face relations have the most impact on their views of Americans (FB3). SP4 said, 'If you wanted to know about any countries or any people in those countries, I think face-to-face, it makes you more clear'.

Despite the limited impact of Facebook friendships on their views, the participants do see face-to-face cultural exchange and educational programmes as helping to improve views and relations. The participants also recognised the relational side of conflicts, the important role of narratives, and the way people engage with one another to the process of peace. They noted that education is the most effective way to combat wrong narratives, including religious intolerance, which was discussed as a problem in Libya (FB6). However, education does not have to be formal education, it can also include opportunities that just bring people together in everyday activities where they can build relationships and learn from one another in the process. FB7 put a high value on collaborative cultural activities like joint programs in art, sport, and education, which can 'show the Americans the real Libyans who hate war and violence, who wants to live in peace and share their culture with the rest of the world'. The participants see cultural exchange activities as a kind of citizen diplomacy when it promotes understanding and trust between people. As such, both face-to-face and online cultural exchange are seen as valuable because they help get views much closer (FB1). This is consistent with the critical peace literature by Richmond (2008b) that recognises the important role that people play in reframing identity narratives. Change must involve citizens not only as brokers of peaceful relations but also in helping to educate one another, dispelling wrong thoughts and creating open-mindedness. This is especially important with extremist groups' active efforts to cause conflicts between citizens and states around divisive topics like populism, ethnicity and religion. These programs were seen as helpful in building promoting understanding and trust. However, the participants also recognise that more effort should be made to reach the average citizen rather than more elite members of society. The participants noted that the average citizen does not always know about cultural exchange opportunities that are facilitated by NGOs and the embassy, nor do they have access to them because of the distance that is required for them to travel to get to the embassy. This is where Facebook becomes valuable. It is accessible for anyone located anywhere as long as they have internet connection. Whereas, face-to-face exchange programmes are limited to a small number of people which means that it is often the well-connected and elite people within society that end up participating in such exchanges. SP2 said, 'The problem, what I have concern about is the normal Libyan woman and man. That's what I'm concerned about, not us'. With online modalities of virtual exchange, large numbers of people are able to learn and interact within the restrictions of money, travel and size limits. So, there would be a value in developing more video-linked exchange opportunities where people can interact in a face-to-face manner.

The participants put a high value on citizen diplomacy initiatives, and the role of civil society organisations have in fostering better relations between states and citizens. FB1 said, "It is very effective to get the views much closer". This is consistent with Former US Secretary of State Hillary Clinton's view of citizen diplomacy, which advocated the need to 'leverage civilian power by connecting businesses, philanthropists, and citizens' groups with partner governments to perform tasks that governments alone cannot' (Clinton, 2010). There is a recognition that part of the way you help improve relations between states is to provide assistance to them. The participants shared a preference for civil society assistance, because living under a dictator has made them distrustful of government in general. During Gaddafi's time in power, they had no civil society organisations in Libya. However, when Libya opened up and those organisations finally arrived and were involved in capacity-building programmes in Libya, they were received very positively because they were seen as having altruistic motives. FB1 said, 'I think America has already begun changing Libyan's views of America through programmes from the embassy and volunteers who come to help us. However, we're looking forward to getting more help'.

Helping Libya during its time of need is seen as a very important gesture of friendship and diplomacy. The participants expressed the need for more help from civil society programmes facilitated by NGOs for the provision of capacity-building programmes. The participants discussed the significant need for support in all things like the economy, army, police, education, health and improving cultural relations and how capacity building programs like this could improve relations between the US and Libya (FB5). Capacity-building programmes are seen as essential to rebuilding and ensuring a strong democratic society is established in Libya, which the participants see as important to internal stability and peace. Some of the participants also noted disappointment with civil society organisations pulling out of Libya when things became unstable. The willingness of civil society organisations to help with the provision of these services plays an important role in how the American people are viewed by the Libyan people. What this indicates is that friendship is not just about talk, but also about action. In personal relations, we expect our friends to help us in our time of need, and this is similar in relations between states. As such, the participants in this study suggest that more on-the-ground and face-to-face initiatives are necessary to improve relations further.

To sum up, the participants in this study see the value of Facebook friendship groups in promoting understanding about one another's countries, histories, culture and even politics. These Facebook groups serve as a kind of virtual exchange of sorts where people can begin to learn about one another and build relations. For many of the participants, these groups have provided information that they did not know about Americans previously, and for others, it has had some impact on dispelling stereotypes that they had based on media and their governments' portrayals. The participants recognise the value of these groups in beginning the process of relating to one another, but in the end, they are seen as more of a default relationship when face-to-face relations are not possible. Instead, the participants put a much higher value on face-to-face relations in improving their views of Americans. In particular, they value citizen initiatives such as cultural exchange programmes and capacity-building projects where citizens can cooperate with one another on shared goals and educate the people in a variety of areas. These kinds of projects are seen as valuable by creating a natural environment of learning from one another, which is helpful in building trust. The participants in this study agreed that Americans helping Libya in their time of need can have the biggest impact on improving relations between Americans and Libyans.

(iii) How and through what modes of reasoning/narratives do transnational citizen-led Facebook friendship groups between Libyans and Americans affect Libyans' views of American foreign policy?

Much of the increase in US public diplomacy funding following 9/11 was based on the view that terrorists attacked the US because America had an image problem (Van Ham, 2003; Peterson, 2002). President George W. Bush supported the view that this image problem was related to a perception of differing values between Americans and citizens of Muslim-majority countries (Bush, 2001). As a result, Bush advocated the expansion of public diplomacy efforts to promote a positive image abroad, especially in the Middle East. Citizen diplomats were encouraged to be a part of this process of improving the US image abroad 'one handshake at a time' (State Department, n.d).

Historically, public diplomacy was state-centric and focused primarily on messaging. However, Joseph Nye (2011) and McClory (2017) assert that with a devolution of power from state to non-state actors came a recognition of the important role that citizens play in public diplomacy efforts. In practice, the US State Department put this into action, even dedicating a section of their website to encourage citizen diplomats to assist in efforts to shape foreign policy through promoting positive relations with people of different countries (State Department, n.d.). In this perspective, relations between people are seen as directly connected to relations between states. By enlisting citizen diplomats in the process of promoting understanding about America, its culture and its values, the belief was that it would also improve foreign publics' views of the country as a whole, its government and even its foreign policy. The belief is that if people have better views of a country, they are less likely to want to attack a country, which then contributes to peaceful relations between countries. In this way, these public diplomacy initiatives recognise that citizens' views matter, not just because they are part of a state, but because in modern international affairs, it is citizens that are causing many of the conflicts.

In regard to relations between America and Libya, the participants in this study suggest that the historically strained relations between these countries have to do with problems between the Libyan and American governments. This is despite the fact that a good deal of the strained relations were a result of terror attacks against civilians by Libyans. The participants recounted how relations between Libya and the US were good during the 50's and 60's, while King Idris Senussi was in power (FB4 and FB32). However, when Muammar Gaddafi took power in Libya relations between America and Libya began to deteriorate. FB3 said, 'The past government used to cause conflicts with America that caused bad reputation to all Libyans'. However, US foreign policy was seen as the main reason for the strained relations, rather than differing values (FB6). Part of the negative views of US foreign policy related to the US support of Israel (SP3), which several participants described as their enemy. Others shared that they perceived the US as engaging in terrorism around the world and questioned the unjust involvement in wars in Iraq (FB3 and FB16).

The historical memory of past conflicts between Libya and America has also had an impact on Libyans' views of American foreign policy. The participants most frequently noted the US air raid on Tripoli and Benghazi in 1986 and the subsequent US and UN sanctions against Libya as a result of Gaddafi's involvement in state-sponsored terrorism. FB8 said, 'The resulting sanctions on Libya after Lockerbie accident. Normal Libyans were suffering and not the leaders. Also, it was not based on sound evidence'. The fact that this participant referred to the Lockerbie terror attack as an accident is quite problematic and shows the ongoing struggle among Libyans to accept that the country of Libya is associated with such acts, even though the participants discussed how they suffered at the hands of Gaddafi as well. This is likely due to the fact that this same participant shared that it was the Libyan people that suffered the most as a result of the sanctions against Libya and not Gaddafi. This shows that it is difficult to separate the impact of a foreign policy decision on a state from its citizens, especially when sanctions are involved. The sanctions caused Libya to be treated as an enemy when they were relegated to outsider status within the international community. The participants shared that the Libyan people were impacted more by this than the Libyan government, which made it very personal to the people and impacted the way they saw the US government.

The US travel ban was discussed most frequently as a factor contributing to Libyans' negative views of US foreign policy. The participants expressed a view that Trump's travel ban is a declaration by the US government that it sees the Libyan people as enemies. FB1 said, 'It's undoubtedly unfair and this makes the American policy disgusting and can't gain other cultural people's trust'. The fact that the ban impacts Libyan citizens makes it deeply personal to the respondents, and it is perceived as inherently unfair to single them out while the US government continues to allow travel for people from countries that export terrorism. The participants exhibited very strong emotions concerning the travel ban because it has impacted their ability to travel to and from the US. In addition, this travel ban has significantly increased their distrust of the American government. FB28 maintained, 'I hope American department gives visa to Libyans to travel there and the reverse for its citizens because this decision has a big impact on our relation'. This is consistent with the assertion of Bially Mattern (2005) that language used between actors directly impacts social reality. However, in the case of the travel ban, it is not just language but actual policy that is impacting relations.

These statements by these participants suggest that citizen-led friendships between Libyans and Americans have no impact on Libyans' views of the US government and its foreign policy. The participants shared positive views of the American people. FB3 said, 'The American people are naïve, innocent, very nice, and you can use all other kinds of words. We know them very well. But American politics is something different'. The participants in this study consistently contended that they separate their views of the American people and the American government and its foreign policy. Instead, participants indicate that the only way to improve their views of American foreign policy is for the US government to change their foreign policy. They also discussed the fact that the problems they have with the US are not related to differing values, cultures or religions, but instead to the US government and its foreign policy (FB9).

Despite the participants' problems with US foreign policy, they still recognise the important role that the US government plays as a leader in international affairs, and they desire that the US expand its efforts to help Libya rebuild after the revolution and develop a strong democracy. As such, the participants spent a significant amount of time discussing the ways they want the US government to engage in Libya. In addition, there was a lot of discussion of how the US government could improve the ways they are viewed in Libya by doing more to help Libya rebuild. FB2 noted that 'Libyan people were hoping that the US government will continue to support Libya and help rebuild the country after the revolution, but the negativity of the White House disappointed the Libyans when they were looking high at US government'. The participants had very particular views on the types of activities that they believe the US government and civil society actors should be involved in within Libya. Most spoke about the need for some assistance with training and capacity-building, with the majority of respondents preferring the US government to stay out of domestic matters like oil and territorial rights.

Overwhelmingly, despite the desire for US government involvement in Libya, the participants noted a general distrust of the US government. This is due in part to a perception that the US government is engaging in unequal communication with leaders throughout the country. Equal communication is especially important when a country is in the midst of ongoing conflict and where there are regional powers fighting for control. The people do not want to feel like the US government is only interested in friendship or relations with people in certain parts of Libya and not others. This was expressed as especially important to the people in eastern Libya, who were often neglected during Gaddafi's time in power. Specifically, some participants noted that they felt that the US government's representatives were not spending enough time interacting with people in eastern Libya. Lack of inclusive communication and communication with groups that are seen as problematic, like Islamists, has caused some misunderstandings and exacerbated feelings of distrust. However, more importantly, the perceptions of distrust relate to concerns about the US government's motives for involvement in Libya, which they see as motivated by interests in oil. This lack of trust and the need to rebuild trust is supported by the argument from Oelsner and Koschut (2014) that trust-building activities are needed between governments and other actors. This lack of trust also jades the efforts that the US Embassy has been making in Libya to promote good relations.

The participants discussed specific ways the US government could build trust with Libyans. FB20 suggested that one way to improve trust in Libya for the US government is for the US government to communicate with the leaders of the three regions in Libya in an intensive and fair manner, which has been lacking since the US Embassy pulled out of Libya. There was also a discussion by FB4 of the desire for the US to rebuild its consulate in eastern Libya and to create a culture centre. However, it is difficult for people to value what gestures and efforts are being made if they question the US government's motivations and long-term commitment. FB1 noted there is a notable effort. However, mistrust taints the views of these efforts. So, more efforts need to be made to foster trust. One of the ways that trust can be fostered is for the US government to commit to staying engaged in Libya during the tough times they are going through. FB4 said, 'Have an open mind and stay'. Seeing a commitment by the US government to help Libya consistently is essential to how the US government is viewed and establishing trust among the people.

One of the most surprising findings in this study was that some of the participants' negative views of the US government and its policy were related the amount of help the US government provided to help Libya rebuild since the Libyan revolution. Historically, the US has developed a reputation as being one of the countries that provide aid and assistance to countries in their time of need. When the US government does not provide as much assistance as the citizens recognise their country's needs, it affects their views of the US government. The participants do recognise the complex security situation in Libya but feel abandoned after the US government, and many US-sponsored NGOs pulled out of Libya after the assassination of Ambassador Chris Stevens. The US government's 'light footprint' approach to engagement in Libya after the revolution has been perceived more as neglect and abandonment. The participants recognise the US government's role as a leader in the world and expected the US government to do more to help rebuild and promote stability in Libya. The participants expressed a desire for cooperation with both the public and private sectors in the US in implementing widespread capacity-building programmes throughout Libya. These kinds of partnerships would likely have a positive impact on the participants' views of the US government and its foreign policy by showing solidarity between countries. Consistent with Koschut and Oelsner's (2014) arguments, these gestures of support and goodwill would help to foster trust between the countries by showing that the US government cares about Libya, its people and its future.

To sum up, the participants in this study tend to separate their views of the US government from the American people. The participants shared that their negative views of the US government are based on its foreign policy decisions, which have treated Libya as enemies like the past sanctions and the travel ban. The participants recognise that there is a need for more inclusive communication and commitment to long-term capacity-building programs within Libya if trust is to be developed with the US government. Part of that will require intentional efforts by the US government to show that they are committed to helping Libya through its ongoing issues, which is evidenced by its posture toward Libya and willingness to commit to ongoing relations with Libya during its time of difficulty. In addition, it will require a commitment to change its policies, like the travel ban, which the participants see as treating the Libyan people as enemies.

6.4 Conclusion

As can be seen, the empirical data supports the premise that the language and behaviour that actors use in international relations do have an impact on the attitudes and views of citizens, which in turn impacts relations between states. Friendship groups and other cultural exchanges provide a necessary forum for dialogue and cultural understanding. Aristotle's friendship framework provides a useful way to look at friendships in the context of transnational citizen-led Facebook friendship groups between Libyans and Americans. The participants value friendships and believe it is possible for Libyans and Americans to develop deeper, or more virtuous forms of friendships that Aristotle idealises, despite cross-cultural differences. However, in the context of the Facebook friendships explored in this study, the friendships that are happening fit more specifically in the utility and pleasure categories. In these relationships, the group members learn about one another and promote understanding and respect, which is an essential building block of trust. It is through these processes of dialogue and socialising that participants are engaging in the process of reframing identity narratives they have about one another's people, culture and country. If participants are open-minded, they can learn a great deal about each other which helps to expand the participants' worldview. This process of knowing one another and being known is seen as vital to being a global citizen. The way people choose to relate to one another will impact the quality of relations within the international society. Using negative and enemy language and behaviour causes negative feelings for the people on the receiving end of that language and behaviour. Whereas, constructing relations around positive and friendly language and behaviour causes similar prosocial language and behaviour on the part of those on the receiving end. This positive behaviour results in more positive images that people have of one another and one another's states. As a result, fostering positive life-giving relations between citizens can have an impact on peaceful relations between states. However, fostering positive relations between citizens will have little impact on relations between states if the leaders of those states are not also engaging in positive diplomacy informed by what is (perceived as) reasonable foreign policy. These diplomatic practices run on parallel tracks and must go hand in hand. This research shows that communication and behaviour is vital in international relations and that treating states and citizens with enmity actually undermines public diplomacy efforts designed to attract and portray positive images of a state. This causes negative feelings and views among citizens and can contribute to tensions and conflict. In the end, people are at the centre of international relations and at a time when much of diplomatic practice is being eroded by the uncivil discourse of leaders, citizens must stand up and take their place in combating negative images through fostering positive life-giving relations in the international arena. Facebook friendship groups like the ones explored in this study, are a good place to start to build peaceful relations.

Chapter 7

Conclusion

7.1 Introduction

The aim of this research was to understand how Facebook friendships between Libyan and American citizens impact Libyans' views of the American people and American foreign policy. The broader aim of this book was to use a case study approach to understand how the concept of 'friend' can be understood in the context of transnational citizen-led Facebook friendship groups and how citizens use Facebook friendships to redefine identity narratives for the purpose of fostering more peaceful relations between their states. To do this, this book has used the Aristotelian framework on utility, pleasure and virtue friendships to understand political friendships that happen in the context of transnational citizen-led Facebook friendship groups between Libyans and Americans. This book has filled a gap in research by providing empirical data on citizen diplomacy and people-to-people friendships and how these relations impact citizens' views. This chapter provides a review of what has been discussed in each of the previous chapters, sets out conclusions and recommendations based on the empirical findings and ends with recommendations for further research and reflections on this research. This book starts with an introductory chapter which discusses the rationale and aim of this study, the epistemological assumptions undergirding the research design and a brief overview of the subsequent chapters. The second chapter involves a review of the literature on the evolution of the topic of public diplomacy and an explanation of where this book is positioned regarding the existing literature. The third chapter extends the argument for the socially constructed nature of views of friend and enemy in IR and discusses the ways that friendships between people can be used to foster peace in international society. In the fourth chapter, there is a discussion of the methodology and the epistemological views undergirding this study and the reasons for choosing focus group interviews of Libyans as the way of gaining insights into the meaning that the participants give to their reasons for participating in Facebook friendship groups with Americans. In the fifth chapter, there is a description of the historical conflict between Libya and the US and how this history informs a decision to explore ways to facilitate more peaceful relations between those countries. The sixth chapter includes the report of the findings from both the face-to-face and Facebook focus group interviews of the Libyan participants, with those findings organised under the overarching themes that were identified in the analysis. In the seventh chapter, the findings and themes are interpreted, synthesised and explained in relation to the theoretical literature on public diplomacy and friendship. Finally, the eighth chapter is this conclusion chapter, where the overall book is reviewed, conclusions are drawn, and recommendations for further research are given.

The purpose of the empirical sections of this case study was to explore, using a sample of the words of Libyan citizens, their perspectives on the significance of Facebook friendships between Libyans and Americans. The following paragraphs include a discussion of the major findings and conclusions drawn from this research.

7.2 Empirical conclusions

The first major finding of this research is that the participants in these focus group interviews put a high value on friendships and see them as a normal part of social and relational life, however, they recognise that there are different kinds of friendship, with some being based on usefulness and others for pleasure. The participants recognise that it can be difficult to reach the deeper more virtuous forms of friendships with people and that it takes time and trust to build these relations. A conclusion that can be drawn is that friendships can look different in different contexts and that sometimes friendships are more utilitarian in nature and other times simply based on the joy of being with another person. Needing supportive relationships with other people is part of what it means to be human. However, the ability to trust and understand one another is an essential part of friendship and a necessary factor in seeing relations move from an acquaintance to a deeper virtuous friendship level. A further and related conclusion is that the process of making and nurturing friendships is an ongoing effort and not always easy; therefore, it is something that people must continue to work at.

The second finding is that there are some similarities and differences between same-culture and cross-cultural friendships. In both, people need to share something in common with the other person to create a foundation to build upon. However, cross-cultural friendships include an added element of helping people gain insights about another person's culture. Different perspectives on culture and religion can make the process of making friendship between Americans and Libyans more challenging, but these differences do not need to serve as a barrier so long as the people respect one another and are willing to adapt their behaviour where appropriate so as not to offend another person's beliefs. A conclusion that can be drawn from this is that cross-cultural friendships are a valuable thing to have because they provide the same support and joy that same-cultural friendships do while providing the added benefit of opening people's eyes to different cultures, which is essential to expanding a person's worldview.

The study's third major finding is that open-mindedness and mutual respect are the keys to successful cross-cultural friendships. A conclusion that can be drawn from this finding is that open-mindedness is the glue that holds friendships together within the midst of difference. This is a kind of collective virtue or goodness that exists among people who are able to bridge the difference that exists between people of different cultures. Open-minded people are ones that seek to learn about different cultures and educate themselves rather than making quick judgements about others that create barriers. Being open-minded allows individuals to build upon commonalities, to educate themselves on their differences and respect other people amid their differences. A further conclusion can be drawn that the internet provides more opportunities than existed in the past to learn about other cultures, promote understanding and develop more peaceful relations between countries that have a history of conflict. However, people must be willing to want to learn and challenge the limited narratives that they are exposed to. A related conclusion is that to combat close-mindedness and to facilitate positive interpersonal relationships between people of different cultures, efforts should be made to facilitate mutual learning about each other's cultures.

The study's fourth finding is that technology, the internet and social media change the way people communicate and develop friendships. Facebook provides opportunities for people all over the world to connect, network and socialise with one another. A conclusion can be drawn that online friendships are definitely different from face-to-face friendships. Instead of being seen as friendships in the traditional sense, Facebook friends are considered more of an acquaintance when someone does not also have a physical world relationship with the other person. They fit within the utility and pleasure categories of Aristotelian friendships. A further conclusion can be drawn that Facebook provides a valuable medium to bridge the cultural divide between people from different countries, however, these relationships are inferior to face-to-face friendships. Face-to-face friendships allow people to become more intimate with one another, which translates into deeper friendships and greater levels of understanding between people, especially people from other cultures.

A fifth finding is that media, both traditional and social, can impact people's views of people from other cultures both negatively and positively. Traditional media tends to focus on reporting on bad things rather than good things, which impacts people's views. A conclusion can be drawn that more efforts need to be made to use media to provide more truthful representations of people from other cultures, which includes highlighting the positive things and dispelling myths. Social media provides an opportunity for citizens themselves to be engaged in the process of promoting understanding between cultures, dispelling myths, and building trust, which can help to improve relations between countries. This means understanding and trust are vital to the positive views of citizens in other states. These positive views are an important element of peaceful relations between states.

The sixth finding is that cultural exchange programmes are the most helpful way to promote trust and understanding which helps to improve relations between Libyans and Americans. Programmes that facilitate mutual exchange and learning on both sides are seen as the most valuable, and more efforts should be made to include average citizens, not just elites, because participation in exchange programmes can have a compounding effect when people share about their experiences with others. A conclusion can be drawn that more cultural exchange opportunities would be advantageous to relations between Libyans and Americans.

The study's seventh finding is that trust-building and inclusive communication between countries is essential to improving understanding between people of different cultures. Libya has three main regions, Tripolitania, Cyrenaica and Fezzan, each with its own regional identity and history. During Gaddafi's time in power, he caused particular strife for the people of Cyrenaica leaving them deeply suspicious of foreign policy initiatives and outreach that is limited to Tripolitania. A conclusion can be drawn that to foster trust among the people of Libya, outreach efforts should be targeted to all regions of Libya. Taking time to understand the unique regional cultures and histories will help to facilitate the building of trust.

The eighth finding is that Libyans' views of the US government are tied to the amount of help the US provides in capacity-building and education programmes. The US government's perception as a leader in the international arena comes with certain perceived responsibilities, one of which is to help countries develop and stabilise. For Libya, this is a significant need since the revolution and the further destabilisation of the security situation caused by instability, ongoing conflicts and fights for power. A conclusion that can be drawn is that if the US government wants to improve their image in Libya and relations between Libya and the US, the government should be more actively involved in promoting capacity-building and education programmes that help Libya to stabilise and develop. A further conclusion is that the Libyan people value cooperation between Libya and the US, and therefore, a needs assessment and joint plan for long-term projects would be beneficial to show a commitment to long-term positive relations between Libya and the US

The ninth finding builds on the last finding and that is that civil society organisations are seen more favourably by the Libyans in this study because they tend to distrust governments. There is a desire to see more civil society programmes instituted in Libya to facilitate capacity-building and education programmes. A conclusion that can be drawn is that the participants would like to see US-based NGOs and educational institutions facilitate capacity-building and education projects in Libya that focus not just on service delivery but also on relationship and trust-building between Libyans and Americans. Furthermore, having these NGOs engaging in long-term capacity-building projects in Libya will begin to help the country rebuild and bring Libyans and Americans together in a face-to-face environment where they can promote understanding and foster peaceful relations between the two countries.

The tenth and final finding is one of the most important because it indicates that the strained relations between Libya and the US and the image problem that the US government has are directly related to negative views of US foreign policy, not the values of citizens. This contradicts the US government's perspective that views of differing values are what influenced the terrorist attacks on 9/11 and subsequent terrorist attacks against US interests since then. This perspective catalysed the US government to significantly increase its values-based public diplomacy efforts following 9/11. However, other research has called this approach into question. For example, Zogby (2004) did survey research into people's views in the Middle East and North Africa and found that views of differing values were not the source of tensions or negative views of the US. Similarly, the Libyan people in this study made it clear that they tend to separate their views of the American people from their views of US foreign policy. They do not dislike America because of its culture or even religion. They dislike US foreign policy and perceive it as unjust and the main reason for conflicts in the Middle East and North Africa. Therefore, a conclusion that can be drawn is that if the US government wants to improve its image in Libya, it should recognise how its foreign policy decisions impact the Libyan people. The people are especially negatively impacted by foreign policy decisions that single all Libya citizens out for what is perceived as unfair treatment, like the travel ban. In addition, the US could improve its foreign policy by communicating better. One useful step is to recognise that the Libyans in this study desire that US government communicate equally with Libyans throughout all the different regions of Libya and help the Libyan people understand the rationale for its foreign policies. They also desire that the US government listen to the Libyan citizens' concerns about US foreign policy rather than just engaging in one-way messaging. As has been consistently mentioned in the literature, dialogue is preferred over monologue, and it will take the US government a lot further in establishing respect, trust and goodwill, which are necessary for long-term positive relations.

7.3 Recommendations

The researcher offers recommendations based on the findings, analysis and conclusions of this study. The recommendations that follow are for Libyan and American citizens and the US government.

1. Efforts should be made by both state and non-state actors to foster more online and offline friendships between their states, especially among average citizens, which are focused on promoting understanding.
2. Libyans and Americans could benefit from increasing the use of social media to combat inappropriate narratives about people and other countries that contribute to conflicts and instead focus their efforts on promoting positive narratives that foster peaceful relations.
3. The US government could benefit from facilitating more face-to-face exchanges between Libyan and American people from all walks of life which the participants in this study see as most helpful to building bridges of understanding that are stable enough to weather conflicts.
4. The US government should focus its efforts on using more dialogic focused public diplomacy approaches where they are listening to foreign publics as much as they are sharing information.
5. The US government should refrain from promoting enemy images of foreign publics through its discourse and policies and instead focus on friendly language.
6. The US government should increase funding for NGOs and universities to engage in capacity-building and education projects in Libya.
7. The US government should review its foreign policy priorities and ensure that they are fair, just and inclusive if they want to be perceived favourably among foreign publics.

7.4 Recommendations for further research

The researcher recommends that further research be conducted into ways to promote more peaceful relations between states through gaining the insights of citizens in those states. Most of the IR research is either historical or focused on relations between governments, while much of the peace research is still largely focused on intrastate conflicts. There is a strong case for more cross-fertilisation among these sub-fields, especially with the critical shift toward emphasising the regularised and commonplace interactions within Peace Studies and the insights from conflict resolution scholars on ways to transform and move beyond conflicts. Scholars are calling for more emancipatory research, which lends itself to making changes within governments and society. As such, there is a need for additional theoretical, methodological and empirical research in this area both to provide an understanding into what works and to test theories.

In addition, since conflicts can be very context-specific and negative views can be connected to historical relations, it would be useful for researchers to conduct some comparative case studies among the public diplomacy target audiences' perceptions in different countries. This would provide some useful information on the kinds of public diplomacy activities that can be standardized and those that need to be adapted based on the context.

7.4.1 Theoretical recommendations

Theoretically, more research is needed into friendship in IR based on all the different ways it is conceptualised. In addition, there is a particular need for studying friendship as a social process between actors, including citizens, especially in International Relations and Peace and Conflict Studies. This should include further exploration of all the various ways people interact with other people in international relations. This research should focus on language and behaviour. A particular focus should be made to gather data on face-to-face interactions between people, because these interactions are seen as more valuable. There is also a need for further conceptualisation of friendship as a social process between states in IR as well, rather than limiting the social process discussion to states that are part of security communities or special relationships. Further, there is also a need for more theoretical exploration of the role of citizens as agents of states in IR. This includes a further conceptualisation of both state-sponsored and non-state-led citizen diplomacy in international relations.

7.4.2 Methodological recommendations

The use of focus groups to collect data is uncommon in IR research. This is surprising, considering the shift to more interpretive approaches. Since it is not used very often, in doing this research I encountered a fair amount of scepticism about this method. This is despite the fact that it has been used by qualitative researchers in other disciplines for many years. The relational turn in IR calls for more relational research methods, and focus group interviews are, by definition, a relational process. It is an especially useful methodology for constructivist/interpretivist scholars doing research into social processes of identity construction. More research studies that use focus group interviews would be valuable in understanding how actors construct meaning together. In addition, the use of the innovative methodology of Facebook focus group interviews provides alternatives to other approaches of data collection on social media or where in-person interviews are not possible. Because questions are being asked of participants rather than researchers simply trying to interpret discourse in Facebook posts, the information gained is much deeper, and the insights more significant. In addition, the ability to translate posts allows researchers to collect more bilingual data and give a voice to non-English speaking perspectives, which continues to be an ongoing challenge for IR researchers. As such, more frequent use of Facebook focus group interviews would provide helpful insights on the diverse ways they can be used, which would help to bolster support for the use of this methodology in IR research more broadly.

7.4.3 Empirical recommendations

In regard to the limits of this individual study to the perspectives of Libyans who participate in Facebook friendships with Americans, it would be helpful to gain the insights of Libyan citizens who do not currently participate in Facebook groups and their perspectives of the American people and US foreign policy. This research should involve studies into the impact of face-to-face relations since this was discussed as more impactful than online relations in this study. It would also be helpful for a researcher to conduct similar research among the American members of the Facebook friendship groups to understand their reasons for participating in such groups and what impact those groups have on their perspectives of the Libyan people and the Libyan government. In general, there is a need for more qualitative and quantitative perspectives from citizens on what they think are the most useful ways to foster peaceful relations between countries. It would also be useful to study how other online spaces and social media environments like Instagram, Tiktok, Snapchat, etc. are being used to facilitate positive relations. In addition, for comparison purposes, it would be appropriate to conduct a similar study using the same criteria with people from other countries that participate in transnational friendship groups and learn whether the perspectives of the participants in other cultural contexts lead to similar findings. It would also be very useful to see ethnographic research conducted into citizens' perspectives on the most effective ways to facilitate peace in interstate conflicts since most of the existing studies are looking at intrastate conflicts. Since the Libyan participants in the study spoke a lot about the value of cooperative civil society and face-to-face exchanges, more qualitative and quantitative research into these kinds of projects would also be valuable. Furthermore, it would be equally valuable for another researcher to take the findings in this study and do surveys of larger numbers of people to gain their insights.

While this research was intentionally designed as a very contextual case study about relations between the US and Libya, there are some useful takeaways that may be relevant to further studies. The first is that in diplomacy, history and context matter. Creating a generalized approach to how states engage in public diplomacy can actually be problematic, especially if the approaches are based on generalized narratives which are not founded in research. So, states need to spend more resources to find out what works in public diplomacy rather than engaging in efforts that could actually be counterproductive. In particular, if states are going to focus on relational approaches, they need to ask the people how those approaches impact their views. However, they should also ask the most important question of what the people on the receiving end of public diplomacy initiatives would find most influential to them. What this research has shown is that if you ask your intended audience what works and what doesn't, they will be willing to tell you. These responses should inform diplomatic practice, not the uninformed opinions of governmental leaders.

7.5 Researcher's final reflections

I want to briefly reflect on my experience conducting this research and writing this book. The decision to embark on this research journey was informed by personal experience working in the country of Libya and directing an NGO that facilitated people-to-people exchanges and capacity-building programmes, and by personal curiosity into whether these kinds of citizen initiatives have any real impact. When you engage in cultural exchanges, dialogues and capacity-building programmes, you gain anecdotal insights into their value through your own personal experiences and from the things people say. Through the years of working in Libya, I have had the privilege to meet a large number of Libyans and I consider many of them my personal friends. Some of them are close friends, and others more of acquaintances. However, they all are valuable to me and have taught me a lot about who the Libyan people are and about the country and its history. These friendships have also helped me to grow as a human being and overcome the tragic loss of my brother, as I have identified with others who have experienced similar loss in Libya. The Libyan people welcomed me into their world on many occasions and have shared their lives with me, and for this I am grateful. They have also taught me that difference in things like culture and religion is not something to be feared. Instead, these relationships of difference have much to offer because they expand people's world view. These relations have also taught me a great deal about what it means to be a good human and live the best life I can live.

Over the years, I have learned that the Libyan people really desire to improve relations with Americans and are committed to the process. They are also people who have suffered much through past and ongoing conflicts, but they are resilient, warm and friendly and always willing to extend the hand of friendship. So, I am not surprised to hear the participants say they value the face-to-face over the online exchanges and they desire more of these exchange opportunities. They participate in the online friendship groups as a first step on the friendship continuum but mostly as a default forum for exchange when face-to-face is not possible. These online friendships are helpful but not sufficient to foster long-term peaceful relations. Relationships have to start somewhere. Since there have been some challenges between the US and Libya throughout the years, there is a need for Libyans and Americans to collaborate in combating the efforts of those who desire to cause conflict. That starts with challenging those negative efforts and promoting truth. True understanding comes from sitting with people in more intimate settings and learning from one another over meals or participating in a shared project. That is often where real life and relationships happen. As such, nurturing more face-to-face relations and exchanges would be valuable both personally and politically.

Overall, I think this was a worthwhile study to conduct because it provides much-needed insights into the perspectives of foreign publics on their views of the American people and US foreign policy and efforts to improve those views. However, this research is also valuable because it has given a voice to the perspectives of the Libyan people, which is a demographic that has been often neglected in research in the Middle East and North Africa, yet has been on the receiving end of US foreign policy decisions which many Libyans find unfair. Despite this, many Libyan citizens choose to participate in Facebook friendship groups with American citizens because they recognise the value that citizens can have collectively in engaging in dialogues designed to promote understanding. Relationships matter in Libyan culture, and my having relationships with Libyans certainly helped the process of recruiting participants for the interviews, but even so, there was a level of distrust that I experienced in the process that confirmed that much work still needs to be done in promoting trust between Americans and Libyans. Therefore, as an American, even the process of conducting interviews with Libyans was a helpful exercise in promoting positive relations between the US and Libya. The participants seemed to welcome the opportunity to give their perspectives, and as a researcher, I am glad to be able to provide a forum where their voices can be heard. In the end, the goal of this research is that academics, governments, policymakers, civil society actors, and citizens alike will use the findings of this study not only for understanding but for promoting policies and practices that are the most beneficial in promoting positive relations in the international arena.

References

Adler, E. and Pouliot, V. 2011. International Practices. *International Theory.* 3(1), pp. 1-36.

Aljazeera. 2017. *Haftar and ISIL fighters launch attacks on Tripoli.* [Online]. 2 June. [Accessed 19 August 2019] Available from: https://www.aljazeera.com/news/2017/06/haftar-isil-forces-launch-attacks-libya-170602170049944.html

Aljazeera. 2019. *UN-recognised GNA attacks key Haftar airbase in central Libya.* [Online]. [Accessed 19 August 2019]. Available from: https://www.aljazeera.com/news/2019/07/recognised-gna-attacks-key-haftar-airbase-central-libya-190727135849634.html

Allan, G. 1979. *A Sociology of Friendship and Kinship.* London: George Allen and Unwin.

Amity: The Journal of Friendship Studies. [no date]. About the Journal. [Online]. [Accessed 20 November 2019]. Available from: https://amityjournal.leeds.ac.uk/about/

Annis, D. 1987. The Meaning, Value and Duties of Friendship. *American Philosophical Quarterly.* 24, pp. 349-356.

Arendt, H. 1970. *On Violence.* California: Harcourt Brace Jovanovich.

Arendt, H. 1989. *The Human Condition.* Chicago: Chicago University Press.

Arendt, H. 1990. Philosophy and Politics. *Social Research.* 57(1), pp. 73-103.

Aristotle. 1996. *Eudemian Ethics.* Cambridge: Harvard Up, for Loeb Classical Editions.

Aristotle. 1994. *The Nichomachean Ethics.* Harmondsworth, UK: Penguin.

Aspen Institute. 2019. Virtual Exchange and Learning Impact Report. *Stevens Initiative.* [Online]. [Accessed 13 January 2020]. Available from: https://www.stevensinitiative.org/wp-content/uploads/2019/11/Virtual-Exchange-Impact-and-Learning-Report.pdf

Assad, A. 2018. Al-Sirraj: Manchester bomber's brother to be extradited from Libya to the UK by end of 2018. *Libya Observer.* [Online]. 15 November. [Accessed 17 November 2018]. Available from: https://www.libyaobserver.ly/news/al-sirraj-manchester-bombers-brother-be-extradited-libya-uk-end-2018

Banks, R. 2011. A Resource Guide to Public Diplomacy Evaluation. *CPD Perspectives on Public Diplomacy.* Paper 9. Los Angeles: Figueroa Press.

Barbour, R. 2007. *Doing Focus Groups.* London: Sage.

Barbour, R. and Kitzinger, J. eds. 1999. *Developing focus group research: Politics, theory and practice.* Thousand Oaks, CA: Sage.

Barker, C. 2005. *Cultural Studies: Theory and Practice.* London: Sage.

BBC. 2015. *Timeline: Lockerbie bombing.* [Online]. 15 October. [Accessed 7 December 2018]. Available from: https://www.bbc.co.uk/news/uk-scotland-34541363

BBC. 2016. *Guide to key Libyan Militias*. [Online]. 11 January. [Accessed 9 September 2019]. Available from: https://www.bbc.co.uk/news/world-middle-east-19744533

Beer, F. 1990. The Reduction of War and the Creation of Peace. In: Smoker, P., Davies, R. and Munske, B. eds. *A Reader in Peace Studies*. Oxford Pergamon Press.

Berenskoetter, F. 2007. Friends, There Are No Friends? An Intimate Reframing of the International. *Millennium: Journal of International Studies*. 35(3), pp. 647-76.

Berenskoetter, F. 2014. Friendship, Security, and Power. In Koschut, S. and Oelsner, A. eds. *Friendship and International Relations*. Houndsmills: Palgrave.

Berenskoetter, F. and Van Hoef, Y. 2017. Friendship and Foreign Policy. *Oxford Encyclopedia of Foreign Policy Analysis*.

Bevir, M. and Daddow, O. 2015. Interpreting foreign policy: National, comparative and regional studies. *International Relations*. 29(3), pp. 273-287.

Bially Mattern, J. 2005. *Ordering International Politics*. New York: Routledge.

Bially Mattern, J. 2011. A Practice Theory of Emotion for International Relations. In Adler, E. and Pouliot, V. eds. *International Practices*. pp. 63-86. Cambridge: Cambridge University Press.

Blanchard, C. 2018. *Libya: Transition and U.S. Policy. Congressional Research Service*. [Online]. 3 May. [Accessed 17 November]. Available from: https://digital.library.unt.edu/ark:/67531/metadc306489/m1/1/high_res_d/RL33142_2014May22.pdf

Bloomberg, L. and Volpe, M. 2016. *Completing Your Qualitative Dissertation*. Thousand Oaks, CA: Sage.

Bloor, M., Frankland, J., Thomas, M. and Robson, K. 2001. *Focus groups in social research*. London: Sage.

Boduszynski, M. 2015. The eternal dimension of Libya's troubled transition: the international community and democratic knowledge transfer. *The Journal of North African Studies*. 20(5), pp. 735-753.

Bollier, D. 2003. *The Rise of Netpolitik: How the Internet is Changing International Politics and Diplomacy*. Washington, DC: The Aspen Institute.

Bouvier, G. 2015. What is a discourse approach to Twitter, Facebook, YouTube and other social media: connecting with other academic fields? *Journal of Multicultural Discourses*, 10(2), pp. 149-162.

Boyd, D. and Ellison, N. 2007. Social Network Sites: Definition, History, and Scholarship. *Journal of Computer-Mediated Communication*. 13, pp. 210-230.

Boyd-Judson, L. 2011. *Strategic Moral Diplomacy: Understanding the Enemy's Moral Universe*. Sterling, VA: Kumarian Press.

Boyne, W. 2008. The Years of Wheelus. *Airforce Magazine*. [Online]. January. [Accessed 19 September 2019]. Available from: http://www.airforcemag.com/MagazineArchive/Pages/2008/January%202008/0108wheelus.aspx

Braun, B., Schindler, S. and Wille, T. 2018. Rethinking agency in International Relations: performativity, performances and actor-networks. *Journal of International Relations and Development*. 22, pp. 787-807.

Braun, V. and Clarke, V. 2013. *Successful qualitative research: A practical guide for beginners*. London: Sage.

Brennan, J. 2016. Testimony of CIA Director John Brennan before the *Select Senate Committee on Intelligence*, 9 February.

Brewer, J. 2010. *Peace Processes: A Sociological Approach*. London: Polity.

Brigham, S. 2010. The American-Soviet Walks: Large-Scale Citizen Diplomacy at Glasnost's Outset. *Peace & Change*. 35, pp. 594-625.

Brown, C. 2001. Our side: critical theory in international relations. In: Jones, W. *Critical theory and world politics*. Boulder, Colorado: Lynne Rienner Publishers.

Brown, J. 2010. Public Diplomacy: "Out" for the U.S., "In" Overseas?" Huffington Post. [Online]. 11 November. [Accessed 12 December 2019]. Available from: https://www.huffpost.com/entry/public-diplomacy-out-for_b_788931

Brown, E. 2011. Strong and Weak Ties: Why Your Weak Ties Matter. *Social Media Today*. [Online]. 30 June. [Accessed 25 February 2020]. Available from: https://www.socialmediatoday.com/content/strong-and-weak-ties-why-your-weak-ties-matter

Brown, K. 2017. The challenges in measuring public diplomacy. In: McClory, J. ed. *The Soft Power 30 Report*. USC Center for Public Diplomacy, pp.119-122.

Brunhorst, H. 2005. *From civic friendship to a global legal community*. Cambridge, Massachusetts: Massachusetts Institute of Technology.

Bueger, C. and Gadinger, F. 2014. *International Practice Theory: New Perspectives*. Basingstoke, UK: Palgrave MacMillan.

Burns, T. 1953. Friends, Enemies and the Polite Fiction. *American Sociological Review*. 18, pp.654-662.

Bush, G. 2001. Bush Press Conference. 11 October. *Washington Post*. [Online]. [Accessed 5 July 2019]. Available from: https://www.washingtonpost.com/wp-srv/nation/specials/attacked/transcripts/bush_text101101.html??noredirect=on

Castanno, E., Sacchi, S. and Gries, P. 2003. The Perception of Other in International Relations: Evidence for the Polarizing Effect of Entitativity. *Political Psychology*. 24(3), pp. 449-468.

Central Intelligence Agency. 1975. *Memorandum on Libya-Soviet Relations*. [Online]. 20 June. [Accessed 19 September 2019]. Available from: https://www.cia.gov/library/readingroom/docs/CIA-RDP79B01737A002100190001-8.pdf

Central Intelligence Agency. 2019. *Libya: The World Factbook*. [Online]. [Accessed 19 September 2019]. Available from: https://www.cia.gov/library/publications/the-world-factbook/geos/ly.html

Chan, D. and Cheng, G. 2004. A comparison of offline and online friendship qualities at different stages of relationship development. *Journal of Social and Personal Relationships*. 21(3), pp. 305-320.

Chiu, L. and Knight, D. 1999. How useful are focus groups for obtaining the views of minority groups? In: Barbour, R. and Kitzinger, J. eds. *Developing Focus Group Research: Politics, Theory and Practice*. London: Sage, pp. 99-112.

Cho, Y. 2009. Conventional and Critical Constructivist Approaches to National Security. *The Korean Journal of International Relations*. 40(3).

Chomsky, N. 1992. Language in the service of propaganda. *Chronicles of Dissent*. Sterling, Scotland: AK Press, pp. 1-32.

Chorin, E. 2012. *Exit the Colonel: The Hidden History of the Libyan Revolution.* New York: Public Affairs.

Clinton, H. 2010. Leading through Civilian Power. *Foreign Affairs* 89. [Online]. [Accessed 16 October 2017]. Available from: http://www.foreignaffairs.com/ articles/66799/hillary-rodham-clinton/leading-through-civilian-power

Cocking, D. and Kennett, J. 1998. Friendship and the Self. *Ethics.* 108, pp. 502-527.

Cocking, D. Van Den Hoven, J. and Timmermans, J. 2012. Introduction: One thousand friends. *Ethics and Information Technology.* 14, pp. 179-184.

Colonomos, A. 2001. Non-state actors as moral entrepreneurs: A transnational perspective on ethical networks. In: Josselin, G. and Wallace, W. eds. *Non-state Actors in World Politics.* New York: Palgrave, pp. 76-89.

Cornut, J. 2015. The Practice Turn in International Relations Theory. *Oxford Encyclopedia of International Relations.*

Council on Foreign Relations. 2001. Improving the US Public Diplomacy Campaign in the War Against Terrorism. [Online]. 3 November. [Accessed 5 July 2019]. Available from: https://cfrd8-files.cfr.org/sites/default/files/pdf/ 2003/09/public_diplomacy.pdf

Cowan, G. and Arsenault, A. 2008. Moving from Monologue to Dialogue to Collaboration: The Three Layers of Public Diplomacy. *The ANNALS of the American Academy of Political and Social Science.* 616(1), pp. 10-30.

Cull, N. 2006. 'Public Diplomacy' Before Gullion: The Evolution of a Phrase. 18 April. *USC Public Diplomacy.* University of Southern California.

Cull, N. 2011. Wikileaks, Public Diplomacy 2.0 and the State of Digital Public Diplomacy. *Place Branding and Public Diplomacy.* 7(1), pp. 1-8.

Cull, N. 2013. The Long Road to Public Diplomacy 2.0: The Internet in the use of public diplomacy. *International Studies Review.* 15, pp. 123-139.

Dahlgren, P. 1988. What's the meaning of this? Viewers' plural sense-making of TV news. *Media, Culture and Society.* 10, pp. 285-301.

Das, R. 2009. Critical Social Constructivism: Culturing Identity, (In) Security, and the State in International Relations Theory. *The Indian Journal of Political Science.* 70(4), pp. 961-982.

Denzin, N. and Lincoln, Y. eds. 2013a. *Strategies of qualitative inquiry.* Thousand Oaks, CA: Sage.

Denzin, N. and Lincoln, Y. 2013b. *Collecting and interpreting qualitative materials.* Thousand Oaks, CA: Sage.

D'Hooghe, I. 2015. *China's Public Diplomacy.* Leiden, Netherlands: Brill.

Digenarro, C. and Dutton, W. 2007. Reconfiguring friendships: Social relationships and the Internet. *Information, Communication and Society.* 10, pp. 591-618.

Digesar, P. 2016. *Friendship Reconsidered and How It Matters to Politics.* New York: Columbia University Press.

Digital Age. 2017. The role of social media in international relations. [Online]. 4 October. [Accessed 31 December 2019]. Available from: https://blogs.unsw. edu.au/thedigitalage/blog/2017/10/the-role-of-social-media-in-international- relations/

Diplomatic and Consular Program (D&CP). [no date]. *Public Diplomacy, Resource Summary,* p.57. [Online]. [Accessed 16 October 2016]. Available from: http:// www.state.gov/documents/organization/181074.pdf

Dolan, F. 2000. Arendt on philosophy and politics. In: Villa, D. ed. *The Cambridge Companion to Hannah Arendt.* Cambridge and New York: Cambridge University Press.

Duvall, R. and Chowdhury, A. 2011. Practices of Theory. In. Adler, E. and Pouliot, V. eds. *International Practices*, pp.335-354. Cambridge: Cambridge University Press.

Elder, A. 2014. Excellent online friendships: An Aristotelian defense of social media. *Ethics and Information Technology.* 16, pp. 287-297.

Ellis, V. 2012. Cultural Diplomacy: does it work? *Ditchley Foundation.* [Online]. [Accessed 25 February 2020]. Available from: https://www.ditchley.com/past-events/past-programme/2010-2019/2012/cultural-diplomacy

Esselmont, T. 2016. As Syrian deaths mount, world's 'responsibility to protect' takes a hit: experts. *Reuters* [Online]. 25 October. [Accessed 24 July 2019]. Available from: https://www.reuters.com/article/us-mideast-crisis-syria-law/as-syrian-deaths-mount-worlds-responsibility-to-protect-takes-a-hit-experts-idUSKCN12O2S3

European Consortium on Political Research. 2010. *Critical Peace and Conflict Studies.* [Online]. [Accessed 15 November 2019]. Available from: https://ecpr.eu/StandingGroups/StandingGroupHome.aspx?ID=42

Eznack, L. 2013. Let's Stay Friends: Relational Repair in Friendly International Relations. *The Polish Quarterly of International Affairs.* 4, pp. 55-76.

Fairclough, N. and Wodak, R. 1997. Discourse Analysis. In: Van Dijk, T. ed. *Discourse as Social Interaction. Discourse Studies: A Multidisciplinary Introduction.* London: Sage, pp. 258-284.

Farrands, C. 2001. Touching friendship beyond friendship: Friendship and citizenship in global politics. *Alternatives: Global, Local, Political.* 26(2), pp. 143-173.

Fernbeck, J. 2007. Beyond the diluted community concept: a symbolic interactionist perspective on online social relations. *New Media and Society.* 9(1).

Finnemore, M. and Sikkink, K. 1998. International Norm Dynamics and Political Change. *International Organization.* 52(4), pp. 887-917.

Fisher, A. 2011. Looking at the Man in the Mirror: Understanding the Power and Influence in Public Diplomacy. In: Fisher, A. and Lucas, S. eds. *Trials of Engagement: The Future of US Public Diplomacy.* Leiden: Martinus Nijhoff Publishing.

Fitzpatrick, K. 2011. *U.S. Public Diplomacy in a Post-9/11 World. From Messaging to Mutuality.* USC Center on Public Diplomacy.

Fitzpatrick, K. 2013. Public Diplomacy and Ethics: From Soft Power to Social Conscience. In: Zaharna, R. et al. eds. *Relational, Networked and Collaborative Approaches to Public Diplomacy.* New York: Routledge, pp. 29-43.

Friedman, M. 1989. Friendship and Moral Growth. *Journal of Value Inquiry.* 23, pp. 3-13.

Friedman, M. 1993. *What are friends for? Feminist Perspectives on Personal Relationships and Moral Theory.* Ithaca: Cornell University Press.

Fregonese, S. 2012. Urban politics 8 years on: Hybrid sovereignties, the everyday and geographies of peace. *Geography Compass.* 6(5), pp. 290-303.

Freire, P. 1972. *Pedagogy of the Oppressed.* Harmondsworth: Penguin.

Freire, P. 2014. *Pedagogy of the Oppressed 30ᵗʰ Anniversary Edition.* USA: Bloomsbury Publishing.

Fulda, A. 2018. The Emergence of Citizen Diplomacy in European Union-China Relations: Principles, Pillars, Pioneers, Paradoxes. *Diplomacy & Statecraft.* 30(1), pp. 188-216.

Fullerton, J. and Kendrick, A. 2006. *Advertising's War on Terrorism: The Story of the U.S. State Department's Shared Values Initiative.* Spokane: Marquette Books.

Galtung, J. 2012. Positive and negative peace. In: Weber, C. and Johanson, J. eds. *Peace and Conflict Studies: A Reader.* Oxon: Routledge.

Gamson, W. 1992. *Talking Politics.* Cambridge: Cambridge University Press.

Gauntlett, D. 2004. *Media, Gender and Identity: An Introduction.* London: Routledge.

Gibson, L. 2019. Can the US Embassy in Libya bridge the divide with Facebook? [Online]. 3 June. [Accessed 25 October 2019]. Available from: https://www.uscpublicdiplomacy.org/blog/can-us-embassy-libya-bridge-divide-faceboo

Glassman, J. 2008. Public Diplomacy 2.0: A New Approach to Global Engagement. *U.S. Department of State.* [Online]. 1 December. [Accessed 13 January 2020]. Available from: https://2001-2009.state.gov/r/us/2008/112605.htm

Glassman, J. 2011. *Jim Glassman Public Diplomacy 2.0.* [Online]. [Accessed 16 October 2016]. Available from: https://www.youtube.com/watch?v=Gyyq AZKa8Cw

Gomati, A. 2014. Khalifa Haftar: Fighting Terrorism or Pursuing Political Power? *Aljazeera.* [Online]. 10 June. [Accessed 10 September 2019]. Available from: https://www.aljazeera.com/indepth/opinion/2014/06/khalifa-hifter-operation-dignity-20146108259233889.html

Graffigna, G. and Bosio, A. 2006. The influence of setting on findings produced in qualitative health research: A comparison between face-to-face and online discussion groups about HIV/AIDS. *International Journal of Qualitative Methods.* 5 Article 5.

Greenbaum, T. 1998. Why focus group deserves to be the most respected of all qualitative research tools. *The Handbook for Focus Group Research.* Thousand Oaks, CA: Sage.

Gregory, B. 2012. American Public Diplomacy. In: Sharp, P. and Wiseman, G. eds. *American Diplomacy.* Leiden and Boston: Martinus Nijhoff.

Greavette, G. 2005. *Great aspirations: The fall and rise of Muammar Qaddafi.* Unpublished doctoral dissertation, Tri-University History Program, Wilfrid Laurier University, Ontario.

Gusterson, H. 1993. Realism and the International Order after the Cold War. *Social Research.* 60(2), pp. 279-300.

Habermas, J. 1990. *Moral Consciousness and Communicative Action.* Cambridge: Polity Press.

Habermas, J. 1994. *The Past as Future.* Cambridge: Polity Press.

Hain, P. 2001. The End of Foreign Policy? *Speech to the Royal Institute of International Affairs,* Chatham House, London, 22 January.

Hall, P. and Bach-Lombardo, J. 2017. The New Network Effect: A Model for Influence. In: McClory, J. ed. *The Soft Power 30 Report.* USC Center for Public Diplomacy, pp. 91-93.

Handlemann, S. 2012. Two Complementary Settings of Peace-making Diplomacy: Political-Elite Diplomacy and Public Diplomacy. *Diplomacy & Statecraft.* 23(1), pp. 162-178.

Hare-Mustin, R. and Marecek, J. eds. 1990. *Making a Difference: Psychology and the Construction of Gender.* New Haven CT: Yale University Press.

Hasan, M. 2018. *Blowback: How the bombing of Libya in 2011 led to terror attacks in Britain.* 28 February. The Intercept [Online]. [Accessed 17 November 2018]. Available from: https://theintercept.com/2018/02/26/libya-bombing-gaddafi-uk-terror-attacks/

Hayden, C. 2013. Facilitating the Conversation: The 2012 U.S. Presidential Election and Public Diplomacy Through Social Media. *American Behavioral Scientist.* 57(11), pp. 1623-1644.

Helland, E. 2017. Virtual exchange and the evolution of citizen diplomacy. In: McClory, J. ed. *The Soft Power 30 Report.* USC Center for Public Diplomacy, pp. 96-100.

Henrikson, A. 2005. Professor of Diplomatic History. [Online]. April. [Accessed 2 April 2018]. Available from: http://pdaa.publicdiplomacy.org/?page_id=6

Hocking, B. 2005. Rethinking the New Public Diplomacy. In: Melissen, J. ed. *The New Public Diplomacy.* London: Palgrave, pp. 23-43.

Hopf, T. 2010. The Logic of Habit in International Relations. *European Journal of International Relations.* 16(4), pp. 539-561.

Hsu, S. 2018. *Libyan militia leader to be sentenced in 2012 attacks that killed US Ambassador.* Washington Post [Online]. 27 June. [Accessed 12 December]. Available from: https://www.washingtonpost.com/local/public-safety/libyan-militia-leader-to-be-sentenced-in-2012-benghazi-attacks-that-killed-us-ambassador/2018/06/27/55782e5c-789a-11e8-aeee-4d04c8ac6158_story.html?utm_term=.1a97b58a3319

Hughes, K. 2005. *The Mission of Public Diplomacy.* US Department of State. [Online]. 22 July. [Accessed 9 November 2019]. Available from: https://2001-2009.state.gov/r/us/2005/49967.htm

Human Rights Watch. 2019. *Libya: Spiralling Militia Attacks May Be War Crimes.* [Online]. 8 September 2014. [Accessed 19 September 2019]. Available from: https://www.hrw.org/news/2014/09/08/libya-spiraling-militia-attacks-may-be-war-crimes

Humphrey, M., Umbach, M. and Clulow, Z. 2019. The political is personal: an analysis of crowd sourced political ideas and images from a Massive Open Online Course. *Journal of Political Ideologies.* 24(2), pp. 121-138.

Hutter H. 1978. *Politics as Friendship.* Waterloo, Ontario, Canada: Wilfrid Laurier University Press.

Institute for Cultural Diplomacy. [no date]. *What is Cultural Diplomacy?* [Online]. [Accessed 7 November 2019]. Available from: http://www.culturaldiplomacy.org/index.php?en_culturaldiplomacy

Institute for Multi-track Diplomacy. [no date]. *Cyprus: Leadership in Conflict Resolution.* [Online]. [Accessed 19 August 2019]. Available from: https://www.imtd.org/cyrus-leadership-in-conflict-resolu

Institute for Multi-Track Diplomacy. [no date]. *Multi-track Diplomacy.* [Online]. [Accessed 19 August 2019]. Available from: https://www.imtd.org/mission

Iosifidis, P. and Wheeler, M. 2016. Public Diplomacy 2.0 and the Social Media. In: *Public Spheres and Mediated Social Networks in the Western Context and Beyond.* London: Palgrave, MacMillan.

Jabri, V. 2007. *War and the Transformation of Global Politics.* London: Palgrave.

Jackson, P. 2016. *The Conduct of Inquiry in International Relations.* London and New York: Routledge.

Jankowski, N.W. 2002. Creating Community with Media: History, Theories and Scientific Investigation. In: Lievrouw, L. and Livingstone, S. eds. *The Handbook of New Media,* pp. 34-49. London: Sage.

Josselin, D. and Wallace, W. 2001. Non-state actors in world politics: a framework. In: Josselin, D. and Wallace, W. eds. *Non-state Actors in World Politics.* New York: Palgrave.

Kaldor, M. 2003. The Idea of Global Civil Society. *International Affairs.* 79(3), pp. 583-593.

Kaliarnta, S. 2016. Using Aristotle's theory of friendship to classify online friendships: A critical counterview. *Ethics and Information Technology.* 18, pp. 65-79.

Kant, I. 1996. *Metaphysical Principles of Virtue.* Cambridge: Cambridge University Press.

Kant, I. 1997. *Lectures on Ethics.* Cambridge: Cambridge University Press.

Kawczynski, D. 2011. *Seeking Gaddafi: Libya, the West and the Arab Spring.* London: Biteback.

Keck, M. and Sikkink, K. 1998. *Activists beyond Borders: Advocacy Networks in International Politics.* New York: Cornell University Press.

Keller, A. 2006. Justice, Peace and History. In: Allan, P. and Keller, A. eds. *What is a Just Peace?* Oxford: Oxford University Press.

King, P. 2007a. Friendship in Politics. *Critical Review of International Social and Political Philosophy.* 10(2), pp. 125-145.

King, P. 2007b. Friendship in Politics. In: King, P. and Smith, G. eds. *Friendship in Politics.* London and New York: Routledge, pp. 9-29.

Kirkpatrick, K. 2011. *US Public Diplomacy in a Post-9/11 World: From messaging to mutuality.* USC Center for Public Diplomacy. Los Angeles: Fuquera Press.

Kitzinger, J. and Barbour, R.1999. The Challenge and Promise of Focus Groups. In: Barbour, J. and Kitzinger, J. eds. *Developing Focus Group Research.* London: Sage.

Koschut, S. 2014. Transatlantic Conflict Management Inside-out: The Impact of Domestic Norms on Regional Security Practices. *Cambridge Review of International Affairs.* 27(2), pp. 339-361.

Koschut, S. and Oelsner, A. 2014. Conclusion. In: Koschut, S. and Oelsner, A. eds. *Friendship and International Relations.* Houndsmills: Palgrave.

Kratochwil, F. 1989. *Rules, Norms, and Decisions.* Cambridge: Cambridge University Press.

Kuzel, A. 1992. Sampling in qualitative inquiry. In: Crabtree, B. and Miller, W. eds. *Doing Qualitative Research.* Newbury Park, CA: Sage, pp. 31-44.

Langhorne, R. 2005. The Diplomacy of Non-State Actors. *Diplomacy & Statecraft,* 16(2), pp. 331-339.

Lemke, J. 1995. *Textual Politics: Discourse and Social Dynamics*. London, UK: Taylor and Francis.

Lenczowski, J. 2011. *Full Spectrum Diplomacy and Grand Strategy: Reforming the Structure and Culture of US Foreign Policy*. Plymouth, UK: Lexington Books.

Leonard, M. and Alakeson, V. 2000. *Going Public: Diplomacy for the Information Society*. London: Foreign Policy Centre/Central Books.

Leonard, M., Stead, M., and Smewing, C. 2002. *Public Diplomacy*. London: Foreign Policy Centre.

Li, L. 2010. Performing Bribery in China-Guanxi Practice, Corruption with a Human Face. *Journal of Contemporary China*. 20(68), pp. 1-20.

Libya Observer. 2017. *East Libya government bans Americans from entering Libya*. [Online]. 27 September. [Accessed 1 October 2018. Available from: https://www.libyaobserver.ly/news/east-libya-government-bans-americans -%E2%80%9Centering-libya%E2%80%9D

Lijadi, A. and van Schalkwyk, J. 2015. Online Facebook Focus Group Research of Hard-to-Reach Participants. *International Journal of Qualitative Methods*, pp. 1-9.

Ling, C. 2004. Communication in Intercultural Relationships. In: Gudykunst, W. and Mody, B. eds. *Handbook of International and Intercultural Communication*. Thousand Oaks, CA: Sage.

Linklater, A. 1982. *Men and citizens in the theory of international relations*. London, UK: MacMillan

Linklater, A. 1994. *Men and citizens in the theory of international relations*. Basingstoke, UK: MacMillan.

Linklater, A. 2001. The Changing Contours of Critical International Relations Theory. In: Jones, W. *Critical Theory and World Politics*. Boulder, Colorado: Lynne Rienner Publishers, Inc.

Lord Carter of Coles. 2005. *Lord Carter Coles: Public Diplomacy Review. House of Commons Affairs Committee*. [Online]. [Accessed 8 February 2018]. Available from: https://publications.parliament.uk/pa/cm200506/cmselect/cmfaff/903/903.pdf

Lu, C. 2000. The One and Many Faces of Cosmopolitanism. *The Journal of Politcal Philosophy*. 8(2), pp. 244-267.

Lu, C. 2009. Polltlcal Friendships Among Peoples. *Journal of International Political Theory*, 5(1), pp. 41-58.

Lyndon B. Johnson School of Public Affairs. 2010. *Public Diplomacy Model for Assessment and Performance*. Policy Research Report Project Number 170. Austin: University of Texas.

Lynch, M. 2000. *The Dialogue of Civilisations and International Public Spheres*. Sage Publications. 29(2), p. 323.

Lyotard, J. and Thebaud, J. 1985. *Just Gaming*. Manchester: Manchester University Press.

MacGinty, R. 2014. Everyday Peace: Bottom-up and Local Agency in Conflict Societies. *Security Dialogue*. 45(6), pp. 391-412.

MacGinty, R. 2019. Circuits, the everyday and international relations: Connecting the home to the international and transnational. *Cooperation and Conflict.* pp. 1-20.

MacIntyre, A. 1985. *After Virtue.* London: Duckworth.

Malinarich, N. 2001. *Flashback: The Berlin disco bombing.* BBC News [Online]. 13 November. [Accessed 1 December 2018]. Available from: http://news.bbc.co.uk/1/hi/world/europe/1653848.stm

Marshall, J. 1949. International Affairs: Citizen Diplomacy. *The American Political Science Review,* 43(1), pp. 83-90.

Marshall, C. and Rossman, G. 2015. *Designing qualitative research.* Thousand Oaks, CA: Sage.

Martin, I. 2015. The United Nations' Role in the First Year of Transition. In: Cole, P. and McQuinn, B. *The Libyan Revolution and Its Aftermath.* New York: Oxford University Press, Kindle Edition.

Maxwell, J. 2013. *Qualitative Research Design: An interactive approach.* Thousand Oaks, CA: Sage.

Mays, N. and Pope, C. 1995. Rigour and qualitative research. *British Medical Journal.* 311, pp. 109-112.

McClory, J. ed. 2017. *The Soft Power 30 Report.* USC Center for Public Diplomacy.

McClory, J. ed. 2019. *The Soft Power 30 Report.* USC Center for Public Diplomacy.

McCourt, D. 2016. Practice Theory and Relationalism as the New Constructivism. *International Studies Quarterly.* [Online]. 28 September. [Accessed 21 May 2019]. Available from: https://www.isanet.org/Publications/ISQ/Posts/ID/5333/Practice-Theory-and-Relationalism-as-the-New-Constructivism

McDonald, J. Further Exploration of Track Two Diplomacy. 1991. In: Kreisburg, L. and Thorson, S. eds. *Timing the De-Escalation of International Conflicts.* Syracuse, NY: Syracuse University Press. pp. 201-220.

McFall, M. 2012. Real character-friends: Aristotelian friendship, living together, and technology. *Ethics and Information Technology.* 14, pp. 221-230.

Mead, G. 1934. *Mind, Self and Society from the Standpoint of a Social Behaviorist.* Chicago: University of Chicago Press.

Melissen, J. 2005. *The New Public Diplomacy.* London: Palgrave.

Melissen, J. 2005. The New Public Diplomacy: Between Theory and Practice. In: Melissen, J. ed. *The New Public Diplomacy.* London: Palgrave, pp. 3-23.

Merriam, S. 2009. *Qualitative research: A guide to design and implementation.* San Francisco: Jossey-Bass.

Miles, M. and Huberman. A. 1994. *Qualitative data analysis: An expanded sourcebook.* Thousand Oaks, CA: Sage.

Miller, E. and Truitte, K. 2017. Filling the Vacuum in Libya. *Foreign Affairs.* [Online]. 18 July. [Accessed 19 September 2019]. Available from: https://www.foreignaffairs.com/articles/libya/2017-07-18/filling-vacuum-libya

Miller, W. and Mousavian, S. 2013. *Iran nuclear talks: Citizen diplomacy would build trust. Christian Science Monitor.* [Online] 45 April. [Accessed 18 August 2019]. Available from: https://www.csmonitor.com/Commentary/Opinion/2013/0405/Iran-nuclear-talks-Citizen-diplomacy-would-build-trust

Mitchell, A. 2011. Quality/control: International peace interventions and 'the everyday'. *Review of International Studies.* 37(4), pp. 1623-1645.

More, T. 1956. *Utopia,* reproduced in Wolfes and Martin, *The Anglo-American Tradition in Foreign Affairs: Readings on Thomas More to Woodrow Wilson.* New Haven: Yale Community Press.

National Democratic Institute. 2013. *Seeking Security: Public Opinion Survey in Libya.*

Navari, C. 2011. The concept of practice in the English School. *European Journal of International Relations.* 17(4), pp .611-630.

Nelson, B. 1973. Civilisational Complexes and Inter-Civilisational Relations. *Sociological Analysis.* 74(1), pp. 79-105.

Nordin, A. and Smith, G. 2018a. Friendship and the new politics: beyond community. *Journal of Global Discourse.* 8(4), pp. 615-632.

Nordin, A. and Smith, G. 2018b. Reintroducing relational ontologies in international relations: relational ontologies from China to the West. *International Relations of the Asia-Pacific.* 18(3), pp. 369-396.

Northern, R. and Pack, J. 2013. The role of outside actors. In: Pack, J. ed. *The 2011 Libyan Uprisings and the Struggle for the Post-Qadhafi Future.* New York: Palgrave MacMillan, pp. 113-150.

Nye, J. 2004. *Soft Power.* New York: Public Affairs.

Nye, J. 2008. Public Diplomacy and Soft Power. *The ANNALS of the American Academy of Political and Social Science.* 616(1), pp. 94-109.

Nye, J. 2010. The Pros and Cons of Citizen Diplomacy. *NYTimes.* [Online]. 5 October. [Accessed 10 October 2017]. Available from: http://www.nytimes.com/2010/10/05/opinion/05iht-ednye.html

Nye, J. 2011. *The Future of Power.* New York: Public Affairs.

Nye, J. 2019. American soft power after Trump. In: McClory, J. *The Soft Power 30 Report.* USC Center on Public Diplomacy.

Oelsner, A. 2014. The Construction of International Friendship in South America. In: Koschut, S. and Oelsner, A. *Friendship and International Relations.* Houndsmills: Palgrave.

Oelsner, A. and Koschut, S. 2014. A Framework for the Study of International Friendship. In: Koschut, S. and Oelsner, A. eds. *Friendship and International Relations.* Houndsmills, Basingstoke, Hampshire; New York: Palgrave.

Oelsner, A. and Vion, A. 2011. Friends in the region: a comparative study on friendship building in regional integration. *International Politics.* 48(1), pp. 129-151.

Oelsner, A. 2007. Friendship, Mutual Trust and the Evolution of Regional Peace in the International System. *Critical Review of International Social and Political Philosophy.* 10(2), pp. 257-279.

Onuf, N. 1998. Constructivism: A User's Manual. In: Kulbalkova, V., Onuf, N. and Kowert, P. eds. *International Relations in a Constructed World.* Armonk, NY: M.E. Sharpe, pp. 58-78.

Padilla, R.V. 1993. Using dialogical research methods in group interviews. In: Morgan, D. ed. *Successful Focus Groups: Advancing the State of the Art.* London: Sage, pp. 153-166.

Paine, R. 1969. In search of friendship. *Man.* 4, pp. 505-524.

Papacharissi, Z. 2002. The Real/Virtual Dichotomy in Online Interaction: A Meta-Analysis of Research on New Media Uses and Consequences. *Paper presented at the International Association of Mass Communication Researchers annual convention*, July, Barcelona, Spain.

Patsias, C. and Patsias, S. 2014. Social Forums and Friendship: A New Way of Contemplating the Notion of Friendship in International Relations. In: Koschut, S. and Oelsner, A. *Friendship and International Relations*. Houndsmills: Palgrave, pp. 163-181.

Patton, M. 2015. *Qualitative research and evaluation methods*. Thousand Oaks, CA: Sage.

Perrigo, B. 2017. How the US Used Jazz as a Cold War Secret Weapon. *Time*. [Online]. 22 December. [Accessed 26 August 2019]. Available from: https://time.com/5056351/cold-war-jazz-ambassadors/

Peterson, P. 2002. Public Diplomacy and the War on Terrorism. *Foreign Affairs*. [Online]. September/October. [Accessed 5 July 2019]. Available from https://www.foreignaffairs.com/articles/2002-09-01/public-diplomacy-and-war-terrorism

Pigman, G. 2010. *Contemporary Diplomacy*. Cambridge: Polity Press.

Plato. 1987. *The Republic*. 2nd ed. Trans. Desmond Lee. New York: Penguin Books.

Pouliot, V. 2004. The essence of constructivism. *Journal of International Relations and Development*. 7(3), pp. 319-336.

Proedrou, F. and Frangonikolopoulos, C. 2012. Refocusing Public Diplomacy: The Need for Strategic Discursive Public Diplomacy. *Diplomacy & Statecraft*, 23(4), pp. 728-745.

Public Diplomacy Association of America. 2017. U.S. Image Under Trump Declines Sharply. [Online]. 1 July. [Accessed 31 December 2019]. Available from: https://pdaa.publicdiplomacy.org/?p=1548

Qin, Y. 2009. Quanxi Benwei Yu Guocheng Jiangou: Jiang Zhongguo Linian Zhiru Guoji Lilun [Relationship and Processional Construction: Bringing Chinese Ideas into International Relations Theory]. *Zhongguo she-hui kexue*. 30(4), pp. 5-20.

Rampton, S. 2007. Shared Values Revisited. *The Center for Media and Democracy's PR Watch*. [Online]. 17 October. [Accessed 16 October 2017]. Available from: http://www.prwatch.org/node/6465.

Richmond, O. 2008a. Reclaiming Peace in International Relations. *Millennium Journal of International Studies*. 36(3), pp. 439-470.

Richmond, O. 2008b. *Peace in International Relations*. London: Routledge.

Richmond, O. 2011. *A Post-Liberal Peace*. Oxon: Routledge.

Richmond, O. 2012. *Peace in International Relations*. London and New York: Routledge.

Risse, T. 2000. 'Let's Argue': Communicative Action in World Politics. *International Organization*. 54(1), pp. 1-39. Robert Wood Johnson Foundation. [no date]. *Qualitative Research Guidelines Project*. [Online]. [Accessed 28 September 2018]. Available from: http://www.qualres.org/HomeCrit-3518.html

Ronfeldt, D. and Arquilla, J. 1999. What If There is a Revolution in Diplomatic Affairs? paper presented as part of 'Virtual Diplomacy: A Revolution in Diplomatic Affairs'. *United States Institute for Peace*. [Online]. 18 February

1999. [Accessed 19 January 2018]. Available from: https://www.webharvest. gov/peth04/20041018110436/http://www.usip.org/virtualdiplomacy/public ations/reports/ronarqISA99.html

Rorty, R. 1989. *Contingency, irony and solidarity.* Cambridge: Cambridge University Press.

Roshchin, E. 2006. The Concept of Friendship from Princes to States. *European Journal of International Relations.* 12(4), pp. 599-624.

Ruggie, J. 1998. *Constructing the World Polity.* New York: Routledge.

Sanger, D. 2012. Even with a 'Light Footprint' It's Hard to Sidestep the Middle East. *NY Times.* 12 November. [Accessed 19 September 2019]. Available from: https://www.nytimes.com/2012/11/18/world/middle-east-challenges-obamas -light-footprint.html

Saudi Gazette. 2012. Group using social media to bridge cultural divide. [Online]. 26 December. [Accessed 31 December 2019]. Available from: http://saudi gazette.com.sa/article/26361

Saunders, F. 1995. Modern Art Was CIA 'Weapon'. *The Independent.* [Online]. 21 October. [Accessed 20 November 2017]. Available from: http://www.independent. co.uk/news/world/modern-art-was-cia-weapon-1578808.html

Saunders, H. 2013. The Relationship Paradigm and Sustained Dialogue. In: Zaharna, R. et al. eds. *Relational, Networked and Collaborative Approaches to Public Diplomacy.* New York: Routledge, pp. 132-143.

Schmitt, C. 1996. *The Concept of the Political.* Trans. Schwab, G. Chicago: The University of Chicago Press.

Schmitt, C. 2004. *The Theory of the Partisan.* East Lansing: Michigan State University Press.

Schneider, C. 2005. Culture communicates: US diplomacy that works. In: Melissen, J. ed. *The New Public Diplomacy.* London: Palgrave Macmillan pp. 147-168.

Schroeder, J. and Risen, J. 2014. Peace through Friendship. *NYTimes.* [Online]. 22 August. [Accessed 16 March 2018]. Available from: https://www.nytimes. com/2014/08/24/opinion/sunday/peace-through-friendship.html

Schultz, A. 1967. *The Phenomenology of the Social World.* Evanston, IL: Northwestern University Press.

Schwartz-Shea, P. and Yanow, D. 2012. *Interpretive Research Design.* New York: Routledge.

Schwartzenbach, S. 2009. *On Civic Friendship: Including Women in the State.* New York: Columbia University Press.

Scott-Smith, G. 2014. Introduction: Private Diplomacy Making the Citizen Visible. *New Global Studies,* 8(1), pp.1-7.

Searle, J. 1995. *The Construction of Social Reality.* New York: Free Press.

Sengupta, K. 2012. Revealed: Inside story of US envoy's assassination. *Independent.* [Online]. 14 September. [Accessed 20 September 2019]. Available from: https:// www.independent.co.uk/news/world/politics/revealed-inside-story-of-us- envoys-assassination-8135797.html

Seo, H. 2013. The Virtual Last Three Feet. In: Zaharna, R. ed. *Relational, Networked and Collaborative Approaches to Public Diplomacy.* New York: Routledge.

Sharp, P. 2005. Revolutionary States, Outlaw Regimes and the Techniques of Public Diplomacy. In: Melissen, J. ed. *The New Public Diplomacy*, pp. 106-123.

Sharp, R. 2012. The obstacles against reaching the highest level of Aristotelian friendship online. *Ethics and Information Technology*. 14, pp. 231-239.

Shay, A. 2013. Israel's New Peer-to-Peer Diplomacy. *The Hague Journal of Diplomacy*. Leiden: Martinus Nijhoff Publishing. 7(4), pp. 473-482.

Shear, M. and Nixon, R. 2017. Trump's Travel Ban to Be Replaced by Restrictions Tailored to Certain Countries. *NYTimes*. [Online]. 21 September. [Accessed 17 November 2018]. Available from: https://www.nytimes.com/2017/09/22/us/politics/trump-travel-ban-replacement-restrictions.html

Shi-xu. 2014. *Chinese discourse studies*. Basingstoke: Palgrave Macmillan

Sipress, A. and Mintz, J. 2003. Libya Accepts responsibility for bombing over Lockerbie. *Washington Post*. [Online]. 1 May. [Accessed 7 December 2018]. Available from: https://www.washingtonpost.com/archive/politics/2003/05/01/libya-accepts-responsibility-for-bombing-over-lockerbie/7865ce94-c723-4458-beff-f1841bc5cdaa/?utm_term=.eeed26aff76e

Skeggs, B. 1997. *Formations of Class and Gender: Becoming Respectable*. London: Sage.

Smith, G. 2011. *Friendship and the Political*. Charlottesville, VA: Imprint Academic.

Smith, G. 2014. Friendship, State and Nation. In: Koschut, S. and Oelsner, A. eds. *Friendship and International Relations*. Houndsmills: Palgrave.

Smith, L. 2017. Digital Diplomacy and the power of citizen networks and advocacy organizations. In: McClory, J. ed. *The Soft Power 30 Report*. USC Center for Citizen Diplomacy, pp. 88-90.

Smith, W. 2017. Cosmopolitanism. *Oxford Research Encyclopedia*. Oxford University Press.

Snow, N. 2009. The Resurgence of U.S. Public Diplomacy after 9/11. *The Impact of 9/11 on Media, Arts and Entertainment. The Day that Changed Everything*. New York: Palgrave MacMillan.

Stake, R. 1995. *The art of case study research*. Thousand Oaks, CA: Sage.

Stanley, L. 2016. Using Focus Groups in political science and international relations. *Politics*. 36(3), pp. 236-249.

Sterling-Folker, J. and Shinko, R. 2005. Discourses of Power: Traversing the Realist-Postmodern Divide. *Millennium*. 33.

Stewart, D. and Shamdasani, P. 1990. *Focus groups: Theory and practice*. Applied social research methods series. Thousand Oaks, CA: Sage.

Stewart, K. and Williams, M. 2005. Researching online populations: The use of online focus groups for social research. *Qualitative Research*. 5, pp. 395-416.

Tarrow, S. 2005. *The New Transactional Activism*. Cambridge: Cambridge University.

Telfer, E. 1970. Friendship. *Proceedings of the Aristotelian Soceity*. 71, pp. 223-241.

The New Arab. 2019. *Haftar launched 37 attacks on health facilities in Libya: UN*. [Online] 16 August. [Accessed 19 August 2019] Available from: https://www.alaraby.co.uk/english/news/2019/8/16/haftar-launched-37-attacks-on-health-facilities-in-libya

The White House. 2017. *Fact Sheet: Proclamation on Enhancing Vetting Capabilities and Processes for Detecting Attempted Entry into the United States by Terrorist or Other Public-Safety Threats.* 24 September.

Thomlison, T. 2000. An Interpersonal Primer with Implications for Public Relations. In: Ledingham, J. and Bruning, S. eds. *Public Relations as Relationship Management: A Relational Approach to the Study and Practice of Public Relations.* Mahway, NJ: Lawrence Erlbaum.

Turse, N. 2015. Last Year America Sent Special Forces Into Almost 70% of the World. *Mother Jones.* [Online]. 21 January. [Accessed 20 September 2019]. Available from: https://www.motherjones.com/politics/2015/01/special-ops -almost-70-percent-world-countries/

United Nations. 2015. *UNSMIL and Int'l Community Consultations on Support to Future Libyan Government of National Accord.* [Online]. 26 August. [Accessed 20 September 2019]. Available from: https://unsmil.unmissions. org/unsmil-and-int%E2%80%99l-community-consultations-support-future -libyan-government-national-accord

United Nations. 2017. *Report of the Secretary-General of the United Nations Support Mission in Libya.* (22 August). [Online]. S/Res/2017/726. [Accessed 18 September 2019. Available from: https://www.securitycouncilreport.org/ atf/cf/%7B65BFCF9B-6D27-4E9C-8CD3-CF6E4FF96FF9%7D/s_2017_726.pdf

United Nations Security Council. 2011. *Resolution 1973 on Libya.* (17 March). [Online]. S/Res/2011/ 1973. [Accessed 8 June 2018]. Available from: https:// www.securitycouncilreport.org/atf/cf/%7B65BFCF9B-6D27-4E9C-8CD3-CF 6E4FF96FF9%7D/Libya%20S%20RES%201973.pdf

United Nations Security Council. 2015. *Unanimously Adopting Resolution 2259.* [Online]. 23 December. [Accessed 3 September 2019]. Available from: https:// www.un.org/press/en/2015/sc12185.doc.htm

United States Department of State. 2016. *Terrorist Designations of ISIL-Yemen-Saudi Arabia, and ISIL-Libya.* [Online].19 May. [Accessed 8 June 2019]. Available from: https://2009-2017.state.gov/r/pa/prs/ps/2016/05/257388.htm

United States Department of State. [no date]. *You Are A Citizen Diplomat.* [Online]. [Accessed August 19, 2019]. Available from: https://diplomacy.state.gov/you-are-a-diplomat

United States Information Agency (USIA). [no date]. Archive website. [Online]. [Accessed 25 October]. Available from: https://www.archives.gov/research/ guide-fed-records/groups/306.html

USC Center for Public Diplomacy. [no date]. What is Public Diplomacy? [Online]. [Accessed 31 December 2019]. Available from: https://www.uscpublicdiplomacy. org/page/what-is-pd

Van der Zweerde, E. 2007. Friendship and the Political. In: King, P. and Smith, G. eds. *Friendship in Politics.* London and New York: Routledge, pp. 31-49.

Vandewalle, D. 2012. *A History of Modern Libya.* Cambridge: Cambridge University Press.

Van Ham, P. 2005. Power, Public Diplomacy and the Pax Americana. In: Melissen, J. ed. *The New Public Diplomacy.* London: Palgrave, pp. 47-66.

Van Ham, P. 2013. Social Power in Public Diplomacy. In: Zaharna, R. et al. eds. *Relational, Collaborative and Networked Approaches to Public Diplomacy.* New York: Routledge.

Van Hoef, Y. and Oelsner, A. 2018. Friendship and Positive Peace: Conceptualising Friendship in Politics and International Relations. *Politics and Governance.* 6(4), pp. 115-124.

Van Noort, C. 2011. *Social Media Strategy: Bringing Public Diplomacy 2.0 to the next level.* Washington, D.C.: Netherlands Embassy.

Veltman, A. 2004. Aristotle and Kant on Self-Disclosure in Friendship. *The Journal of Value Inquiry.* 38, pp. 225-239.

Viltard, Y. 2009. Que faire de la rhétorique de l'amitié en Relations Internationales? *Raisons Politiques.* 33(1), pp.127-147.

Waldhauser, T. 2018. U.S. AFRICOM Commander Gen. Thomas Waldhauser. *Testimony before the Senate Armed Services Committee. 31 March.*

Walhof, D. 2006. Friendship, otherness and Gadamer's politics of solidarity. *Political Theory.* 34(5), pp. 569-593.

Walker, R. 1994. Social Movements/World Politics. *Millennium: Journal of International Studies.* 23(3), pp. 669-700.

Wallis, J. and Richmond, O. 2017. From Constructivist to critical engagements with peacebuilding: implications for hybrid peace. *Third World Thematics: A TWQ Journal.* 2(4), pp. 422-445).

Wayne, A. 2019. *Trump spoke to Libyan strongman threatening Tripoli.* Bloomberg [Online]. 19 April. [Accessed 19 August 2019] Available from https://www.bloomberg.com/news/articles/2019-04-19/trump-haftar-libya

Weber, M. 1919. *Politics As a Vocation.* Munich: Duncker & Humboldt.

Weldes, J., Laffey, M., Gusterson, H. and Duvall, R. 1999. *Cultures of Insecurity: States, Communities and the Production of Danger.* Minnesota: University of Minnesota Press.

Wendt, A. 1987. The Agent Structure Problem in International Relations Theory. *International Organization.* 41(1), pp. 335-370.

Wendt, A. 1994. Collective identity formation and the international state. *American Political Science Review.* 88(2), pp. 384-396.

Wendt, A. 1999. *Social Theory of International Politics.* Cambridge: Cambridge University Press.

West, C. and Zimmerman, D. 1991. Doing Gender. *Gender and Society.* 1, pp. 125-51.

Whelan, M. 2017. Ugly rhetoric first. In: McClory, J. ed. *The Soft Power 30.* USC Center for Public Diplomacy, pp. 64-67.

Wight, C. 1999. They Shoot Dead Horses, Don't They? Locating Agency in the Agent-structure Problematique. *European Journal of International Relations.* 5(1), pp. 109-142.

Wight, C. 2006. *Agents, Structures and International Relations—Politics as Ontology.* New York: Cambridge University Press.

Wike, R., Stokes, B., Poushter, J. and Fetterolf, J. 2017. U.S. Image Suffers as Publics Around the World Question Trump's Leadership. *Pew Research Center.* [Online]. 26 June. [Accessed 2 January 2020]. Available from: https://www.

pewresearch.org/global/2017/06/26/u-s-image-suffers-as-publics-around-world-question-trumps-leadership/

Wilkinson, S. 1999. How useful are focus groups in feminist research? In: Barbour, R. and Kitzinger, J. eds. *Developing Focus Group Research*. London: Sage.

Williams, P. 2015. *Everyday Peace? Politics, citizenship and Muslim lives in India*. West Sussex: John Wiley & Sons.

Wiseman, G. 2012. Distinctive characteristics of American diplomacy. In: Sharp, P. and Wiseman, G. eds. *American Diplomacy*. Leiden: Martinus Nijhoff Publishing, pp. 1-25.

Wolfers, A. and Martin, L. 1956. *The Anglo-American Tradition in Foreign Affairs: Readings on Thomas More to Woodrow Wilson*. New Haven: Yale Community Press.

Woods, K. 2013. Civic and Cosmopolitan Friendship. *Res Publica*. 19, pp. 81-94.

Zaharna, R. 2009. Mapping out a spectrum of public diplomacy initiatives: Information and relational communication frameworks. In: Snow, N. & Taylor, P. eds. *Public diplomacy*. London: Routledge, pp .86-100.

Zaharna, R. 2010. *Battles to Bridges: U.S. Strategic Communication and Public Diplomacy after 9/11*. Basingstoke, UK: Palgrave Macmillan.

Zaharna, R. 2012. *The Cultural Awakening in Public Diplomacy*. Los Angeles, CA: Figueroa Press.

Zaharna, R., Fisher, A. and Arsenault, A. 2013. Introduction. In: Zaharna, R. et al. eds. *Relational, Networked and Collaborative Approaches to Public Diplomacy*. New York: Routledge.

Zakaria, T. and Stewart, P. 2011. *After the fall, U.S. concerned about Libya weapons*. [Online]. 22 August. [Accessed 2 September 2019]. Available from: https://www.reuters.com/article/us-libya-usa-weapons/after-the-fall-u-s-concerned-about-libyan-weapons-idUSTRE77L7C220110822

Zatepilina-Monacell, O. 2012. High stakes: U.S. nonprofit organizations and the U.S. standing abroad. *Public Relations Review*. [Online] 38(3), pp. 471-476. [Accessed: 31 October 2016]. Available from: http://www.sciencedirect.com/science/article/pii/S0363811112000318

Zhao, T. 2006. Rethinking empire from Chinese concept 'All-under-Heaven' (Tianxia). *Social Identities*. 12(1), pp. 29-41.

Zhao, S., Grassmuck, S., and Martin, J. 2008. Identity construction on Facebook: Digital empowerment in anchored relationships. *Computers in Human Behavior*, 24, pp. 1816-1836.

Zogby International. 2004. *Impressions of America: How Arabs View America; How Arabs Learn About America*. Utica, NY.

Focus Group Interviews cited

Facebook (FB). 2018. *Facebook Focus Group*. Interviewed by Lisa Gibson. August.

Speaker (SP). 2018. *Denver Focus Group*. Interviewed by Lisa Gibson. 28 March.

Further Reading

Braun, V. and Clarke, V. [no date]. *Questions about thematic analysis*. [Online]. [Accessed 3 October 2018]. Available from: https://www.psych.auckland.ac.nz/en/about/our-research/research-groups/thematic-analysis/frequently-asked-questions-8.html

Braun, V. and Clarke, V. 2006. Using thematic analysis in psychology. *Qualitative Research in Psychology*. 3(2), pp. 77-101.

Burman, E. and Parker, I. (eds). 1993. *Discourse Analytic Research: Repertoires and Readings of Texts in Action*. London: Routledge.

Causey, C. and Howard, P. 2013. Delivering Digital Public Diplomacy. In: Zaharna, R. et al. eds. *Relational, Networked, and Collaborative Approaches to Public Diplomacy*. New York: Routledge, pp. 144-156.

Flyvbjerg, B. 2006. Five Misunderstandings About Case-Study Research. *Qualitative Inquiry*. 12(2).

Appendices

Table A.2 Data extracts from face-to-face focus group and Facebook focus group interviews, with codes applied.

Data extract	Coded for
We are human beings. I mean, we have to socialise. It's part of our sociology. Friendship, I think it depends. There are many categories, like friendship without benefit, friendship with benefit . . . like this. I prefer friendship without benefit (SP3).	Meaning of friendship Categories of friendship
Friendship is a trustful alliance, mutual cooperation and standing for each other against the life issues (FB18).	Meaning of friendship
It's difficult when you get in friendship. That's why I told you it starts as a just get to know people to have someone and then go on to deep friendship (SP2).	True friendship
What would I like about different cultures other than my personal curiosity, it's that you're gonna learn something (SP2).	Friendship with other cultures Cultural learning and curiosity
Friendship means that you have something in common. It does not matter whether the person is from your country or not (FB10).	Friendship with other cultures
Friends with different cultures is amazing. Not just the friendship is about knowledge, probing your mind, understanding how they're thinking, you can build mind and like many Americans, how they view is different. As we get more...let's say a belief on what's called global citizenship (SP2).	Challenging worldview Becoming open-minded
Some people are more interested in learning more about other cultures because their desire or curiosity or how much they love their foreign friends can motivate them to learn these friends' cultures (FB28).	Open-mindedness and curiosity is needed
I think it's challenging in a different culture. To my experience with friendship here with Americans, they're kind of older people, not so young and they really have experience with multi-cultures (SP1).	Cross-cultural challenges
I think that the American people have different mentalities can create apparent barriers between religious, cultural and countries (FB2).	Cross-cultural challenges
Actually, I have a lot of friends, American and different religions too but when I'm meeting, we just talk like humans, not focus about the religions and different cultures. This is dependent on my religion too, because my religion focuses on be respectful of religions and all the people (SP5).	Respecting all people and religions
When someone made any bad things, they think religion is bad. But some of them in America, what I found, most of them or many people are open so they know all the religions have some good and bad people (SP4).	Religion has good and bad people
I think it's very wrong to continue to teach and speak about hate for others who are not Muslims, this issue has to be addressed in every mosque (FB4).	Religion has good and bad people Open-mindedness and curiosity is necessary
Media is sometimes showing only the bad things; they don't show any good things (SP4).	Media influences views
Media Media Media! It's responsible for making bad reputation about other countries about other people and it's really good in picturing them retarded or barbarian (FB18).	Media influences views

I think the main reason is religion-driven and language driven (SP1).	Differences between friendships with own culture and other cultures
But the barrier thing about the religion when we meet with American friends, my American friend when they invite me to dinner, they don't drink because they know I can't sit at a table with drinks. So they usually try to adjust where to go when I am with them—which is in a way amazing, actually and respectful (SP2).	Adapting behaviour Cross-cultural challenges
The media, the internet . . . social media opens new doors (SP2).	Social media bridges divide
Due to technology the distance does not affect the ability to make friendships with Americans (FB 22).	Social media bridges the divide Social media can facilitate relationships
From my experience, I think social media helped me a lot. I got a lot of American friends; we do a lot of work publishing articles, editing stuff. . . We never met face-to-face. With social media I know a lot of people around the States (SP3).	Social media can facilitate relationships
I started the Libyan American Friendship Association to have a good relationship with the United States and many political people, business, culture and education (SP3).	Social media bridges the divide Cultural understanding and learning
For example, different cultures, different story, different material, different all things, but you can compare and you can learn from them (SP6).	Cultural understanding and learning
They make the whole world as a small village we can tour via the internet in just a few hours (FB1).	Cultural understanding and learning
To be clear, Facebook is not changing my views of Americans. Facebook has changed the way we communicate (FB2).	Facebook changes way we communicate
From social media, I think best stereotype was about the American people in my life. I think most of us, we were thinking American people, it's not gonna be easy to make communication with them. But we found it completely different (SP4).	Dispelling stereotypes
It had an impact before having American friends like all American seemed to be as their policy: unfair, tyrant and aggressive (FB1).	Dispelling stereotypes
I believe FB helped in widening the communication between people from different backgrounds and perspectives but at a superficial level (FB8).	Limits of social media
Because to be honest, if you wanted to know about any countries or any people in those countries, I think face to face, it makes you more clear. Because like, when we see Facebook or this stuff, sometimes I cannot imagine if this is truth or not (SP4).	Face-to-face has more impact
Online friends are different from face-to-face. I have had experience with these two types of friendships. There is a real contact I feel with face-to-face friends because we share dialogues, food visits. So we have understood the nature of each. Whereas online friendships are friendships in the default world we can't feel (FB2).	Face-to-face has more impact
Joint programs in art, sport, education, etc. show Americans the real Libyans who hate war and violence who wants to live in peace and share their culture with the rest of the world (FB7).	Cultural exchange promotes understanding
I want the normal people, the ones who come from a farm or suburban to understand that nobody hates us (SB2).	Cultural exchange promotes understanding
Communicate with the three regions of Libya in an intensive and fair manner (FB20).	Inclusive communication
Understanding the importance of regional and national identity will result in strong friendly relationship (FB19).	Inclusive communication Trust-building

Have an open mind and stay (FB4).	Trust-building
Without facilitating trust the future between Libyan and American people will take long time even if the politician come to an agreement (FB6).	Trust-building
I think America has already begun to changing the Libyans' view of American through the programmes are set from American embassy and the volunteers who come to help us. However, we are looking for more help (FB1).	America helping Libya impacts views
I was lucky to be selected by the US Embassy to participate in the International Visitor Program between the two countries. These type of programs are very useful, interesting and promotes good relations between countries (FB7).	Cultural exchange promotes understanding
Individual initiatives are more effective in changing the negative views between countries than what governments can do especially when people get benefits from these projects such as a work or a scholarship (FB1).	Civil society is more effective than government
I believe more NGOs; it is not the US embassy (SP3).	Civil society is more effective than government
Through education information silos has to be knocked down (FB6).	Educational programmes
It is a long process but countries like Indonesia succeeded in it by education. If education is strong enough and you have all the other tools for that like non-profit organization and if the media help with those open-mindedness things. You have the tools. Even the mosque is important (SP2).	Becoming open-minded
No, but they don't care about this. If they catch an American citizen in Libya they will kill him. Just to get revenge. They don't care; if he's American. . . They don't appreciate like us (SP1).	Closed-mindedness breeds conflict
People in cultures could be friends despite the politics, because governments can change but people don't (SP2).	Separate views of people from government
I believe the only thing that effect people in Libya was the political policy of your government with Israel, which we talk about usually. It's the main topic. This is a very big factor (SP3).	American foreign policy affects views
I found that governments have more to do with this than religious and cultural differences if the two countries agreed at high level people will develop friendship and business as well. I actually interview three of my family and they all agreed on that (FB9).	American foreign policy affects views
Yes, here in Denver. They said, "He's not gonna kick me, he's gonna kick you out because you are black." They said many bad things. I was surprised (SP4).	Trump's election influence on views
I don't know why but there are some of American people who voted for him. So that scares me a little bit because after Obama I thought, Oh my God, these people are amazing because the first African-American president for 8 years; it was amazing (SP2).	Trump's election influence on views
American raid in 1986 and blockage for ten years (FB1).	Historical memory
The implemented sanctions on Libya after Lockerbie accident. Normal Libyans were suffering and not the leader (FB8).	Historical memory
I lost my sister and I couldn't go home. If I go home I would lose my studies. Is this freedom? (SP4).	Travel ban
I think the Trump travel ban is a new type of racism (FB3).	Travel ban

Participant Information Sheet

Title of Study: **Transnational Citizen-led Friendship Groups as a Public Diplomacy Strategy between Libya and the US.**

Name of Researcher(s): Lisa Gibson

We would like to invite you to take part in our research study. Before you decide we would like you to understand why the research is being done and what it would involve for you. Talk to others about the study if you wish. Ask us if there is anything that is not clear.

What is the purpose of the study?

The purpose of this study is to learn about whether friendship between Libyans and Americans has any effect on Libyans' views toward Americans and/or American foreign policy.

Why have I been invited?

You are being invited to take part because you are a Libyan. We are inviting groups of 4-10 participants like you to participate in focus groups.

Do I have to take part?

It is up to you to decide whether or not to take part. If you do decide to take part you will be given this information sheet to keep and be asked to sign a consent form. If you decide to take part you are still free to withdraw at any time and without giving a reason. This would not affect your legal rights.

What will happen to me if I take part?

This focus group will take place in a group setting. The researcher will ask a question and then allow time for the participants in the group to answer the questions, which may include discussing among themselves. The participants are not required to disclose anything that they are not comfortable disclosing. The role of the researcher is primarily to ask questions and observe. There is no right or wrong answer. Instead, the researcher is interested in the participant's personal views on the questions asked. The face-to-face focus group will be recorded. The focus group should last approximately one hour and a half.

Expenses

Participants will receive a $10 Amazon gift card.

What are the possible benefits of taking part?

We cannot promise the study will help you but the information we get from this study may help explain ways that US foreign and diplomacy can improve and help to foster more positive and peaceful relations between Americans and Libyans.

What if there is a problem?

If you have a concern about any aspect of this study, you should ask to speak to the researchers who will do their best to answer your questions. The researchers contact details are given at the end of this information sheet.

Will my taking part in the study be kept confidential?

We will follow ethical and legal practice and all information about you will be handled in confidence.

All information which is collected about you during the course of the research will be kept **strictly confidential**, stored in a secure and locked office, and on a password protected database.

What will happen if I don't want to carry on with the study?

Your participation is voluntary and you are free to withdraw at any time, without giving any reason, and without your legal rights being affected. If you withdraw then the information collected so far cannot be erased and this information may still be used in the project analysis.

Who has reviewed the study?

All research in the School of Politics and International Relations is looked at by independent group of people, called a Research Ethics Committee, to protect your interests. This study has been reviewed and given favourable opinion by the School of Politics and International Relations Research Ethics Committee.

Further information and contact details

Lisa Gibson
Email Lisa.Gibson@nottingham.ac.uk
+447803062096

Consent form

Project title: Transnational citizen led Facebook friendship groups as a public diplomacy strategy between the US and Libya.

Researcher: Lisa Gibson - Lisa.Gibson@nottingham.ac.uk

Supervisors: Oliver Daddow - Oliver.Daddow@nottingham.ac.uk and Neville Wylie - Neville.Wylie@nottingham.ac.uk

Please read this form and sign it once the above named or their designated representative has explained fully the aims and procedures of the study to you.

- I voluntarily agree to take part in this study.

- I confirm that I have been given a full explanation by the above named and that I have read and understand the information sheet given to me which is attached.

- I have been given the opportunity to ask questions and discuss the study with the researcher on all aspects of the study and have understood the advice and information given as a result.

- I authorise the researcher to disclose the results of my participation in the study but not my name.

- I understand that information about me recorded during the study will be kept in a secure database.

- I agree to the use of anonymised quotes in publications

- I understand that I can ask for further instructions or explanations at any time.

- I understand that I am free to withdraw from the study at any time up to three months after completion of the interview, without having to give a reason for withdrawing.

- I understand that focus groups using the chat feature on Facebook are not secure, but after those online focus groups take place the information will be stored in a secure location.

Email signature   Date

Ethical approval

your study. This includes proving appropriate information sheets and consent forms, and ensuring confidentiality in the storage and use of data. Any significant change in the question, design or conduct over the course of the research should be notified to the Research Ethics Committee and may require a new application for ethics approval.

Signed: Lisa
Gibson

Date:
11 December
2017

If submitted by a student please pass to your supervisor for signature

Supervisor's Comments: | I am satisfied with Lisa's ethical reflections and proposed courses of action taken to safeguard participants in the research.

Name of supervisor:
Oliver Daddow

Signature of supervisor:

Date:
11 December 2017   12 December 2017

Name   *Andrew Benham*   Name

(Chair of REC or representative)   (Chair of REC or representative)

Signed   Signed

Date   2↓.12.17   Date

Index

A

Abedi, Ramadan, 93
agency, 5
al Megrahi, Abdel Basset, 86
Al Qaeda, 93
Al Senussi, Idris, 85
Algeria, 93
Allan, G., 69
al-Sarraj, Fayez, 92, 93
Arendt, H., 73, 75, 138
Aristotelian friendship typology, 8, 21, 70
Aristotle, 77, 126, 127, 128, 129, 132, 133, 135
Arsenault, A., 38, 39, 40, 135, 139
authentic dialogue, 39

B

Barbour, R., 16
Belmokhtar, Mokhtar, 93
Benghazi, 86, 113, 117, 120
Berenskoetter, F., 8, 63, 67, 68, 125, 138
Blanchard, C., 88, 89, 90, 92
Bollier, D., 52
Boyd, D., 139
Boyd-Judson, L., 40
broadcast-focused activities, 32
Brown, K., 59, 60
Burns, T., 69
Bush, George W., 11, 33, 117, 124, 143

C

capacity-building programmes, 113, 142, 152
Chan, D., 80
Cheng, G., 80
citizen diplomacy, 41, 43, 44, 48
citizen-led Facebook forums, 138
citizen-led Facebook friendship, 51
citizen-led friendship groups states relations through, 9
citizen-led public diplomacy, 10, 20, 22
civil society programmes, importance, 115, 152
clicktivism, 52
Clinton, Hillary, 47, 54, 141
close-mindedness, 102, 103, 151
Cocking, D., 71, 80, 131
Colonomos, A., 48
communication
    as post-sovereign peace, 4
    cross-cultural, 33, 55
    importance, 37, 38, 76, 145
    inclusive, 112, 147, 152
    networks and, 41
    online, 53, 54, 78
    promoting understandings, 6
    relationships and, 31
    transnational, 52, 56
constructivist approach, 63
Cowan, G., 38, 40, 135, 139
critical peace, 3, 4
critical social constructivism, 3, 4

www.ingramcontent.com/pod-product-compliance
Lightning Source LLC
Chambersburg PA
CBHW072130020426
42334CB00018B/1735